GREAT ILLUSTRATED CLASSICS

To the Reader.

This Figure, that thou here feeft put,
    It was for gentle Shakefpeare cut;
Wherein the Grauer had a ftrife
    with Nature, to out-doo the life:
O, could he but haue drawne his wit
    As well in fraffe, as he hath hit
His face; the Print would then furpaffe
    all, that was euer writ in braffe.
But, fince he cannot, Reader, looke
    Not on his Picture, but his Booke.

B. I.

Martin Droeshout's portrait of Shakespeare appears on the title page of the first folio of "Mr. William Shakespeare's Comedies, Histories, & Tragedies; Published according to the True Original Copies" and printed in London in 1623. Ben Jonson's verse "To the Reader" was printed on the facing page.

THREE TRAGEDIES

Julius Caesar, Hamlet, Macbeth

BY WILLIAM SHAKESPEARE

With biographical illustrations and pictures
of the setting of the plays, together
with introductions by
John Masefield

NEW YORK · DODD, MEAD & COMPANY

The texts for these plays are from the *New Clarendon Shakespeare* editions and are used by permission of the Clarendon Press, Oxford, England.

LIBRARY OF CONGRESS CATALOG CARD NUMBER: 65-21869
PRINTED IN THE UNITED STATES OF AMERICA

CONTENTS

INTRODUCTION   ix

CHRONOLOGY   xix

JULIUS CAESAR   1

   Introduction   3

   Dramatis Personæ   9

   The Play   10

HAMLET, Prince of Denmark   95

   Introduction   97

   Dramatis Personæ   105

   The Play   106

MACBETH   229

   Introduction   231

   Dramatis Personæ   237

   The Play   238

GLOSSARY   315

ILLUSTRATIONS

The Martin Droeshout portrait of Shakespeare   *Frontispiece*

	FACING PAGE
Shakespeare's birthplace	10
Roman statue of Julius Caesar	13
The Roman Forum	44
The death of Caesar	77
The "Flower" portrait of Shakespeare	108
Kronborg Castle at Elsinore	117
Ophelia	132
The duel scene in *Hamlet*	141
The Globe Theatre	172
The Shakespeare monument	205
Macbeth and Lady Macbeth	236
"Screw your courage"	245
The towers of Glamis Castle	260
Stratford-on-Avon	269
The Shakespeare statue in the Church at Stratford	300

INTRODUCTION

SHAKESPEARE AND STRATFORD

STRATFORD-ON-AVON, the poet's destiny and present place of pilgrimage, is a small prosperous country town in the English midlands. It stands on a ground rising slightly above the Avon's western bank. The country near it is mainly flat pasture, with miles of hilly sheep-walk to the south, good orchard land to the south-west, and low hilly woodland, once forest, to the north.

The name Stratford is frequent in England. It occurs where a Roman road (in this case a road to Alcester) comes to a ford through a river. Many coins and traces of the Romans have been found in the district.

Till the coming of the canals, and, later, of the railways, the English rivers were much used for the carriage of heavy goods. Some twenty years after Shakespeare's death, the Avon was made navigable as far as Stratford for small sea-going vessels from the Bristol Channel. As late as the year 1800, the town "had the appearance of a small sea-port."

From very early times the ford gave the place importance as well as a name. Half a dozen roads or tracks converged upon it. In the reign of King Henry the Seventh, a bridge was built to supplement the ford; this bridge also has since been supplemented.

In the Middle Ages, Stratford became a prosperous market town: it was incorporated; it had a mayor and aldermen, a well-endowed good school, and a splendid Church. It had several fairs in each year.

In Shakespeare's time, it was probably in the main a long street, with a few lesser streets or lanes crossing it: most of the houses were small, well-built and two-storied, with attics under the pitched roofs. As much timber was used in the building and thatch in the roofing the town suffered much from fires, then and later.

The countryside, being good pasture, raised beef and dairy cattle: much barley was grown thereabout. England, then, fed her people; usually with rude abundance, though in cold wet seasons the scarcity was sometimes like famine. The work of the district, then, was farming. The work of the town depended on farming: there were smiths, maltsters, millers, butchers, salters, skinners, spinners, weavers, tanners, boot- and shoe-makers, many carters and carriers, hewers and sawyers of wood.

There were fisheries in the river, yielding coarse fish and eels. Guns of precision were not then frequent, but many people hawked when the weather permitted. There were deer-parks in the district, from which the deer strayed or were driven. Men hunted, or went fowling, for food; the arts of the hunter and fowler were very well known.

In this town, with property in the town and near it, the poet's father, John Shakespeare, lived with his wife Mary. John Shake-speare was a man of the middle class, then prosperous, by various country crafts and trades; he has been called a grazier; a butcher; a maltster: he may have been all these things.

William Shakespeare the poet, his third child and first son, was baptised in Stratford Church on April 26th, 1564. It has been assumed that he was born on April 23rd.

It has been assumed that he was born in a room on the first floor at the western end of a detached double dwelling on the north side of Henley Street. The house, or a part of it, was then the property of John Shakespeare. The double dwelling has long since been converted into one: it is now a show-place. There is no evidence that the poet was born there; the Church's Register proves the baptism.

The baptism raises the question of religion. England at that time was sloughing the Middle Ages and those allegiances that had once given a Roman unity to much of Europe. There was then a bitter and growing hostility to many ancient ways and sympathies. Shakespeare's parents were conforming Protestants: we know no more of their faiths than that. Their son was brought up as a conforming Protestant, and no doubt remained so, and was buried as one.

We know nothing of his childhood. It is assumed that he went to a school in Stratford, and learned enough Latin to get pleasure from some classical tales and histories. It is certain that he heard and was stirred by many tales of ghosts, fairies and witches: the popular imagination was always stronger in him than anything to be learned in a school. It is certain that the active life of the countryside, the farming, shepherding and hunting life, with its works and games, delighted him. It is certain, too, that during his quite early childhood his father's prosperity ceased, and some years of poverty (if not of want, of frequent anxiety) lay on the home.

Of the home, we know nothing, except that place and inmates were dear to him; he held by them and returned to them.

Of the amusements of the place no doubt he had a fair share; he learned something of music and singing; he learned very much about hounds, hawking and hunting, as any robust active boy will in a country place.

It is likely that from time to time he saw plays performed in Stratford by companies of strolling actors.

There is some early, credible tradition that his first work was to help a butcher, perhaps his father, and that he disliked butchery.

Being a robust, active lad with the violet in his blood he married at the age of eighteen a woman named Anne or Agnes Hathaway, whose daughter, Susanna, was born less than six months later (May, 1583). In January, 1585, twins were born to him, a son, Hamnet, who died in 1596, and a daughter, Judith, who survived him.

He was, then, nearly twenty-one, with a wife and three little children, in an impoverished household, with no very lively nor likely prospects, and, according to the often quoted story, in some trouble for poaching venison.

How far he had gone at that time in his passion and practice in poetry we do not know.

At this point, he disappears, we know not what he did, nor where he went. We can feel fairly sure that he had heard more than he had read, that he did not in the least know what he could do, nor, perhaps, with great clearness, what he wished to do.

Most people today suppose that at this time in his life he had not been given any great enlightenment as to the power within him and the opportunity without. Light had not been put to the faggot; he was a man of slow and late development.

To the people of Stratford, he may have seemed the son of a man in misfortune, and unlikely to rise above his father's ill-luck. He had made an intemperate marriage with one whom they knew better than we and did not seem to settle down to a country employment. The talk about the venison, whoever spread it, and whenever it may have been spread, is much such gossip as the evil invent about the unlucky and the idle repeat, in any countryside. We may suppose that Stratford had little good to say of the young man.

Today, when we think of the young man we know a side of him not then shewn to the world. We know what he became. We see some at least of the constant elements in him, though much of him remains as utter a mystery as it was to Stratford in 1585.

We know now that Shakespeare, if he had not a deep religious sense, had a righteous mind. The beauty of the right course, the evil of the wrong course, is clear in each play. From the very first, there is an insistence upon truth, of every kind, as the life in human affairs, the enduring thing.

We see, now, that he found a truth in human affection as in other things, that he was a true man. Whatever miseries had fallen on the house, and doubtless many had fallen, yet it was his house, and for him to lessen them. What man has stood more nobly by his people? He may have left Stratford with small hopes and few prospects, but he left with a purpose that stood firm, to restore his house, comfort his parents, and establish his family where they belonged. There was greatness in the purpose and magnificence in the achievement, but never presumption in either. Consider the rightness and justice of his chosen motto

Non sans droict.

I wish that we could know more about him as he was when he left Stratford, what poetry meant much to him, what his hopes and ambitions were. Poetry, hopes and ambitions may all have been almost unknown to him.

We must suppose that he was an active, cheerful, sensitive young man, with a mind somewhat given to wanton joking and imagery, with a joyous knowledge of country things and with a future not only unsure but ominous.

As such, he went out to seek his fortune, to find what he could do, and then to learn how to do it. It is probable that in his wildest moment he had no dream, no thought, of how he would return to Stratford and how he would abide there in later centuries.

Some have supposed that he became a lawyer's clerk, a soldier, a sailor, this, that and the other thing. Some have supposed that he became a page or servant in the house of a nobleman or country justice. "How otherwise," these people ask, "could he have acquired his knowledge of the professions and of the manners of the great?"

Lawyers have assured me that his knowledge of law was that of many civilians of the time. I judge that his knowledge of war came from Holinshed and Plutarch, from what he had seen of the impressment of men, and from the frequent stage practice in historical plays. He learned of the sea in the Pool below London Bridge, just enough for his very slight use of her.

As to his sense of the manners (and frequent want of manners) in people of position, we may grant that he was intelligent and sensitive, observant of all things, watchful for character, and that his life, whatever it was, gave him opportunity for seeing.

A luminous mind, concentrated upon a subject, perceives with great perfection. Imagination, being much neglected in the modern world, is little understood. We wonder why writers have not tried to show that Shakespeare must have been, at odd times, a witch, a murderer, a claimant of the crown (English or French), and a woman.

It is certain that when he was twenty-five or twenty-six he was writing remarkable poetical tales, and other lesser poems. Soon after this, we know not how nor when, he became one of a company of actors. It is likely that as a beginner he walked on as one of a crowd, was one of the dead in a stage-battle, and from this came to be Third Murderer, and Messenger.

It is suggested by the malignancy of an enemy, that he was put to many odd jobs, and could do them.

It was found that, among the odd jobs this young poet could be set to, was the writing of scenes in the patch-work historical plays then very popular. Very soon, it was found that he had unusual talent for this, great fertility of invention, and match-less powers of work. In a year or two, he was famous as a writer of plays. Being a man of good presence, pleasant manners, as well as varied genius, he became eminent in his company as actor and poet, as shareholder and co-director. Though he won no outstanding fame as an actor, he was no doubt a popular reliable leading actor, best (it is thought) in what are called "character parts."

Through most of his active life he was with Richard Burbage, one of the great actors of the time, in the most famous of the companies then acting.

His life may be briefly told as follows:

He became rich, he re-established his family, applied for and was granted a coat of arms, bought the house and grounds known as New Place, in Stratford; invested in other property in London and near his home; and after a brief prosperous time of quiet, died and was buried at Stratford. He died on the 23rd of April, 1616, aged fifty-two years. The cause of his death is not known. His wife and two daughters survived him.

Though Shakespeare was a public figure for more than twenty years, known by face, voice, manner and reputation to thousands in London and elsewhere, little is recorded of him. His old homes and theatres in London have been destroyed; and the fires that took them have taken books and papers that might have told us much. The Great Fire of London must have been very fatal in this way. The letters, diaries and memoirs of most of the City must have perished then.

Setting aside the gossip gathered long after he was dead from surviving village idiots, hoping, perhaps, for reward, there are the words of the intelligent. Aubrey learned of him that he was "a handsome well-shap't man." Another wrote of him that "he had the Phantsie very strong." Put together, these seem a fair portrait of man and mind.

Next, as to his human relationships. Though much has been destroyed, the evidence is out-spoken in his praise. If, as seems certain, Henry Chettle refers to him, it begins early (in 1592) and is eloquent.

> . . . his demeanour no less civil, than he excellent in the quality he professes. Besides, divers of worship have reported his uprightness of dealing, which argues his honesty, and his facetious grace in writing, that approves his art.

In the verses printed below the engraved portrait in the first folio, 1623, Ben Jonson, who knew him well, and had to compress his commendation within small space, calls him "gentle." In the same Book, the same great man, in all the nobleness of his nature, issued such praise as few poets have ever given to a brother poet.

The lines are well known; they are often quoted; and must not figure here. I can only quote the great lapidary heading:

To the memory of my beloved
The Authour
Mr. William Shakespeare
And
What he hath left us.

What other of our great poets has won such an inscription from a comparable brain? Chaucer, indeed, won the loving praise of Hoccleve; Wordsworth, the enthusiasm of Coleridge; but the above, and the pages that follow, are on another level. When Ben Jonson was touched to the heart he spoke with splendour.

There are two portraits of Shakespeare accepted fairly generally as likely to be attempts at likenesses, if not very like him. One of these is the coloured half-length bust on the chancel wall in Stratford Church. This was made by one Gerard Janssen, a sculptor and mason of repute. It was placed in the Church within seven years of the poet's death.

I do not know whether Janssen ever drew or modelled Shakespeare during his life, nor whether he knew him. Presumably he had some lively image to work from, for the bust is the image of a man with much vitality of mind. The stone face is that of an alert and sunny man, energetic and effective.

The other portrait is that engraved for the title-page of the first folio, published in 1623. This is by one Martin Droeshout, who was only fifteen when Shakespeare died and may have been about twenty-two when he wrought the engraving. I do not know if he had ever seen Shakespeare, nor from what image, sketch or portrait he worked. It represents an unusual man.

A few (doubtless the earliest) impressions from this engraving show a face of delicate sensitiveness; much of this grace was quickly lost as the plate wore and was retouched.

We may assume that Ben Jonson knew Droeshout, and saw both the plate and the earliest impressions, and that from some first, early, unlettered proof, he wrote the well-known lines "To the Reader."

These lines suggest that the engraver had done his best, and had really made a likeness of the face that Ben Jonson knew well.

Besides these two portraits there is a painting now at Stratford, supposed by some to be the original of the engraving, and by others to be a later painting from the engraving. It is said that the late William Morris said that "it must be like Shake-speare, because it isn't like a man."

The face is like the face in the engraving, and mingles (like the plays) an extra-ordinary common-ness with an extra-ordinary un-common-ness.

There is no evidence to show that it is a portrait of Shake-speare.

There are many other supposed portraits of him, also with-out evidence. The bust and the engraving alone have some like-lihood of being based upon some record made during his life.

CHRONOLOGY

Shakespeare's biographical dates are based upon existing official records. The dates of his plays can only be approximate.

1564, April 26. Christening of Shakespeare at Stratford parish church.

1582, November 27. License for Marriage of Shakespeare to Anne Hathaway.

1583, May 26. Christening of Susanna Shakespeare.

1585, February 2. Christening of Hamnet and Judith Shakespeare.

1590–91. *Henry VI.*

1592. *Richard III, Titus Andronicus.*

1593–94. *Venus and Adonis, Comedy of Errors, Two Gentlemen of Verona, Taming of the Shrew, Love's Labour's Lost, Sonnets, The Rape of Lucrece.*

1595. *Romeo and Juliet, Richard II.*

1596. August 11. Burial of Hamnet Shakespeare.
A Midsummer Night's Dream, King John.

1597. *Merchant of Venice, Part 1 Henry IV.*

1598. *Part 2 Henry IV, Merry Wives.*

1599. Opening of Globe Theatre. *Henry V, Much Ado.*

1600. *As You Like It, Twelfth Night.*

1601. September 8. Burial of the poet's father, John Shakespeare.
Julius Caesar(?), Hamlet.

1602. *Troilus and Cressida(?).*

1603. *All's Well, Measure for Measure.*

1604. *Othello.*

1605. *Timon of Athens.*

1606. *King Lear, Macbeth.*

1607, June 5. Marriage of Shakespeare's daughter Susanna to John

Hall in Stratford. *Antony and Cleopatra, Coriolanus.*

1608, February 21. Christening of Shakespeare's granddaughter, Elizabeth Hall. The only grandchild born in the poet's lifetime.

1608, September 9. Burial of the poet's mother, Mary Shakespeare. *Pericles.*

1609, May 20. Registration of *Sonnets. Cymbeline.*

1610. Probable Migration of Shakespeare to Stratford. *The Winter's Tale.*

1611. *The Tempest.*

1612. *Henry VIII.*

1613, June 29. The Globe burned down during a perfomance of *Henry VIII. Two Noble Kinsmen(?).*

1616, April 23. Death of Shakespeare.

April 25. Burial of 'Will. Shakspere, gent.'

Julius Caesar

Julius Caesar

INTRODUCTION

Written. 1601 (?)

Produced. (?)

Published, in the first folio, 1623

Source of the Plot. The lives of Antonius, Brutus and Julius Caesar in Sir Thomas North's *Plutarch.*

A tragedy of Julius Caesar, now lost, was performed by Shakespeare's company in 1594. Shakespeare must have known this play.

The Fable. Cassius, fearing that Julius Caesar is about to extinguish all trace of Republican rule in Rome, persuades Brutus and others to plot a change. They decide to murder Caesar.

On the morning chosen for the murder, Caesar is warned by many omens not to stir abroad. He is persuaded to ignore the omens. He goes to the Senate House, and is there killed. Mark Antony, his friend, obtains leave from the murderers to make a public oration over the corpse.

In his speech he so inflames the populace against the murderers that they are compelled to leave Rome.

Joining himself to Octavius, he takes the field against Brutus and Cassius, and helps to defeat them at Philippi.

Cassius is killed by his servant when he sees that all is lost. Brutus, seeing the battle go against him, kills himself.

Somewhere in what Dante calls "Nel mezzo del cammin," in the middle of our Way of Life, at about thirty-five, an age often fatal to men of talent, Shakespeare stepped into splendour and opened its doors to us, so that we might behold glories of a kind new to men.

3

We do not know what had kept this new world from him until then, nor why he had not been exhausted by the mass of work written by him since he came into the theatre, nor what it was, what happiness of mood or moment, that opened the door: but certainly a door opened to a power such as no poet has known; he entered in might and declared his joy with ecstasy.

Critics and scholars are in fair agreement that it was with this play that the new power was first shown.

The men who went to see it could not have guessed that they were going to a new revelation. Even now, after three and a half centuries, men have not yet declared how wonderful this revelation was.

Nothing in the least like it had been shown to men until then: nothing comparable has appeared in Europe (or elsewhere) since. It takes us into a new world, more enduring than this, in which all imaginative men may live.

Readers, and those who go to see this play, should remember that Shakespeare's design was not quite that of the ancient nor of the modern playwright, though his concern, like theirs, in all his high attempts, is the working out of a Justice for a wrong committed.

A Greek playwright, working on such a fable, might have shewn Caesar too ambitious, too neglectful of divine and human warnings, and ended the action at the murder. A chorus of ancient Senators, or, perhaps, of Gaulish and British slaves, would then have chanted something noble about the results of pride and the mysterious movings of the gods. Possibly, the Greek would have preferred to take Brutus as his theme; making a trilogy of high endeavour and ambition, shewing Brutus in friendship with Caesar through the first play; angry with, and killing him, in the second; finding his mistake, and killing himself in the third. After this there might have come some brief satyr play, and so an end.

A modern playwright would probably know too much about modern theatrical difficulties to attempt any tragic rendering of the theme: but if he did, he would perhaps be told that the public expected a happy ending. He would perhaps be urged to try a film; a Julius Caesar play, with the conspirators all ready to murder him, and then a brave, loving, lovely slave-girl contriving to get him safely away to Capri, to live happily ever after. If, resisting this temptation, the playwright still chose to kill Caesar in the Senate-house, his curtain would have to fall a minute after the murder, with some political comment proper to modern times.

Shakespeare's design was more like the Greek trilogy than the other methods. He meant to put into one play a great act and its consequences. Long before, he and his fellows had put the usurpation of Bolingbroke and its consequences into eight plays: but since then power had come to him, and progress had come to the theatre. This play runs for two and a half acts after Caesar is killed: the greater play of *Macbeth* is made upon much the same plan.

In both plays, the great act, on which all turns, is the murder of the head of a State. In neither case is Shakespeare deeply interested in the victim, nor is he at any pains to make him attractive to the audience. Duncan, in *Macbeth,* is a too trusting, generous gentleman; Caesar, in this play, is a touchy man of affairs whose head is turned. Shakespeare's imagination broods on the fact that the killers were deluded into murder, Macbeth by an envious wife and the belief that Fate meant him to be king, Brutus by an envious friend and the belief that he was saving Rome. In both cases the killers show base personal ingratitude and treachery. In both plays, an avenging justice makes even the scales. The mind of the poet follows them from the moment when the guilty thought is prompted, through the agony, hysteria and blindness of dreadful acts, to the horror of unhappy failure till Fate's just sword falls. His imagination is most keenly stirred just as ours is, by the great event, the murder of the victim: but his subject is not the murder, nor yet the tragical end of a ruler. His subject in both plays is the working of Fate who prompts to murder, uses the murderer, and then destroys him.

From this summary of a great conception, let the reader turn to the great work, to see how simply yet how grandly it is opened, and how nobly the power proceeds.

Caesar is subtly and then loudly warned: Brutus is loudly and then subtly warned, in each case, in vain. As in *Macbeth,* an effect of storm preludes the crime. Then, as all warnings have been in vain, Caesar and the conspirators are in the Senate House, and one of the most marvellous acts ever written has begun.

As it is of a piece, in the one great mood, all seen in its clearness and relation, with the mastery of power, I do not doubt that it was written in one day; such a day as even Shakespeare not often knew. It is of a perfection beyond praise. The thing is superb, and unalterable.

The anxiety of the conspirators, lest they have been betrayed by Popilius, is anguish to the audience, for one wonderful moment. The entry there, of Popilius, using his few ambiguous words, is beyond praise. An instant later, the anguish of the audience is for Caesar, and this anguish is artfully maintained by three minutes of skill, in which Metellus, Brutus and Cassius plead for the banished Publius Cimba, and Caesar replies.

After the appeal of Cassius, Caesar begins a speech more than a minute long, a fine speech, comparing himself to the Pole Star. The suspense of the audience is so great for him at this moment, that I doubt if anyone ever knows what he talks about. A player acting Caesar might at this moment talk about the weather, or substitute a speech of Jaques, Hamlet or Macbeth; few, if any would notice, if he gave the right cue-lines at the end. The audience is in anguish for him, and thinks only of the smilers with the knives hid. More than once, I have heard men in London audiences cry out "Look out, Caesar," during this speech; and I have heard of one brave fellow, in New York, who cried out "I'll not sit by and see murder done," and leaped on to the stage to save him.

The murder is done: there follows a scene of hysteria and indirection among the killers, during which Brutus, the least bloody of them, suggests and does the savage thing (long afterwards condemned as blackguardly in the Laxdale Saga and there called the rite of "hale, enjoy hands"). A moment later, he, the most reasonable of the killers, suggests and causes the foolish thing, the admission of Mark Antony.

This entrance of Mark Antony begins another great scene, truly noble. Mark Antony enters upon the Senate, on the floor of which his friend and ally Caesar still lies dead, to confront the killers, who will probably kill him, but on whom he hopes to avenge his friend, if life be given. I know no scene in poetry more anxious. Any least slip in beauty of bearing would bring his instant death; and the audience is aghast for him for ten terrible matchless minutes.

As for the later scene, with the funeral oration over Caesar, it is unlike anything in poetry. In the theatre it is often marred by the interruptions of the crowd, during the first few minutes. Surely this is an error in the production. The crowd is stunned, cowed and frightened, with only a few revolutionary supporters in it. Such a crowd should be ominously still: Brutus's long, cold, intellectual rhetoric could only have made it more ominous and stiller. It is the speech that makes the fire: it is after the speech that the rage runs: all the skill of the theatre can then direct a great scene of popular madness out for blood.

In the modern theatre, of course, the next two acts are anticlimax and epilogue. They were the heart of the play when Shakespeare first gave it to the Globe. The great scenes of the play, then, were the dispute between Brutus and Cassius; the emergence of the figure of Octavius Caesar; the coming of Caesar's ghost; and the rightful and awful deaths of the conspirators. All those four matters were of deep importance to Shakespeare and his fellows.

We do not know who first played Brutus and Cassius, but we do know that the dispute scene was wonderfully done, memorable and splendid. Shakespeare was plainly already bent on writing his *Antony and Cleopatra;* that was to follow at the Globe, and follow soon. The audience had to be prepared for that great clash in the Roman world between the plain blunt man that loved his friends and a subtle wonderful man who loved himself: something of the two natures together had to be shown; if only to encourage the players to the theme. As for the Ghost, that foreteller of coming doom; all belief is for the Ghost; all know that doom falls, and most of us, before doom falls, learn something of an unseen world. The deaths at the end taught the Elizabethans of that world's justice: the skill of the players touched the justice with pity and forgiveness.

The verse has added many quotations to popular speech, such as the wonderful line

It is the bright day that brings forth the adder . . .

Among much other splendour, are these lines, spoken by Brutus, to show to after ages something of what Shakespeare knew about the unseen world that holds us.

Between the acting of a dreadful thing
And the first motion, all the interim is
Like a phantasma or a hideous dream:
The Genius and the mortal instruments
Are then in council; and the state of man,
Like to a little kingdom, suffers then
The nature of an insurrection.

DRAMATIS PERSONÆ

JULIUS CAESAR

OCTAVIUS CAESAR,
MARCUS ANTONIUS,
M. AEMILIUS LEPIDUS,
} Triumvirs after the Death of Julius Caesar

CICERO,
PUBLIUS,
POPILIUS LENA,
} Senators

MARCUS BRUTUS,
CASSIUS,
CASCA,
TREBONIUS,
LIGARIUS,
DECIUS BRUTUS,
METELLUS CIMBER,
CINNA,
} Conspirators against Julius Caesar

FLAVIUS and MARULLUS, Tribunes

ARTEMIDORUS, a Sophist of Cnidos

A SOOTHSAYER

CINNA, a Poet

ANOTHER POET

LUCILIUS, TITINIUS, MESSALA, YOUNG CATO, and VOLUMNIUS, Friends to Brutus and Cassius

VARRO, CLITUS, CLAUDIUS, STRATO, LUCIUS, DARDANIUS, Servants to Brutus

PINDARUS, Servant to Cassius

CALPHURNIA, Wife to Caesar

PORTIA, Wife to Brutus

SENATORS, CITIZENS, GUARDS, ATTENDANTS, &c.

SCENE. *During a great part of the Play, at Rome; afterwards, Sardis and near Philippi*

9

Act 1

Scene I.   Rome. A Street

Enter FLAVIUS, MARULLUS, *and certain* COMMONERS.

FLAVIUS. Hence! home, you idle creatures, get you home.
Is this a holiday? What! know you not,
Being mechanical, you ought not walk
Upon a labouring day without the sign
Of your profession? Speak, what trade art thou?

FIRST COMMONER. Why, sir, a carpenter.

MARULLUS. Where is thy leather apron, and thy rule?
What dost thou with thy best apparel on?
You, sir, what trade are you?

SECOND COMMONER. Truly, sir, in respect of a fine workman,
I am but, as you would say, a cobbler.

MARULLUS. But what trade art thou? Answer me directly.

SECOND COMMONER. A trade, sir, that, I hope, I may use with
a safe conscience; which is, indeed, sir, a mender of bad soles.

MARULLUS. What trade, thou knave? thou naughty knave,
what trade?

SECOND COMMONER. Nay, I beseech you, sir, be not out with
me: yet, if you be out, sir, I can mend you.

MARULLUS. What meanest thou by that? Mend me, thou saucy
fellow!

SECOND COMMONER. Why, sir, cobble you.

FLAVIUS. Thou art a cobbler, art thou?

SECOND COMMONER. Truly, sir, all that I live by is with the
awl: I meddle with no tradesman's matters, nor women's mat-

10

The house in which Shakespeare was supposedly born in 1564

ters, but with awl. I am, indeed, sir, a surgeon to old shoes;
when they are in great danger, I recover them. As proper men
as ever trod upon neat's leather have gone upon my handiwork.
   FLAVIUS. But wherefore art not in thy shop to-day?
Why dost thou lead these men about the street?
   SECOND COMMONER. Truly, sir, to wear out their shoes, to get
myself into more work. But, indeed, sir, we make holiday to see
Caesar and to rejoice in his triumph.
   MARULLUS. Wherefore rejoice? What conquest brings he
      home?
What tributaries follow him to Rome
To grace in captive bonds his chariot wheels?
You blocks, you stones, you worse than senseless things!
O you hard hearts, you cruel men of Rome,
Knew you not Pompey? Many a time and oft
Have you climb'd up to walls and battlements,
To towers and windows, yea, to chimney-tops,
Your infants in your arms, and there have sat
The livelong day, with patient expectation,
To see great Pompey pass the streets of Rome:
And when you saw his chariot but appear,
Have you not made a universal shout,
That Tiber trembled underneath her banks,
To hear the replication of your sounds
Made in her concave shores?
And do you now put on your best attire?
And do you now cull out a holiday?
And do you now strew flowers in his way,
That comes in triumph over Pompey's blood?
Be gone!
Run to your houses, fall upon your knees,
Pray to the gods to intermit the plague
That needs must light on this ingratitude.
   FLAVIUS. Go, go, good countrymen, and, for this fault,
Assemble all the poor men of your sort;
Draw them to Tiber banks, and weep your tears

Into the channel, till the lowest stream
Do kiss the most exalted shores of all.

[Exeunt all the COMMONERS.

See whe'r their basest metal be not mov'd;
They vanish tongue-tied in their guiltiness.
Go you down that way towards the Capitol;
This way will I. Disrobe the images
If you do find them deck'd with ceremonies.

MARULLUS. May we do so?
You know it is the feast of Lupercal.

FLAVIUS. It is no matter; let no images
Be hung with Caesar's trophies. I'll about
And drive away the vulgar from the streets:
So do you too where you perceive them thick.
These growing feathers pluck'd from Caesar's wing
Will make him fly an ordinary pitch,
Who else would soar above the view of men
And keep us all in servile fearfulness.   *[Exeunt.*

Scene II.   The Same. A Public Place

Enter, in procession, with music, CAESAR; ANTONY, *for the
course;* CALPHURNIA, PORTIA, DECIUS, CICERO, BRUTUS, CASSIUS,
and CASCA; *a great crowd following, among them a* SOOTH-
SAYER.

CAESAR. Calphurnia!

CASCA.   Peace, ho! Caesar speaks.

[Music ceases.

CAESAR.   Calphurnia!

CALPHURNIA. Here, my lord.

CAESAR. Stand you directly in Antonius' way
When he doth run his course. Antonius!

ANTONY. Caesar, my lord.

CAESAR. Forget not, in your speed, Antonius,
To touch Calphurnia; for our elders say,

A statue of Julius Caesar in the
Palazzo dei Conservatori in Rome

The barren, touched in this holy chase,
Shake off their sterile curse.
ANTONY.   I shall remember:
When Caesar says 'Do this,' it is perform'd.
CAESAR. Set on; and leave no ceremony out.   [*Music.*
SOOTHSAYER. Caesar!
CAESAR. Ha! Who calls?
CASCA. Bid every noise be still: peace yet again!
                                        [*Music ceases.*
CAESAR. Who is it in the press that calls on me?
I hear a tongue, shriller than all the music,
Cry 'Caesar.' Speak; Caesar is turn'd to hear.
SOOTHSAYER. Beware the ides of March.
CAESAR.   What man is that?
BRUTUS. A soothsayer bids you beware the ides of March.
CAESAR. Set him before me; let me see his face.
CASSIUS. Fellow, come from the throng; look upon Caesar.
CAESAR. What sayst thou to me now? Speak once again.
SOOTHSAYER. Beware the ides of March.
CAESAR. He is a dreamer; let us leave him: pass.
          [*Sennet. Exeunt all but* BRUTUS *and* CASSIUS.
CASSIUS. Will you go see the order of the course?
BRUTUS. Not I.
CASSIUS. I pray you, do.
BRUTUS. I am not gamesome: I do lack some part
Of that quick spirit that is in Antony.
Let me not hinder, Cassius, your desires;
I'll leave you.
CASSIUS. Brutus, I do observe you now of late:
I have not from your eyes that gentleness
And show of love as I was wont to have:
You bear too stubborn and too strange a hand
Over your friend that loves you.
BRUTUS.   Cassius,
Be not deceiv'd: if I have veil'd my look,
I turn the trouble of my countenance

Merely upon myself. Vexed I am
Of late with passions of some difference,
Conceptions only proper to myself,
Which give some soil perhaps to my behaviours;
But let not therefore my good friends be griev'd,—
Among which number, Cassius, be you one,—
Nor construe any further my neglect,
Than that poor Brutus, with himself at war,
Forgets the shows of love to other men.

CASSIUS. Then, Brutus, I have much mistook your passion;
By means whereof this breast of mine hath buried
Thoughts of great value, worthy cogitations.
Tell me, good Brutus, can you see your face?

BRUTUS. No, Cassius; for the eye sees not itself,
But by reflection, by some other things.

CASSIUS. 'Tis just:
And it is very much lamented, Brutus,
That you have no such mirrors as will turn
Your hidden worthiness into your eye,
That you might see your shadow. I have heard,
Where many of the best respect in Rome,—
Except immortal Caesar,—speaking of Brutus,
And groaning underneath this age's yoke,
Have wish'd that noble Brutus had his eyes.

BRUTUS. Into what dangers would you lead me, Cassius,
That you would have me seek into myself
For that which is not in me?

CASSIUS. Therefore, good Brutus, be prepar'd to hear;
And, since you know you cannot see yourself
So well as by reflection, I, your glass,
Will modestly discover to yourself
That of yourself which you yet know not of.
And be not jealous on me, gentle Brutus:
Were I a common laughter, or did use
To stale with ordinary oaths my love
To every new protester; if you know

That I do fawn on men and hug them hard,
And after scandal them; or if you know
That I profess myself in banqueting
To all the rout, then hold me dangerous.   [*Flourish and shout.*

   BRUTUS. What means this shouting? I do fear the people
Choose Caesar for their king.

   CASSIUS.   Ay, do you fear it?
Then must I think you would not have it so.

   BRUTUS. I would not, Cassius; yet I love him well.
But wherefore do you hold me here so long?
What is it that you would impart to me?
If it be aught toward the general good,
Set honour in one eye and death i' the other,
And I will look on both indifferently;
For let the gods so speed me as I love
The name of honour more than I fear death.

   CASSIUS. I know that virtue to be in you, Brutus,
As well as I do know your outward favour.
Well, honour is the subject of my story.
I cannot tell what you and other men
Think of this life; but, for my single self,
I had as lief not be as live to be
In awe of such a thing as I myself.
I was born free as Caesar; so were you:
We both have fed as well, and we can both
Endure the winter's cold as well as he:
For once, upon a raw and gusty day,
The troubled Tiber chafing with her shores,
Caesar said to me, 'Dar'st thou, Cassius, now
Leap in with me into this angry flood,
And swim to yonder point?' Upon the word,
Accoutred as I was, I plunged in
And bade him follow; so indeed he did.
The torrent roar'd, and we did buffet it
With lusty sinews, throwing it aside
And stemming it with hearts of controversy;

But ere we could arrive the point propos'd,
Casear cried, 'Help me, Cassius, or I sink!'
I, as Aeneas, our great ancester,
Did from the flames of Troy upon his shoulder
The old Anchises bear, so from the waves of Tiber
Did I the tired Caesar. And this man
Is now become a god, and Cassius is
A wretched creature and must bend his body
If Caesar carelessly but nod on him.
He had a fever when he was in Spain,
And when the fit was on him, I did mark
How he did shake; 'tis true, this god did shake;
His coward lips did from their colour fly,
And that same eye whose bend doth awe the world
Did lose his lustre; I did hear him groan;
Ay, and that tongue of his that bade the Romans
Mark him and write his speeches in their books,
Alas! it cried, 'Give me some drink, Titinius,'
As a sick girl. Ye gods, it doth amaze me,
A man of such a feeble temper should
So get the start of the majestic world,
And bear the palm alone.   [*Flourish. Shout.*
    BRUTUS.   Another general shout!
I do believe that these applauses are
For some new honours that are heaped on Caesar.
    CASSIUS. Why, man, he doth bestride the narrow world
Like a Colossus; and we petty men
Walk under his huge legs, and peep about
To find ourselves dishonourable graves.
Men at some time are masters of their fates:
The fault, dear Brutus, is not in our stars,
But in ourselves, that we are underlings.
Brutus and Caesar: what should be in that 'Caesar'?
Why should that name be sounded more than yours?
Write them together, yours is as fair a name;

Sound them, it doth become the mouth as well;
Weigh them, it is as heavy; conjure with 'em,
'Brutus' will start a spirit as soon as 'Caesar.'
Now, in the names of all the gods at once,
Upon what meat doth this our Caesar feed,
That he is grown so great? Age, thou art sham'd!
Rome, thou hast lost the breed of noble bloods!
When went there by an age, since the great flood,
But it was fam'd with more than with one man?
When could they say, till now, that talk'd of Rome,
That her wide walks encompass'd but one man?
Now is it Rome indeed and room enough,
When there is in it but one only man.
O! you and I have heard our fathers say,
There was a Brutus once that would have brook'd
Th' eternal devil to keep his state in Rome
As easily as a king.

BRUTUS. That you do love me, I am nothing jealous;
What you would work me to, I have some aim:
How I have thought of this and of these times,
I shall recount hereafter; for this present,
I would not, so with love I might entreat you,
Be any further mov'd. What you have said
I will consider; what you have to say
I will with patience hear, and find a time
Both meet to hear and answer such high things.
Till then, my noble friend, chew upon this:
Brutus had rather be a villager
Than to repute himself a son of Rome
Under these hard conditions as this time
Is like to lay upon us.

CASSIUS.   I am glad
That my weak words have struck but thus much show
Of fire from Brutus.

BRUTUS. The games are done and Caesar is returning.

CASSIUS. As they pass by, pluck Casca by the sleeve,
And he will, after his sour fashion, tell you
What hath proceeded worthy note to-day.

Re-enter CAESAR *and his Train.*

BRUTUS. I will do so. But, look you, Cassius,
The angry spot doth glow on Caesar's brow,
And all the rest look like a chidden train:
Calphurnia's cheek is pale, and Cicero
Looks with such ferret and such fiery eyes
As we have seen him in the Capitol,
Being cross'd in conference by some senators.

CASSIUS. Casca will tell us what the matter is.

CAESAR. Antonius!

ANTONY. Caesar.

CAESAR. Let me have men about me that are fat;
Sleek-headed men and such as sleep o' nights.
Yond Cassius has a lean and hungry look;
He thinks too much: such men are dangerous.

ANTONY. Fear him not, Caesar, he's not dangerous;
He is a noble Roman, and well given.

CAESAR. Would he were fatter! but I fear him not:
Yet if my name were liable to fear,
I do not know the man I should avoid
So soon as that spare Cassius. He reads much;
He is a great observer, and he looks
Quite through the deeds of men; he loves no plays,
As thou dost, Antony; he hears no music;
Seldom he smiles, and smiles in such a sort
As if he mock'd himself, and scorn'd his spirit
That could be mov'd to smile at any thing.
Such men as he be never at heart's ease
Whiles they behold a greater than themselves,
And therefore are they very dangerous.
I rather tell thee what is to be fear'd
Than what I fear, for always I am Caesar.

Come on my right hand, for this ear is deaf,
And tell me truly what thou think'st of him.

> [*Sennet. Exeunt* CAESAR *and his Train.* CASCA
> *stays behind.*

CASCA. You pull'd me by the cloak; would you speak with me?

BRUTUS. Ay, Casca; tell us what hath chanc'd to-day,
That Caesar looks so sad.

CASCA. Why, you were with him, were you not?

BRUTUS. I should not then ask Casca what had chanc'd.

CASCA. Why, there was a crown offered him; and, being offered him, he put it by with the back of his hand, thus; and then the people fell a-shouting.

BRUTUS. What was the second noise for?

CASCA. Why, for that too.

CASSIUS. They shouted thrice: what was the last cry for?

CASCA. Why, for that too.

BRUTUS. Was the crown offered him thrice?

CASCA. Ay, marry, was 't, and he put it by thrice, every time gentler than other; and at every putting-by mine honest neighbours shouted.

CASSIUS. Who offered him the crown?

CASCA. Why, Antony.

BRUTUS. Tell us the manner of it, gentle Casca.

CASCA. I can as well be hanged as tell the manner of it: it was mere foolery; I did not mark it. I saw Mark Antony offer him a crown; yet 'twas not a crown neither, 'twas one of these coronets; and, as I told you, he put it by once; but, for all that, to my thinking, he would fain have had it. Then he offered it to him again; then he put it by again; but, to my thinking, he was very loath to lay his fingers off it. And then he offered it the third time; he put it the third time by; and still as he refused it the rabblement shouted and clapped their chopped hands, and threw up their sweaty night-caps, and uttered such a deal of stinking breath because Caesar refused the crown, that it had almost choked Caesar; for he swounded and fell down at it: and for mine own part, I durst not laugh, for fear of opening my lips and receiving the bad air.

CASSIUS. But soft, I pray you: what! did Caesar swound?

CASCA. He fell down in the market-place, and foamed at mouth, and was speechless.

BRUTUS. 'Tis very like: he hath the falling-sickness.

CASSIUS. No, Caesar hath it not; but you, and I, And honest Casca, we have the falling-sickness.

CASCA. I know not what you mean by that; but I am sure Caesar fell down. If the tag-rag people did not clap him and hiss him, according as he pleased and displeased them, as they use to do the players in the theatre, I am no true man.

BRUTUS. What said he, when he came unto himself?

CASCA. Marry, before he fell down, when he perceiv'd the common herd was glad he refused the crown, he plucked me ope his doublet and offered them his throat to cut. An I had been a man of any occupation, if I would not have taken him at a word, I would I might go to hell among the rogues. And so he fell. When he came to himself again, he said, if he had done or said any thing amiss, he desired their worships to think it was his infirmity. Three or four wenches, where I stood, cried, 'Alas! good soul,' and forgave him with all their hearts: but there's no heed to be taken of them; if Caesar had stabbed their mothers, they would have done no less.

BRUTUS. And after that he came, thus sad, away?

CASCA. Ay.

CASSIUS. Did Cicero say any thing?

CASCA. Ay, he spoke Greek.

CASSIUS. To what effect?

CASCA. Nay, an I tell you that, I'll ne'er look you i' the face again; but those that understood him smiled at one another and shook their heads; but, for mine own part, it was Greek to me. I could tell you more news too; Marullus and Flavius, for pulling scarfs off Caesar's images, are put to silence. Fare you well. There was more foolery yet, if I could remember it.

CASSIUS. Will you sup with me to-night, Casca?

CASCA. No, I am promised forth.

CASSIUS. Will you dine with me to-morrow?

CASCA. Ay, if I be alive, and your mind hold, and your dinner worth the eating.

CASSIUS. Good; I will expect you.

CASCA. Do so. Farewell, both.   [*Exit.*

BRUTUS. What a blunt fellow is this grown to be!
He was quick mettle when he went to school.

CASSIUS. So is he now in execution
Of any bold or noble enterprise,
However he puts on this tardy form.
This rudeness is a sauce to his good wit,
Which gives men stomach to digest his words
With better appetite.

BRUTUS. And so it is. For this time I will leave you:
To-morrow, if you please to speak with me,
I will come home to you; or, if you will,
Come home to me, and I will wait for you.

CASSIUS. I will do so: till then, think of the world.

[*Exit* BRUTUS.

Well, Brutus, thou art noble; yet, I see,
Thy honourable metal may be wrought
From that it is dispos'd: therefore 'tis meet
That noble minds keep ever with their likes;
For who so firm that cannot be seduc'd?
Caesar doth bear me hard; but he loves Brutus:
If I were Brutus now and he were Cassius
He should not humour me. I will this night,
In several hands, in at his windows throw,
As if they came from several citizens,
Writings all tending to the great opinion
That Rome holds of his name; wherein obscurely
Caesar's ambition shall be glanced at:
And after this let Caesar seat him sure;
For we will shake him, or worse days endure.

[*Exit.*

Scene III. The Same. A Street

Thunder and lightning. Enter, from opposite sides, CASCA,
with his sword drawn, and CICERO.

CICERO. Good even, Casca: brought you Caesar home?
Why are you breathless? and why stare you so?
CASCA. Are not you mov'd, when all the sway of earth
Shakes like a thing unfirm? O Cicero!
I have seen tempests, when the scolding winds
Have riv'd the knotty oaks; and I have seen
The ambitious ocean swell and rage and foam,
To be exalted with the threat'ning clouds:
But never till to-night, never till now,
Did I go through a tempest dropping fire.
Either there is a civil strife in heaven,
Or else the world, too saucy with the gods,
Incenses them to send destruction.
CICERO. Why, saw you any thing more wonderful?
CASCA. A common slave—you know him well by sight—
Held up his left hand, which did flame and burn
Like twenty torches join'd; and yet his hand,
Not sensible of fire, remain'd unscorch'd.
Besides,—I have not since put up my sword,—
Against the Capitol I met a lion,
Who glaz'd upon me, and went surly by,
Without annoying me; and there were drawn
Upon a heap a hundred ghastly women,
Transformed with their fear, who swore they saw
Men all in fire walk up and down the streets.
And yesterday the bird of night did sit,
Even at noon-day, upon the market-place,
Hooting and shrieking. When these prodigies
Do so conjointly meet, let not men say
'These are their reasons, they are natural;'

For, I believe, they are portentous things
Unto the climate that they point upon.

CICERO. Indeed, it is a strange-disposed time:
But men may construe things after their fashion,
Clean from the purpose of the things themselves.
Comes Caesar to the Capitol to-morrow?

CASCA. He doth; for he did bid Antonius
Send word to you he would be there to-morrow.

CICERO. Good-night then, Casca: this disturbed sky
Is not to walk in.

CASCA.   Farewell, Cicero.   [*Exit* CICERO.

    Enter CASSIUS.

CASSIUS. Who's there?

CASCA.   A Roman.

CASSIUS.   Casca, by your voice.

CASCA. Your ear is good. Cassius, what night is this!

CASSIUS. A very pleasing night to honest men.

CASCA. Who ever knew the heavens menace so?

CASSIUS. Those that have known the earth so full of faults.
For my part, I have walk'd about the streets,
Submitting me unto the perilous night,
And, thus unbraced, Casca, as you see,
Have bar'd my bosom to the thunder-stone;
And, when the cross blue lightning seem'd to open
The breast of heaven, I did present myself
Even in the aim and very flash of it.

CASCA. But wherefore did you so much tempt the heavens?
It is the part of men to fear and tremble
When the most mighty gods by tokens send
Such dreadful heralds to astonish us.

CASSIUS. You are dull, Casca, and those sparks of life
That should be in a Roman you do want,
Or else you use not. You look pale, and gaze,
And put on fear, and cast yourself in wonder,

To see the strange impatience of the heavens;
But if you would consider the true cause
Why all these fires, why all these gliding ghosts,
Why birds and beasts, from quality and kind—
Why old men, fools, and children calculate;
Why all these things change from their ordinance,
Their natures, and pre-formed faculties,
To monstrous quality, why, you shall find
That heaven hath infus'd them with these spirits
To make them instruments of fear and warning
Unto some monstrous state.
Now could I, Casca, name to thee a man
Most like this dreadful night,
That thunders, lightens, opens graves, and roars
As doth the lion in the Capitol,
A man no mightier than thyself or me
In personal action, yet prodigious grown
And fearful as these strange eruptions are.

    CASCA. 'Tis Caesar that you mean; is it not, Cassius?

    CASSIUS. Let it be who it is: for Romans now
Have thews and limbs like to their ancestors;
But, woe the while! our fathers' minds are dead,
And we are govern'd with our mothers' spirits;
Our yoke and sufferance show us womanish.

    CASCA. Indeed, they say the senators to-morrow
Mean to establish Caesar as a king;
And he shall wear his crown by sea and land,
In every place, save here in Italy.

    CASSIUS. I know where I will wear this dagger then;
Cassius from bondage will deliver Cassius:
Therein, ye gods, you make the weak most strong;
Therein, ye gods, you tyrants do defeat:
Nor stony tower, nor walls of beaten brass,
Nor airless dungeon, nor strong links of iron,
Can be retentive to the strength of spirit;

But life, being weary of those worldly bars,
Never lacks power to dismiss itself.
If I know this, know all the world besides,
That part of tyranny that I do bear
I can shake off at pleasure. [*Thunder still.*

    CASCA. So can I:
So every bondman in his own hand bears
The power to cancel his captivity.

    CASSIUS. And why should Caesar be a tyrant then?
Poor man! I know he would not be a wolf
But that he sees the Romans are but sheep;
He were no lion were not Romans hinds.
Those that with haste will make a mighty fire
Begin it with weak straws; what trash is Rome,
What rubbish, and what offal, when it serves
For the base matter to illuminate
So vile a thing as Caesar! But, O grief!
Where hast thou led me? I, perhaps, speak this
Before a willing bondman; then I know
My answer must be made: but I am arm'd,
And dangers are to me indifferent.

    CASCA. You speak to Casca, and to such a man
That is no fleering tell-tale. Hold, my hand:
Be factious for redress of all these griefs,
And I will set this foot of mine as far
As who goes furthest.

    CASSIUS. There's a bargain made.
Now know you, Casca, I have mov'd already
Some certain of the noblest-minded Romans
To undergo with me an enterprise
Of honourable-dangerous consequence;
And I do know by this they stay for me
In Pompey's porch: for now, this fearful night,
There is no stir, or walking in the streets;
And the complexion of the element

In favour's like the work we have in hand,
Most bloody, fiery, and most terrible.

CASCA. Stand close awhile, for here comes one in haste.

CASSIUS. 'Tis Cinna; I do know him by his gait:
He is a friend.

Enter CINNA.

Cinna, where haste you so?

CINNA. To find out you. Who's that? Metellus Cimber?

CASSIUS. No, it is Casca; one incorporate
To our attempts. Am I not stay'd for, Cinna?

CINNA. I am glad on 't. What a fearful night is this!
There's two or three of us have seen strange sights.

CASSIUS. Am I not stay'd for? Tell me.

CINNA.   Yes, you are.
O Cassius! if you could
But win the noble Brutus to our party—

CASSIUS. Be you content. Good Cinna, take this paper,
And look you lay it in the praetor's chair,
Where Brutus may but find it; and throw this
In at his window; set this up with wax
Upon old Brutus' statue: all this done,
Repair to Pompey's porch, where you shall find us.
Is Decius Brutus and Trebonius there?

CINNA. All but Metellus Cimber; and he's gone
To see you at your house. Well, I will hie,
And so bestow these papers as you bade me.

CASSIUS. That done, repair to Pompey's theatre. [*Exit* CINNA.
Come, Casca, you and I will yet ere day
See Brutus at his house: three parts of him
Is ours already, and the man entire
Upon the next encounter yields him ours.

CASCA. O! he sits high in all the people's hearts:
And that which would appear offence in us,
His countenance, like richest alchemy,
Will change to virtue and to worthiness.

CASSIUS. Him and his worth and our great need of him
You have right well conceited. Let us go,
For it is after midnight; and ere day
We will awake him and be sure of him.   [*Exeunt.*

Act 2

Scene I.   Rome.   Brutus' Orchard

Enter BRUTUS.

BRUTUS. What, Lucius! ho!
I cannot, by the progress of the stars,
Give guess how near to day. Lucius, I say!
I would it were my fault to sleep so soundly.
When, Lucius, when! Awake, I say! what, Lucius!

Enter LUCIUS.

LUCIUS. Call'd you, my lord?
BRUTUS. Get me a taper in my study, Lucius:
When it is lighted, come and call me here.
LUCIUS. I will, my lord.   [*Exit.*
BRUTUS. It must be by his death: and, for my part,
I know no personal cause to spurn at him,
But for the general. He would be crown'd:
How that might change his nature, there's the question:
It is the bright day that brings forth the adder;
And that craves wary walking. Crown him?—that!
And then, I grant, we put a sting in him,
That at his will he may do danger with.
The abuse of greatness is when it disjoins
Remorse from power; and, to speak truth of Caesar,
I have not known when his affections sway'd
More than his reason. But 'tis a common proof,

28

That lowliness is young ambition's ladder,
Whereto the climber-upward turns his face;
But when he once attains the upmost round,
He then unto the ladder turns his back,
Looks in the clouds, scorning the base degrees
By which he did ascend. So Caesar may:
Then, lest he may, prevent. And, since the quarrel
Will bear no colour for the thing he is,
Fashion it thus; that what he is, augmented,
Would run to these and these extremities;
And therefore think him as a serpent's egg
Which, hatch'd, would, as his kind, grow mischievous,
And kill him in the shell.

> *Re-enter* LUCIUS.

LUCIUS. The taper burneth in your closet, sir.
Searching the window for a flint, I found
This paper, thus seal'd up; and I am sure
It did not lie there when I went to bed.
BRUTUS. Get you to bed again; it is not day.
Is not to-morrow, boy, the ides of March?
LUCIUS. I know not, sir.
BRUTUS. Look in the calendar, and bring me word.
LUCIUS. I will, sir.   [*Exit.*
BRUTUS. The exhalations whizzing in the air
Give so much light that I may read by them.   [*Opens the letter.*
Brutus, thou sleep'st: awake and see thyself.
Shall Rome, &c. Speak, strike, redress!
Brutus, thou sleep'st: awake!
Such instigations have been often dropp'd
Where I have took them up.
'Shall Rome, &c.' Thus must I piece it out:
Shall Rome stand under one man's awe? What, Rome?
My ancestors did from the streets of Rome
The Tarquin drive, when he was call'd a king.
'Speak, strike, redress!' Am I entreated

To speak, and strike? O Rome! I make thee promise;
If the redress will follow, thou receiv'st
Thy full petition at the hand of Brutus!

Re-enter LUCIUS.

LUCIUS. Sir, March is wasted fifteen days.   [*Knocking within.*
BRUTUS. 'Tis good. Go to the gate: somebody knocks.

[*Exit* LUCIUS.

Since Cassius first did whet me against Caesar,
I have not slept.
Between the acting of a dreadful thing
And the first motion, all the interim is
Like a phantasma, or a hideous dream:
The genius and the mortal instruments
Are then in council; and the state of man,
Like to a little kingdom, suffers then
The nature of an insurrection.

Re-enter LUCIUS.

LUCIUS. Sir, 'tis your brother Cassius at the door,
Who doth desire to see you.
BRUTUS.   Is he alone?
LUCIUS. No, sir, there are moe with him.
BRUTUS.   Do you know them?
LUCIUS. No, sir; their hats are pluck'd about their ears,
And half their faces buried in their cloaks,
That by no means I may discover them
By any mark of favour.
BRUTUS.   Let 'em enter.

[*Exit* LUCIUS.

They are the faction. O conspiracy!
Sham'st thou to show thy dangerous brow by night,
When evils are most free? O! then by day
Where wilt thou find a cavern dark enough
To mask thy monstrous visage? Seek none, conspiracy;
Hide it in smiles and affability:

For if thou path, thy native semblance on,
Not Erebus itself were dim enough
To hide thee from prevention.

Enter the Conspirators, CASSIUS, CASCA, DECIUS, CINNA,
METELLUS CIMBER *and* TREBONIUS.

CASSIUS. I think we are too bold upon your rest:
Good morrow, Brutus; do we trouble you?
BRUTUS. I have been up this hour, awake all night.
Know I these men that come along with you?
CASSIUS. Yes, every man of them; and no man here
But honours you; and every one doth wish
You had but that opinion of yourself
Which every noble Roman bears of you.
This is Trebonius.
BRUTUS.   He is welcome hither.
CASSIUS. This, Decius Brutus.
BRUTUS.   He is welcome too.
CASSIUS. This, Casca; this, Cinna;
And this, Metellus Cimber.
BRUTUS.   They are all welcome.
What watchful cares do interpose themselves
Betwixt your eyes and night?
CASSIUS. Shall I entreat a word?   [BRUTUS *and* CASSIUS *whisper.*
DECIUS. Here lies the east: doth not the day break here?
CASCA. No.
CINNA. O! pardon, sir, it doth; and yon grey lines
That fret the clouds are messengers of day.
CASCA. You shall confess that you are both deceiv'd.
Here, as I point my sword, the sun arises;
Which is a great way growing on the south,
Weighing the youthful season of the year.
Some two months hence up higher toward the north
He first presents his fire; and the high east
Stands, as the Capitol, directly here.
BRUTUS. Give me your hands all over, one by one.

CASSIUS. And let us swear our resolution.

BRUTUS. No, not an oath: if not the face of men,
The sufferance of our souls, the time's abuse,
If these be motives weak, break off betimes,
And every man hence to his idle bed;
So let high-sighted tyranny range on,
Till each man drop by lottery. But if these,
As I am sure they do, bear fire enough
To kindle cowards and to steel with valour
The melting spirits of women, then, countrymen,
What need we any spur but our own cause
To prick us to redress? what other bond
Than secret Romans, that have spoke the word
And will not palter? and what other oath
Than honesty to honesty engag'd,
That this shall be, or we will fall for it?
Swear priests and cowards and men cautelous,
Old feeble carrions and such suffering souls
That welcome wrongs; unto bad causes swear
Such creatures as men doubt; but do not stain
The even virtue of our enterprise,
Nor th' insuppressive mettle of our spirits,
To think that or our cause or our performance
Did need an oath; when every drop of blood
That every Roman bears, and nobly bears,
Is guilty of a several bastardy,
If he do break the smallest particle
Of any promise that hath pass'd from him.

CASSIUS. But what of Cicero? Shall we sound him?
I think he will stand very strong with us.

CASCA. Let us not leave him out.

CINNA.   No, by no means.

METELLUS. O! let us have him; for his silver hairs
Will purchase us a good opinion
And buy men's voices to commend our deeds:
It shall be said his judgment rul'd our hands;

Our youths and wildness shall no whit appear,
But all be buried in his gravity.
   BRUTUS. O! name him not: let us not break with him;
For he will never follow any thing
That other men begin.
      CASSIUS.   Then leave him out.
      CASCA. Indeed he is not fit.
      DECIUS. Shall no man else be touch'd but only Caesar?
      CASSIUS. Decius, well urg'd. I think it is not meet,
Mark Antony, so well belov'd of Caesar,
Should outlive Caesar: we shall find of him
A shrewd contriver; and, you know, his means,
If he improve them, may well stretch so far
As to annoy us all; which to prevent,
Let Antony and Caesar fall together.
   BRUTUS. Our course will seem too bloody, Caius Cassius,
To cut the head off and then hack the limbs,
Like wrath in death and envy afterwards;
For Antony is but a limb of Caesar.
Let us be sacrificers, but not butchers, Caius.
We all stand up against the spirit of Caesar;
And in the spirit of men there is no blood:
O! then that we could come by Caesar's spirit,
And not dismember Caesar. But, alas!
Caesar must bleed for it. And, gentle friends,
Let's kill him boldly, but not wrathfully;
Let's carve him as a dish fit for the gods,
Not hew him as a carcass fit for hounds:
And let our hearts, as subtle masters do,
Stir up their servants to an act of rage,
And after seem to chide 'em. This shall make
Our purpose necessary and not envious;
Which so appearing to the common eyes,
We shall be call'd purgers, not murderers.
And, for Mark Antony, think not of him;
For he can do no more than Caesar's arm

When Caesar's head is off.

CASSIUS.   Yet I fear him;
For in the engrafted love he bears to Caesar—

BRUTUS. Alas! good Cassius, do not think of him:
If he love Caesar, all that he can do
Is to himself, take thought and die for Caesar:
And that were much he should; for he is given
To sports, to wildness, and much company.

TREBONIUS. There is no fear in him; let him not die:
For he will live, and laugh at this hereafter.   [Clock strikes.

BRUTUS. Peace! count the clock.

CASSIUS.   The clock hath stricken three.

TREBONIUS. 'Tis time to part.

CASSIUS.   But it is doubtful yet
Whether Caesar will come forth to-day or no;
For he is superstitious grown of late,
Quite from the main opinion he held once
Of fantasy, of dreams, and ceremonies.
It may be, these apparent prodigies,
The unaccustom'd terror of this night,
And the persuasion of his augurers,
May hold him from the Capitol to-day.

DECIUS. Never fear that: if he be so resolv'd,
I can o'ersway him; for he loves to hear
That unicorns may be betray'd with trees,
And bears with glasses, elephants with holes,
Lions with toils, and men with flatterers;
But when I tell him he hates flatterers,
He says he does, being then most flattered.
Let me work;
For I can give his humour the true bent,
And I will bring him to the Capitol.

CASSIUS. Nay, we will all of us be there to fetch him.

BRUTUS. By the eighth hour: is that the uttermost?

CINNA. Be that the uttermost, and fail not then.

METELLUS. Caius Ligarius doth bear Caesar hard,

Who rated him for speaking well of Pompey:
I wonder none of you have thought of him.

BRUTUS. Now, good Metellus, go along by him:
He loves me well, and I have given him reasons;
Send him but hither, and I'll fashion him.

CASSIUS. The morning comes upon's; we'll leave you, Brutus.
And, friends, disperse yourselves; but all remember
What you have said, and show yourselves true Romans.

BRUTUS. Good Gentlemen, look fresh and merrily;
Let not our looks put on our purposes,
But bear it as our Roman actors do,
With untir'd spirits and formal constancy:
And so good morrow to you every one.

         [Exeunt all except BRUTUS.

Boy! Lucius! Fast asleep? It is no matter;
Enjoy the honey-heavy dew of slumber:
Thou hast no figures nor no fantasies
Which busy care draws in the brains of men;
Therefore thou sleep'st so sound.

  Enter PORTIA.

PORTIA.   Brutus, my lord!

BRUTUS. Portia, what mean you? Wherefore rise you now?
It is not for your health thus to commit
Your weak condition to the raw cold morning.

PORTIA. Nor for yours neither. You've ungently, Brutus,
Stole from my bed; and yesternight at supper
You suddenly arose, and walk'd about,
Musing and sighing, with your arms across,
And when I ask'd you what the matter was,
You star'd upon me with ungentle looks.
I urg'd you further; then you scratch'd your head,
And too impatiently stamp'd with your foot;
Yet I insisted, yet you answer'd not,
But, with an angry wafture of your hand,
Gave sign for me to leave you. So I did,

Fearing to strengthen that impatience
Which seem'd too much enkindled, and withal
Hoping it was but an effect of humour,
Which sometime hath his hour with every man.
It will not let you eat, nor talk, nor sleep,
And could it work so much upon your shape
As it hath much prevail'd on your condition,
I should not know you, Brutus. Dear my lord,
Make me acquainted with your cause of grief.

   BRUTUS. I am not well in health, and that is all.

   PORTIA. Brutus is wise, and were he not in health,
He would embrace the means to come by it.

   BRUTUS. Why, so I do. Good Portia, go to bed.

   PORTIA. Is Brutus sick, and is it physical
To walk unbraced and suck up the humours
Of the dank morning? What! is Brutus sick,
And will he steal out of his wholesome bed
To dare the vile contagion of the night,
And tempt the rheumy and unpurged air
To add unto his sickness? No, my Brutus;
You have some sick offence within your mind,
Which, by the right and virtue of my place,
I ought to know of; and, upon my knees,
I charm you, by my once-commended beauty,
By all your vows of love, and that great vow
Which did incorporate and make us one,
That you unfold to me, your self, your half,
Why you are heavy, and what men to-night
Have had resort to you; for here have been
Some six or seven, who did hide their faces
Even from darkness.

   BRUTUS.   Kneel not, gentle Portia.

   PORTIA. I should not need, if you were gentle Brutus.
Within the bond of marriage, tell me, Brutus,
Is it excepted, I should know no secrets

That appertain to you? Am I yourself
But, as it were, in sort or limitation,
To keep with you at meals, comfort your bed,
And talk to you sometimes? Dwell I but in the suburbs
Of your good pleasure? If it be no more,
Portia is Brutus' harlot, not his wife.

 BRUTUS. You are my true and honourable wife,
As dear to me as are the ruddy drops
That visit my sad heart.

 PORTIA. If this were true then should I know this secret.
I grant I am a woman, but, withal,
A woman that Lord Brutus took to wife;
I grant I am a woman, but, withal,
A woman well-reputed, Cato's daughter.
Think you I am no stronger than my sex,
Being so father'd and so husbanded?
Tell me your counsels, I will not disclose 'em.
I have made strong proof of my constancy,
Giving myself a voluntary wound
Here, in the thigh: can I bear that with patience
And not my husband's secrets?

 BRUTUS.   O ye gods!
Render me worthy of this noble wife.   [*Knocking within.*
Hark, hark! one knocks. Portia, go in awhile;
And by and by thy bosom shall partake
The secrets of my heart.
All my engagements I will construe to thee,
All the charactery of my sad brows.
Leave me with haste.   [*Exit* PORTIA.
    Lucius, who's that knocks?

Re-enter LUCIUS *with* LIGARIUS.

 LUCIUS. Here is a sick man that would speak with you.
 BRUTUS. Caius Ligarius, that Metellus spoke of.
Boy, stand aside. Caius Ligarius! how?

LIGARIUS. Vouchsafe good morrow from a feeble tongue.

BRUTUS. O! what a time have you chose out, brave Caius,
To wear a kerchief. Would you were not sick.

LIGARIUS. I am not sick if Brutus have in hand
Any exploit worthy the name of honour.

BRUTUS. Such an exploit have I in hand, Ligarius,
Had you a healthful ear to hear of it.

LIGARIUS. By all the gods that Romans bow before
I here discard my sickness. Soul of Rome!
Brave son, deriv'd from honourable loins!
Thou, like an exorcist, has conjur'd up
My mortified spirit. Now bid me run,
And I will strive with things impossible;
Yea, get the better of them. What's to do?

BRUTUS. A piece of work that will make sick men whole.

LIGARIUS. But are not some whole that we must make sick?

BRUTUS. That must we also. What it is, my Caius,
I shall unfold to thee as we are going
To whom it must be done.

LIGARIUS.   Set on your foot,
And with a heart new-fir'd I follow you,
To do I know not what; but it sufficeth
That Brutus leads me on.

BRUTUS.   Follow me then.   [Exeunt.

Scene II. The Same. Caesar's House

Thunder and lightning. Enter CAESAR *in his night-gown.*

CAESAR. Nor heaven nor earth have been at peace to-night:
Thrice hath Calphurnia in her sleep cried out,
'Help, ho! They murder Caesar!' Who's within?

Enter a SERVANT.

SERVANT. My lord!

CAESAR. Go bid the priests do present sacrifice,

And bring me their opinions of success.

SERVANT. I will, my lord. [*Exit.*

Enter CALPHURNIA.

CALPHURNIA. What mean you, Caesar? Think you to walk
  forth?
You shall not stir out of your house to-day.

CAESAR. Caesar shall forth: the things that threaten'd me
Ne'er look'd but on my back; when they shall see
The face of Caesar, they are vanished.

CALPHURNIA. Caesar, I never stood on ceremonies,
Yet now they fright me. There is one within,
Besides the things that we have heard and seen,
Recounts most horrid sights seen by the watch.
A lioness hath whelped in the streets;
And graves have yawn'd and yielded up their dead;
Fierce fiery warriors fought upon the clouds,
In ranks and squadrons and right form of war,
Which drizzled blood upon the Capitol;
The noise of battle hurtled in the air,
Horses did neigh, and dying men did groan,
And ghosts did shriek and squeal about the streets.
O Caesar! these things are beyond all use,
And I do fear them.

CAESAR.   What can be avoided
Whose end is purpos'd by the mighty gods?
Yet Caesar shall go forth; for these predictions
Are to the world in general as to Caesar.

CALPHURNIA. When beggars die there are no comets seen;
The heavens themselves blaze forth the death of princes.

CAESAR. Cowards die many times before their deaths;
The valiant never taste of death but once.
Of all the wonders that I yet have heard,
It seems to me most strange that men should fear;
Seeing that death, a necessary end,
Will come when it will come.

Re-enter SERVANT.

What say the augurers?

SERVANT. They would not have you to stir forth to-day.
Plucking the entrails of an offering forth,
They could not find a heart within the beast.

CAESAR. The gods do this in shame of cowardice:
Caesar should be a beast without a heart
If he should stay at home to-day for fear.
No, Caesar shall not; danger knows full well
That Caesar is more dangerous than he:
We are two lions litter'd in one day,
And I the elder and more terrible:
And Caesar shall go forth.

CALPHURNIA.　　　　　　Alas! my lord,
Your wisdom is consum'd in confidence.
Do not go forth to-day: call it my fear
That keeps you in the house, and not your own.
We'll send Mark Antony to the senate-house,
And he shall say you are not well to-day:
Let me, upon my knee, prevail in this.

CAESAR. Mark Antony shall say I am not well;
And, for thy humour, I will stay at home.

Enter DECIUS.

Here's Decius Brutus, he shall tell them so.

DECIUS. Caesar, all hail! Good morrow, worthy Caesar:
I come to fetch you to the senate-house.

CAESAR. And you are come in very happy time
To bear my greeting to the senators,
And tell them that I will not come to-day:
Cannot, is false, and that I dare not, falser;
I will not come to-day: tell them so, Decius.

CALPHURNIA. Say he is sick.

CAESAR.　　　　　　　　Shall Caesar send a lie?
Have I in conquest stretch'd mine arm so far

To be afeard to tell greybeards the truth?
Decius, go tell them Caesar will not come.
   DECIUS. Most mighty Caesar, let me know some cause,
Lest I be laugh'd at when I tell them so.
   CAESAR. The cause is in my will: I will not come;
That is enough to satisfy the senate:
But for your private satisfaction,
Because I love you, I will let you know:
Calphurnia here, my wife, stays me at home;
She dreamt to-night she saw my statue,
Which, like a fountain with a hundred spouts,
Did run pure blood; and many lusty Romans
Came smiling, and did bathe their hands in it:
And these does she apply for warnings and portents,
And evils imminent; and on her knee
Hath begg'd that I will stay at home to-day.
   DECIUS. This dream is all amiss interpreted;
It was a vision fair and fortunate:
Your statue spouting blood in many pipes,
In which so many smiling Romans bath'd,
Signifies that from you great Rome shall suck
Reviving blood, and that great men shall press
For tinctures, stains, relics, and cognizance.
This by Calphurnia's dream is signified.
   CAESAR. And this way have you well expounded it.
   DECIUS. I have, when you have heard what I can say:
And know it now: the senate have concluded
To give this day a crown to mighty Caesar.
If you shall send them word you will not come,
Their minds may change. Besides, it were a mock
Apt to be render'd, for some one to say
'Break up the senate till another time,
When Caesar's wife shall meet with better dreams.'
If Caesar hide himself, shall they not whisper
'Lo! Caesar is afraid'?
Pardon me, Caesar; for my dear dear love

To your proceeding bids me tell you this,
And reason to my love is liable.

CAESAR. How foolish do your fears seem now, Calphurnia!
I am ashamed I did yield to them.
Give me my robe, for I will go:

Enter PUBLIUS, BRUTUS, LIGARIUS, METELLUS, CASCA, TRE-
BONIUS, *and* CINNA.

And look where Publius is come to fetch me.

PUBLIUS. Good morrow, Caesar.

CAESAR.   Welcome, Publius.
What! Brutus, are you stirr'd so early too?
Good morrow, Casca. Caius Ligarius,
Caesar was ne'er so much your enemy
As that same ague which hath made you lean.
What is't o'clock?

BRUTUS.   Caesar, 'tis strucken eight.

CAESAR. I thank you for your pains and courtesy.

Enter ANTONY.

See! Antony, that revels long o' nights,
Is notwithstanding up. Good morrow, Antony.

ANTONY. So to most noble Caesar.

CAESAR   Bid them prepare within:
I am to blame to be thus waited for.
Now, Cinna; now, Metellus; what, Trebonius!
I have an hour's talk in store for you;
Remember that you call on me to-day:
Be near me, that I may remember you.

TREBONIUS. Caesar, I will:—[*Aside.*] and so near will I be,
That your best friends shall wish I had been further.

CAESAR. Good friends, go in, and taste some wine with me;
And we, like friends, will straightway go together.

BRUTUS. [*Aside.*] That every like is not the same, O Caesar!
The heart of Brutus yearns to think upon.   [*Exeunt.*

Scene III.   The Same. A Street near the Capitol.

Enter ARTEMIDORUS, *reading a paper.*

Caesar, beware of Brutus; take heed of Cassius; come not near Casca; have an eye to Cinna; trust not Trebonius; mark well Metellus Cimber; Decius Brutus loves thee not; thou hast wronged Caius Ligarius. There is but one mind in all these men, and it is bent against Caesar. If thou be'st not immortal, look about you: security gives way to conspiracy. The mighty gods defend thee! Thy lover,

ARTEMIDORUS.

Here will I stand till Caesar pass along,
And as a suitor will I give him this.
My heart laments that virtue cannot live
Out of the teeth of emulation.
If thou read this, O Caesar! thou mayst live;
If not, the Fates with traitors do contrive.   [*Exit.*

Scene IV.   The Same. Another Part of the same Street, before the House of Brutus

Enter PORTIA *and* LUCIUS.

PORTIA. I prithee, boy, run to the senate-house;
Stay not to answer me, but get thee gone.
Why dost thou stay?

LUCIUS.   To know my errand, madam.

PORTIA. I would have had thee there, and here again,
Ere I can tell thee what thou shouldst do there.
O constancy! be strong upon my side;
Set a huge mountain 'tween my heart and tongue;
I have a man's mind, but a woman's might.
How hard it is for women to keep counsel!
Art thou here yet?

LUCIUS.   Madam, what shall I do?

Run to the Capitol, and nothing else?
And so return to you, and nothing else?
 PORTIA. Yes, bring me word, boy, if thy lord look well,
For he went sickly forth; and take good note
What Caesar doth, what suitors press to him.
Hark, boy! what noise is that?
 LUCIUS. I hear none, madam.
 PORTIA.   Prithee, listen well:
I heard a bustling rumour, like a fray,
And the wind brings it from the Capitol.
 LUCIUS. Sooth, madam, I hear nothing.

  Enter the SOOTHSAYER.

 PORTIA. Come hither, fellow: which way hast thou been?
 SOOTHSAYER. At mine own house, good lady.
 PORTIA. What is 't o'clock?
 SOOTHSAYER.   About the ninth hour, lady.
 PORTIA. Is Caesar yet gone to the Capitol?
 SOOTHSAYER. Madam, not yet: I go to take my stand,
To see him pass on to the Capitol.
 PORTIA. Thou hast some suit to Caesar, hast thou not?
 SOOTHSAYER. That I have, lady: if it will please Caesar
To be so good to Caesar as to hear me,
I shall beseech him to befriend himself.
 PORTIA. Why, know'st thou any harm's intended towards him?
 SOOTHSAYER. None that I know will be, much that I fear may
  chance.
Good morrow to you. Here the street is narrow;
The throng that follows Caesar at the heels,
Of senators, of praetors, common suitors,
Will crowd a feeble man almost to death:
I'll get me to a place more void, and there
Speak to great Caesar as he comes along.   [*Exit.*
 PORTIA. I must go in. Ay me! how weak a thing
The heart of woman is. O Brutus!
The heavens speed thee in thine enterprise.

Sure, the boy heard me: Brutus hath a suit
That Caesar will not grant. O! I grow faint.
Run, Lucius, and commend me to my lord;
Say I am merry: come to me again,
And bring me word what he doth say to thee.

　　　　　　　　　　　　　[Exeunt, severally.

Act 3

Scene I. Rome. Before the Capitol; the Senate Sitting Above

A crowd of People; among them ARTEMIDORUS *and the* SOOTHSAYER. *Flourish. Enter* CAESAR, BRUTUS, CASSIUS, CASCA, DECIUS, METELLUS, TREBONIUS, CINNA, ANTONY, LEPIDUS, POPILIUS, PUBLIUS, *and Others.*

CAESAR. [*To the* Soothsayer.] The ides of March are come.
SOOTHSAYER. Ay, Caesar; but not gone.
ARTEMIDORUS. Hail, Caesar! Read this schedule.
DECIUS. Trebonius doth desire you to o'er-read,
At your best leisure, this his humble suit.
ARTEMIDORUS. O Caesar! read mine first; for mine's a suit
That touches Caesar nearer. Read it, great Caesar.
CAESAR. What touches us ourself shall be last serv'd.
ARTEMIDORUS. Delay not, Caesar; read it instantly.
CAESAR. What! is the fellow mad?
PUBLIUS.   Sirrah, give place.
CAESAR. What! urge you your petitions in the street?
Come to the Capitol.

> CAESAR *goes up to the Senate-House, the rest following. All the Senators rise.*

POPILIUS. I wish your enterprise to-day may thrive.
CASSIUS. What enterprise, Popilius?
POPILIUS.   Fare you well.
> [*Advances to* CAESAR.

46

BRUTUS. What said Popilius Lena?

CASSIUS. He wish'd to-day our enterprise might thrive. I fear
our purpose is discovered.

BRUTUS. Look, how he makes to Caesar: mark him.

CASSIUS. Casca, be sudden, for we fear prevention.
Brutus, what shall be done? If this be known,
Cassius or Caesar never shall turn back,
For I will slay myself.

BRUTUS.   Cassius, be constant.
Popilius Lena speaks not of our purposes;
For, look, he smiles, and Caesar doth not change.

CASSIUS. Trebonius knows his time; for, look you, Brutus,
He draws Mark Antony out of the way.

[*Exeunt* ANTONY *and* TREBONIUS. CAESAR
and the Senators take their seats.

DECIUS. Where is Metellus Cimber? Let him go,
And presently prefer his suit to Caesar.

BRUTUS. He is address'd; press near and second him.

CINNA. Casca, you are the first that rears your hand.

CAESAR. Are we all ready? What is now amiss,
That Caesar and his senate must redress?

METELLUS. Most high, most mighty, and most puissant Caesar,
Metellus Cimber throws before thy seat
A humble heart,—   [*Kneeling.*

CAESAR.   I must prevent thee, Cimber.
These couchings and these lowly courtesies
Might fire the blood of ordinary men,
And turn pre-ordinance and first decree
Into the law of children. Be not fond
To think that Caesar bears such rebel blood
That will be thaw'd from the true quality
With that which melteth fools; I mean sweet words,
Low-crooked curtsies, and base spaniel fawning.
Thy brother by decree is banished:
If thou dost bend and pray and fawn for him,
I spurn thee like a cur out of my way.

Know, Caesar doth not wrong, nor without cause
Will he be satisfied.

METELLUS. Is there no voice more worthy than my own,
To sound more sweetly in great Caesar's ear
For the repealing of my banish'd brother?

BRUTUS. I kiss thy hand, but not in flattery, Caesar;
Desiring thee, that Publius Cimber may
Have an immediate freedom of repeal

CAESAR. What, Brutus!

CASSIUS.   Pardon, Caesar; Caesar, pardon:
As low as to thy foot doth Cassius fall,
To beg enfranchisement for Publius Cimber.

CAESAR. I could be well mov'd if I were as you;
If I could pray to move, prayers would move me;
But I am constant as the northern star,
Of whose true-fix'd and resting quality
There is no fellow in the firmament.
The skies are painted with unnumber'd sparks,
They are all fire and every one doth shine,
But there's but one in all doth hold his place:
So, in the world; 'tis furnish'd well with men,
And men are flesh and blood, and apprehensive;
Yet in the number I do know but one
That unassailable holds on his rank,
Unshak'd of motion: and that I am he,
Let me a little show it, even in this,
That I was constant Cimber should be banish'd,
And constant do remain to keep him so.

CINNA. O Caesar,—

CAESAR.   Hence! Wilt thou lift up Olympus!

DECIUS. Great Caesar,—

CAESAR.   Doth not Brutus bootless kneel?

CASCA. Speak, hands, for me!   [They stab CAESAR.

CAESAR. Et tu, Brute? Then fall, Caesar!   [Dies.

CINNA. Liberty! Freedom! Tyranny is dead!
Run hence, proclaim, cry it about the streets.

CASSIUS. Some to the common pulpits, and cry out,
'Liberty, freedom, and enfranchisement!'

BRUTUS. People and senators, be not affrighted;
Fly not; stand still; ambition's debt is paid.

CASCA. Go to the pulpit, Brutus.

DECIUS.   And Cassius too.

BRUTUS. Where's Publius?

CINNA. Here, quite confounded with this mutiny.

METELLUS. Stand fast together, lest some friend of Caesar's
Should chance—

BRUTUS. Talk not of standing. Publius, good cheer;
There is no harm intended to your person,
Nor to no Roman else; so tell them, Publius.

CASSIUS. And leave us, Publius; lest that the people,
Rushing on us, should do your age some mischief.

BRUTUS. Do so; and let no man abide this deed
But we the doers.

Re-enter TREBONIUS.

CASSIUS. Where's Antony?

TREBONIUS.   Fled to his house amaz'd.
Men, wives and children stare, cry out and run
As it were doomsday.

BRUTUS.   Fates, we will know your pleasures.
That we shall die, we know; 'tis but the time
And drawing days out, that men stand upon.

CASCA. Why, he that cuts off twenty years of life
Cuts off so many years of fearing death.

BRUTUS. Grant that, and then is death a benefit:
So are we Caesar's friends, that have abridg'd
His time of fearing death. Stoop, Romans, stoop,
And let us bathe our hands in Caesar's blood
Up to the elbows, and besmear our swords:
Then walk we forth, even to the market-place;
And waving our red weapons o'er our heads,

Let's all cry, 'Peace, freedom, and liberty!'

CASSIUS. Stoop, then, and wash. How many ages hence
Shall this our lofty scene be acted o'er,
In states unborn and accents yet unknown!

BRUTUS. How many times shall Caesar bleed in sport,
That now on Pompey's basis lies along
No worthier than the dust!

CASSIUS.   So oft as that shall be,
So often shall the knot of us be call'd
The men that gave their country liberty.

DECIUS. What! shall we forth?

CASSIUS.   Ay, every man away:
Brutus shall lead; and we will grace his heels
With the most boldest and best hearts of Rome.

Enter a SERVANT.

BRUTUS. Soft! who comes here? A friend of Antony's.

SERVANT. Thus, Brutus, did my master bid me kneel;
Thus did Mark Antony bid me fall down;
And, being prostrate, thus he bade me say:
Brutus is noble, wise, valiant, and honest;
Caesar was mighty, bold, royal, and loving:
Say I love Brutus, and I honour him;
Say I fear'd Caesar, honour'd him, and lov'd him.
If Brutus will vouchsafe that Antony
May safely come to him, and be resolv'd
How Caesar hath deserv'd to lie in death,
Mark Antony shall not love Caesar dead
So well as Brutus living; but will follow
The fortunes and affairs of noble Brutus
Thorough the hazards of this untrod state
With all true faith. So says my master Antony.

BRUTUS. Thy master is a wise and valiant Roman;
I never thought him worse.
Tell him, so please him come unto this place,
He shall be satisfied; and, by my honour,

Depart untouch'd.

SERVANT.   I'll fetch him presently.   [*Exit.*

BRUTUS. I know that we shall have him well to friend.

CASSIUS. I wish we may: but yet have I a mind

That fears him much; and my misgiving still

Falls shrewdly to the purpose.

    Re-enter ANTONY.

BRUTUS. But here comes Antony. Welcome, Mark Antony.

ANTONY. O mighty Caesar! dost thou lie so low?

Are all thy conquests, glories, triumphs, spoils,

Shrunk to this little measure? Fare thee well.

I know not, gentlemen, what you intend,

Who else must be let blood, who else is rank:

If I myself, there is no hour so fit

As Caesar's death's hour, nor no instrument

Of half that worth as those your swords, made rich

With the most noble blood of all this world.

I do beseech ye, if ye bear me hard,

Now, whilst your purpled hands do reek and smoke,

Fulfil your pleasure. Live a thousand years,

I shall not find myself so apt to die:

No place will please me so, no mean of death,

As here by Caesar, and by you cut off,

The choice and master spirits of this age.

BRUTUS. O Antony! beg not your death of us.

Though now we must appear bloody and cruel,

As, by our hands and this our present act,

You see we do, yet see you but our hands

And this the bleeding business they have done:

Our hearts you see not; they are pitiful;

And pity to the general wrong of Rome—

As fire drives out fire, so pity pity—

Hath done this deed on Caesar. For your part,

To you our swords have leaden points, Mark Antony;

Our arms, in strength of malice, and our hearts

Of brothers' temper, do receive you in
With all kind love, good thoughts, and reverence.

CASSIUS. Your voice shall be as strong as any man's
In the disposing of new dignities.

BRUTUS. Only be patient till we have appeas'd
The multitude, beside themselves with fear,
And then we will deliver you the cause
Why I, that did love Caesar when I struck him,
Have thus proceeded.

ANTONY.   I doubt not of your wisdom.
Let each man render me his bloody hand:
First, Marcus Brutus, will I shake with you;
Next, Caius Cassius, do I take your hand;
Now, Decius Brutus, yours; now yours, Metellus;
Yours, Cinna; and, my valiant Casca, yours;
Though last, not least in love, yours, good Trebonius.
Gentlemen all,—alas! what shall I say?
My credit now stands on such slippery ground,
That one of two bad ways you must conceit me,
Either a coward or a flatterer.
That I did love thee, Caesar, O! 'tis true:
If then thy spirit look upon us now,
Shall it not grieve thee dearer than thy death,
To see thy Antony making his peace,
Shaking the bloody fingers of thy foes,
Most noble! in the presence of thy corse?
Had I as many eyes as thou hast wounds,
Weeping as fast as they stream forth thy blood,
It would become me better than to close
In terms of friendship with thine enemies.
Pardon me, Julius! Here wast thou bay'd, brave hart;
Here didst thou fall; and here thy hunters stand,
Sign'd in thy spoil, and crimson'd in thy lethe.
O world! thou wast the forest to this hart;
And this, indeed, O world! the heart of thee.

How like a deer, strucken by many princes,
Dost thou here lie!

CASSIUS. Mark Antony,—

ANTONY.   Pardon me, Caius Cassius:
The enemies of Caesar shall say this;
Then, in a friend, it is cold modesty.

CASSIUS. I blame you not for praising Caesar so;
But what compact mean you to have with us?
Will you be prick'd in number of our friends,
Or shall we on, and not depend on you?

ANTONY. Therefore I took your hands, but was indeed
Sway'd from the point by looking down on Caesar.
Friends am I with you all, and love you all,
Upon this hope, that you shall give me reasons
Why and wherein Caesar was dangerous.

BRUTUS. Or else were this a savage spectacle.
Our reasons are so full of good regard
That were you, Antony, the son of Caesar,
You should be satisfied.

ANTONY.   That's all I seek:
And am moreover suitor that I may
Produce his body to the market-place;
And in the pulpit, as becomes a friend,
Speak in the order of his funeral.

BRUTUS. You shall, Mark Antony.

CASSIUS.   Brutus, a word with you.
[*Aside to* BRUTUS.] You know not what you do; do not consent
That Antony speak in his funeral:
Know you how much the people may be mov'd
By that which he will utter?

BRUTUS.   By your pardon;
I will myself into the pulpit first,
And show the reason of our Caesar's death:
What Antony shall speak, I will protest
He speaks by leave and by permission,

And that we are contented Caesar shall
Have all true rites and lawful ceremonies.
It shall advantage more than do us wrong.
    CASSIUS. I know not what may fall; I like it not.
    BRUTUS. Mark Antony, here, take you Caesar's body.
You shall not in your funeral speech blame us,
But speak all good you can devise of Caesar,
And say you do 't by our permission;
Else shall you not have any hand at all
About his funeral; and you shall speak
In the same pulpit whereto I am going,
After my speech is ended.
    ANTONY.   Be it so;
I do desire no more.
    BRUTUS. Prepare the body then, and follow us.
                        [*Exeunt all but* ANTONY.
    ANTONY. O! pardon me, thou bleeding piece of earth,
That I am meek and gentle with these butchers.
Thou art the ruins of the noblest man
That ever lived in the tide of times.
Woe to the hand that shed this costly blood!
Over thy wounds now do I prophesy,
Which like dumb mouths do ope their ruby lips,
To beg the voice and utterance of my tongue,
A curse shall light upon the limbs of men;
Domestic fury and fierce civil strife
Shall cumber all the parts of Italy;
Blood and destruction shall be so in use,
And dreadful objects so familiar,
That mothers shall but smile when they behold
Their infants quarter'd with the hands of war;
All pity chok'd with custom of fell deeds:
And Caesar's spirit, ranging for revenge,
With Ate by his side come hot from hell,
Shall in these confines with a monarch's voice
Cry 'Havoc!' and let slip the dogs of war;

That this foul deed shall smell above the earth
With carrion men, groaning for burial.

Enter a SERVANT.

You serve Octavius Caesar, do you not?
SERVANT. I do, Mark Antony.
ANTONY. Caesar did write for him to come to Rome.
SERVANT. He did receive his letters, and is coming;
And bid me say to you by word of mouth—
          [Seeing the body.
O Caesar!—
ANTONY. Thy heart is big, get thee apart and weep.
Passion, I see, is catching; for mine eyes,
Seeing those beads of sorrow stand in thine,
Began to water. Is thy master coming?
SERVANT. He lies to-night within seven leagues of Rome.
ANTONY. Post back with speed, and tell him what hath
 chanc'd:
Here is a mourning Rome, a dangerous Rome,
No Rome of safety for Octavius yet;
Hie hence and tell him so. Yet, stay awhile;
Thou shalt not back till I have borne this corpse
Into the market-place; there shall I try,
In my oration, how the people take
The cruel issue of these bloody men;
According to the which thou shalt discourse
To young Octavius of the state of things.
Lend me your hand.   *[Exeunt, with* CAESAR'S *body.*

Scene II. *The Same. The Forum*

Enter BRUTUS *and* CASSIUS, *and a throng of* CITIZENS.

CITIZENS. We will be satisfied: let us be satisfied.
BRUTUS. Then follow me, and give me audience, friends.
Cassius, go you into the other street,

And part the numbers.
Those that will hear me speak, let 'em stay here;
Those that will follow Cassius, go with him;
And public reasons shall be rendered
Of Caesar's death.

FIRST CITIZEN.   I will hear Brutus speak.

SECOND CITIZEN. I will hear Cassius; and compare their reasons,

When severally we hear them rendered.

[*Exit* CASSIUS, *with some of the* CITIZENS;
BRUTUS *goes into the pulpit.*

THIRD CITIZEN. The noble Brutus is ascended: silence!

BRUTUS. Be patient till the last.

Romans, countrymen, and lovers! hear me for my cause; and be silent, that you may hear: believe me for mine honour, and have respect to mine honour, that you may believe: censure me in your wisdom, and awake your senses, that you may the better judge. If there be any in this assembly, any dear friend of Caesar's, to him I say, that Brutus' love to Caesar was no less than his. If then that friend demand why Brutus rose against Caesar, this is my answer: Not that I loved Caesar less, but that I loved Rome more. Had you rather Caesar were living, and die all slaves, than that Caesar were dead, to live all free men? As Caesar loved me, I weep for him; as he was fortunate, I rejoice at it; as he was valiant, I honour him; but, as he was ambitious, I slew him. There is tears for his love; joy for his fortune; honour for his valour; and death for his ambition. Who is here so base that would be a bondman? If any, speak; for him have I offended. Who is here so rude that would not be a Roman? If any, speak; for him have I offended. Who is here so vile that will not love his country? If any, speak; for him have I offended. I pause for a reply.

CITIZENS. None, Brutus, none.

BRUTUS. Then none have I offended. I have done no more to Caesar, than you shall do to Brutus. The question of his death is enrolled in the Capitol; his glory not extenuated, wherein he

was worthy, nor his offences enforced, for which he suffered
death.

Enter ANTONY *and Others, with* CAESAR's *body.*

Here comes his body, mourned by Mark Antony: who, though
he had no hand in his death, shall receive the benefit of his
dying, a place in the commonwealth; as which of you shall not?
With this I depart: that, as I slew my best lover for the good of
Rome, I have the same dagger for myself, when it shall please
my country to need my death.

    CITIZENS. Live, Brutus! live! live!

    FIRST CITIZEN. Bring him with triumph home unto his house.

    SECOND CITIZEN. Give him a statue with his ancestors.

    THIRD CITIZEN. Let him be Caesar.

    FOURTH CITIZEN.   Caesar's better parts
Shall be crown'd in Brutus.

    FIRST CITIZEN. We'll bring him to his house with shouts and
    clamours.

    BRUTUS. My countrymen,—

    SECOND CITIZEN.   Peace! silence! Brutus speaks.

    FIRST CITIZEN. Peace, ho!

    BRUTUS. Good countrymen, let me depart alone,
And, for my sake, stay here with Antony.
Do grace to Caesar's corpse, and grace his speech
Tending to Caesar's glories, which Mark Antony,
By our permission, is allow'd to make.
I do entreat you, not a man depart,
Save I alone, till Antony have spoke.   *[Exit.*

    FIRST CITIZEN. Stay, ho! and let us hear Mark Antony.

    THIRD CITIZEN. Let him go up into the public chair;
We'll hear him. Noble Antony, go up.

    ANTONY. For Brutus' sake, I am beholding to you.

                           [Goes up.

    FOURTH CITIZEN. What does he say of Brutus?

    THIRD CITIZEN.   He says, for Brutus' sake,
He finds himself beholding to us all.

FOURTH CITIZEN. 'Twere best he speak no harm of Brutus here.

FIRST CITIZEN. This Caesar was a tyrant.

THIRD CITIZEN.   Nay, that's certain:
We are bless'd that Rome is rid of him.

SECOND CITIZEN. Peace! let us hear what Antony can say.

ANTONY. You gentle Romans,—

CITIZENS.   Peace, ho! let us hear him.

ANTONY. Friends, Romans, countrymen, lend me your ears;
I come to bury Caesar, not to praise him.
The evil that men do lives after them,
The good is oft interred with their bones;
So let it be with Caesar. The noble Brutus
Hath told you Caesar was ambitious;
If it were so, it was a grievous fault,
And grievously hath Caesar answer'd it.
Here, under leave of Brutus and the rest,—
For Brutus is an honourable man;
So are they all, all honourable men,—
Come I to speak in Caesar's funeral.
He was my friend, faithful and just to me:
But Brutus says he was ambitious;
And Brutus is an honourable man.
He hath brought many captives home to Rome,
Whose ransoms did the general coffers fill:
Did this in Caesar seem ambitious?
When that the poor have cried, Caesar hath wept;
Ambition should be made of sterner stuff:
Yet Brutus says he was ambitious;
And Brutus is an honourable man.
You all did see that on the Lupecal
I thrice presented him a kingly crown,
Which he did thrice refuse: was this ambition?
Yet Brutus says he was ambitious;
And, sure, he is an honourable man.
I speak not to disprove what Brutus spoke,
But here I am to speak what I do know.

You all did love him once, not without cause:
What cause withholds you then to mourn for him?
O judgment! thou art fled to brutish beasts,
And men have lost their reason. Bear with me;
My heart is in the coffin there with Caesar,
And I must pause till it come back to me.

FIRST CITIZEN. Methinks there is much reason in his sayings.

SECOND CITIZEN. If thou consider rightly of the matter,
Caesar has had great wrong.

THIRD CITIZEN.   Has he, masters?
I fear there will a worse come in his place.

FOURTH CITIZEN. Mark'd ye his words? He would not take the
    crown;
Therefore 'tis certain he was not ambitious.

FIRST CITIZEN. If it be found so, some will dear abide it.

SECOND CITIZEN. Poor soul! his eyes are red as fire with weep-
    ing.

THIRD CITIZEN. There's not a nobler man in Rome than An-
    tony.

FOURTH CITIZEN. Now mark him; he begins again to speak.

ANTONY. But yesterday the word of Caesar might
Have stood against the world; now lies he there,
And none so poor to do him reverence.
O masters! if I were dispos'd to stir
Your hearts and minds to mutiny and rage,
I should do Brutus wrong, and Cassius wrong,
Who, you all know, are honourable men.
I will not do them wrong; I rather choose
To wrong the dead, to wrong myself, and you,
Than I will wrong such honourable men.
But here's a parchment with the seal of Caesar;
I found it in his closet, 'tis his will.
Let but the commons hear this testament—
Which, pardon me, I do not mean to read—
And they would go and kiss dead Caesar's wounds,
And dip their napkins in his sacred blood,

Yea, beg a hair of him for memory,
And, dying, mention it within their wills,
Bequeathing it as a rich legacy
Unto their issue.

FOURTH CITIZEN. We'll hear the will: read it, Mark Antony.

CITIZENS. The will, the will! we will hear Caesar's will.

ANTONY. Have patience, gentle friends; I must not read it:
It is not meet you know how Caesar lov'd you.
You are not wood, you are not stones, but men;
And, being men, hearing the will of Caesar,
It will inflame you, it will make you mad.
'Tis good you know not that you are his heirs;
For if you should, O! what would come of it?

FOURTH CITIZEN. Read the will, we'll hear it, Antony;
You shall read us the will, Caesar's will.

ANTONY. Will you be patient? Will you stay awhile?
I have o'ershot myself to tell you of it.
I fear I wrong the honourable men
Whose daggers have stabb'd Caesar; I do fear it.

FOURTH CITIZEN. They were traitors: honourable men!

CITIZENS. The will! the testament!

SECOND CITIZEN. They were villains, murderers. The will! read
the will.

ANTONY. You will compel me then to read the will?
Then make a ring about the corpse of Caesar,
And let me show you him that made the will.
Shall I descend? and will you give me leave?

CITIZENS. Come down.

SECOND CITIZEN. Descend. [ANTONY comes down.

THIRD CITIZEN. You shall have leave.

FOURTH CITIZEN. A ring; stand round.

FIRST CITIZEN. Stand from the hearse; stand from the body.

SECOND CITIZEN. Room for Antony; most noble Antony.

ANTONY. Nay, press not so upon me; stand far off.

CITIZENS. Stand back! room! bear back!

ANTONY. If you have tears, prepare to shed them now.

You all do know this mantle: I remember
The first time ever Caesar put it on;
'Twas on a summer's evening, in his tent,
That day he overcame the Nervii.
Look! in this place ran Cassius' dagger through:
See what a rent the envious Casca made:
Through this the well-beloved Brutus stabb'd;
And, as he pluck'd his cursed steel away,
Mark how the blood of Caesar follow'd it,
As rushing out of doors, to be resolv'd
If Brutus so unkindly knock'd or no;
For Brutus, as you know, was Caesar's angel:
Judge, O you gods! how dearly Caesar lov'd him.
This was the most unkindest cut of all;
For when the noble Caesar saw him stab,
Ingratitude, more strong than traitors' arms,
Quite vanquish'd him: then burst his mighty heart;
And, in his mantle muffling up his face,
Even at the base of Pompey's statuë,
Which all the while ran blood, great Caesar fell.
O! what a fall was there, my countrymen;
Then I, and you, and all of us fell down,
Whilst bloody treason flourish'd over us.
O! now you weep, and I perceive you feel
The dint of pity; these are gracious drops.
Kind souls, what! weep you when you but behold
Our Caesar's vesture wounded? Look you here,
Here is himself, marr'd, as you see, with traitors.
    FIRST CITIZEN. O piteous spectacle!
    SECOND CITIZEN. O noble Caesar!
    THIRD CITIZEN. O woeful day!
    FOURTH CITIZEN. O traitors! villains!
    FIRST CITIZEN. O most bloody sight!
    SECOND CITIZEN. We will be revenged.
    CITIZENS. Revenge!—About!—Seek!—Burn!
Fire!—Kill!—Slay! Let not a traitor live.

ANTONY. Stay, countrymen!

FIRST CITIZEN. Peace there! Hear the noble Antony.

SECOND CITIZEN. We'll hear him, we'll follow him, we'll die
with him.

ANTONY. Good friends, sweet friends, let me not stir you up
To such a sudden flood of mutiny.
They that have done this deed are honourable:
What private griefs they have, alas! I know not,
That made them do it; they are wise and honourable,
And will, no doubt, with reasons answer you.
I come not, friends, to steal away your hearts:
I am no orator, as Brutus is;
But, as you know me all, a plain blunt man,
That love my friend; and that they know full well
That gave me public leave to speak of him.
For I have neither wit, nor words, nor worth,
Action, nor utterance, nor the power of speech,
To stir men's blood: I only speak right on;
I tell you that which you yourselves do know,
Show you sweet Caesar's wounds, poor poor dumb mouths,
And bid them speak for me: but were I Brutus,
And Brutus Antony, there were an Antony
Would ruffle up your spirits, and put a tongue
In every wound of Casear, that should move
The stones of Rome to rise and mutiny.

CITIZENS. We'll mutiny.

FIRST CITIZEN. We'll burn the house of Brutus.

THIRD CITIZEN. Away, then! come, seek the conspirators.

ANTONY. Yet hear me, countrymen; yet hear me speak.

CITIZENS. Peace, ho!—Hear Antony,—most noble Antony.

ANTONY. Why, friends, you go to do you know not what.
Wherein hath Caesar thus deserv'd your loves?
Alas! you know not: I must tell you then.
You have forgot the will I told you of.

CITIZENS. Most true. The will! let's stay and hear the will.

ANTONY. Here is the will, and under Caesar's seal.

To every Roman citizen he gives,
To every several man, seventy-five drachmas.
SECOND CITIZEN. Most noble Caesar! we'll revenge his death.
THIRD CITIZEN. O royal Caesar!
ANTONY. Hear me with patience.
CITIZENS. Peace, ho!
ANTONY. Moreover, he hath left you all his walks,
His private arbours, and new-planted orchards,
On this side Tiber; he hath left them you,
And to your heirs for ever; common pleasures,
To walk abroad, and recreate yourselves.
Here was a Caesar! when comes such another?
FIRST CITIZEN. Never, never! Come, away, away!
We'll burn his body in the holy place,
And with the brands fire the traitors' houses.
Take up the body.
SECOND CITIZEN. Go fetch fire.
THIRD CITIZEN. Pluck down benches.
FOURTH CITIZEN. Pluck down forms, windows, any thing.
                              [*Exeunt* CITIZENS, *with the body.*
ANTONY. Now let it work: mischief, thou art afoot,
Take thou what course thou wilt!

  Enter a SERVANT.

                              How now, fellow!
SERVANT. Sir, Octavius is already come to Rome.
ANTONY. Where is he?
SERVANT. He and Lepidus are at Caesar's house.
ANTONY. And thither will I straight to visit him.
He comes upon a wish. Fortune is merry,
And in this mood will give us any thing.
SERVANT. I heard him say Brutus and Cassius
Are rid like madmen through the gates of Rome.
ANTONY. Belike they had some notice of the people,
How I had mov'd them. Bring me to Octavius.
                                        [*Exeunt.*

Scene III. The Same. A Street

Enter CINNA, *the Poet.*

CINNA. I dreamt to-night that I did feast with Caesar,
And things unlucky charge my fantasy:
I have no will to wander forth of doors,
Yet something leads me forth.

Enter CITIZENS.

FIRST CITIZEN. What is your name?
SECOND CITIZEN. Whither are you going?
THIRD CITIZEN. Where do you dwell?
FOURTH CITIZEN. Are you a married man, or a bachelor?
SECOND CITIZEN. Answer every man directly.
FIRST CITIZEN. Ay, and briefly.
FOURTH CITIZEN. Ay, and wisely.
THIRD CITIZEN. Ay, and truly, you were best.
CINNA. What is my name? Whither am I going? Where do
I dwell? Am I a married man, or a bachelor? Then, to answer
every man directly and briefly, wisely and truly: wisely I say, I
am a bachelor.
SECOND CITIZEN. That's as much as to say, they are fools that
marry; you'll bear me a bang for that, I fear. Proceed; directly.
CINNA. Directly, I am going to Caesar's funeral.
FIRST CITIZEN. As a friend or an enemy?
CINNA. As a friend.
SECOND CITIZEN. That matter is answered directly.
FOURTH CITIZEN. For your dwelling, briefly.
CINNA. Briefly, I dwell by the Capitol.
THIRD CITIZEN. Your name, sir, truly.
CINNA. Truly, my name is Cinna.
SECOND CITIZEN. Tear him to pieces; he's a conspirator.
CINNA. I am Cinna the poet, I am Cinna the poet.
FOURTH CITIZEN. Tear him for his bad verses, tear him for his
bad verses.

CINNA. I am not Cinna the conspirator.

SECOND CITIZEN. It is no matter, his name's Cinna; pluck but his name out of his heart, and turn him going.

THIRD CITIZEN. Tear him, tear him! Come, brands, ho! fire-brands! To Brutus', to Cassius'; burn all. Some to Decius' house, and some to Casca's; some to Ligarius'. Away! go!   [*Exeunt.*

Act 4

Scene I.   Rome. A Room in Antony's House

ANTONY, OCTAVIUS, *and* LEPIDUS, *seated at a table.*

ANTONY. These many then shall die; their names are prick'd.
OCTAVIUS. Your brother too must die; consent you, Lepidus?
LEPIDUS. I do consent.
OCTAVIUS.   Prick him down, Antony.
LEPIDUS. Upon condition Publius shall not live,
Who is your sister's son, Mark Antony.
ANTONY. He shall not live; look, with a spot I damn him.
But, Lepidus, go you to Caesar's house;
Fetch the will hither, and we shall determine
How to cut off some charge in legacies.
LEPIDUS. What! shall I find you here?
OCTAVIUS. Or here or at the Capitol.   [*Exit* LEPIDUS.
ANTONY. This is a slight unmeritable man,
Meet to be sent on errands: is it fit,
The three-fold world divided, he should stand
One of the three to share it?
OCTAVIUS.   So you thought him;
And took his voice who should be prick'd to die,
In our black sentence and proscription.
ANTONY. Octavius, I have seen more days than you:
And though we lay these honours on this man,
To ease ourselves of divers slanderous loads,
He shall but bear them as the ass bears gold,
To groan and sweat under the business,
Either led or driven, as we point the way;

And having brought our treasure where we will,
Then take we down his load, and turn him off,
Like to the empty ass, to shake his ears,
And graze in commons.

OCTAVIUS. You may do your will;
But he's a tried and valiant soldier.

ANTONY. So is my horse, Octavius; and for that
I do appoint him store of provender.
It is a creature that I teach to fight,
To wind, to stop, to run directly on,
His corporal motion govern'd by my spirit.
And, in some taste, is Lepidus but so;
He must be taught, and train'd, and bid go forth;
A barren-spirited fellow; one that feeds
On abject orts, and imitations,
Which, out of use and stal'd by other men,
Begin his fashion: do not talk of him
But as a property. And now, Octavius,
Listen great things: Brutus and Cassius
Are levying powers; we must straight make head;
Therefore let our alliance be combin'd,
Our best friends made, and our means stretch'd;
And let us presently go sit in council,
How covert matters may be best disclos'd,
And open perils surest answered.

OCTAVIUS. Let us do so: for we are at the stake,
And bay'd about with many enemies;
And some that smile have in their hearts, I fear,
Millions of mischiefs.   [*Exeunt.*

Scene II. *Camp near Sardis. Before Brutus' Tent*

Drum. Enter BRUTUS, LUCILIUS, LUCIUS, *and* SOLDIERS: TITINIUS *and* PINDARUS *meet them.*

BRUTUS. Stand, ho!
LUCILIUS. Give the word, ho! and stand.

BRUTUS. What now, Lucilius! is Cassius near?

LUCILIUS. He is at hand; and Pindarus is come
To do you salutation from his master.

[PINDARUS *gives a letter to* BRUTUS.

BRUTUS. He greets me well. Your master, Pindarus,
In his own change, or by ill officers,
Hath given me some worthy cause to wish
Things done, undone; but, if he be at hand,
I shall be satisfied.

PINDARUS.   I do not doubt
But that my noble master will appear
Such as he is, full of regard and honour.

BRUTUS. He is not doubted. A word, Lucilius;
How he receiv'd you, let me be resolv'd.

LUCILIUS. With courtesy and with respect enough;
But not with such familiar instances,
Nor with such free and friendly conference,
As he hath us'd of old.

BRUTUS.   Thou hast describ'd
A hot friend cooling. Ever note, Lucilius,
When love begins to sicken and decay,
It useth an enforced ceremony.
There are no tricks in plain and simple faith;
But hollow men, like horses hot at hand,
Make gallant show and promise of their mettle;
But when they should endure the bloody spur,
They fall their crests, and, like deceitful jades,
Sink in the trial. Comes his army on?

LUCILIUS. They mean this night in Sardis to be quarter'd;
The greater part, the horse in general,
Are come with Cassius.

BRUTUS.   Hark! he is arriv'd.

[*Low march within.*

March gently on to meet him.

Enter CASSIUS *and* SOLDIERS.

CASSIUS. Stand, ho!

BRUTUS. Stand, ho! Speak the word along.

FIRST SOLDIER. Stand!

SECOND SOLDIER. Sand!

THIRD SOLDIER. Stand!

CASSIUS. Most noble brother, you have done me wrong.

BRUTUS. Judge me, you gods! Wrong I mine enemies?
And, if not so, how should I wrong a brother?

CASSIUS. Brutus, this sober form of yours hides wrongs;
And when you do them—

BRUTUS.   Cassius, be content;
Speak your griefs softly: I do know you well.
Before the eyes of both our armies here,
Which should perceive nothing but love from us,
Let us not wrangle: bid them move away;
Then in my tent, Cassius, enlarge your griefs,
And I will give you audience.

CASSIUS.   Pindarus,
Bid our commanders lead their charges off
A little from this ground.

BRUTUS. Lucilius, do you the like; and let no man
Come to our tent till we have done our conference.
Let Lucius and Titinius guard our door.   [*Exeunt.*

Scene III. *Within the Tent of Brutus*

Enter BRUTUS *and* CASSIUS.

CASSIUS. That you have wrong'd me doth appear in this:
You have condemn'd and noted Lucius Pella
For taking bribes here of the Sardians;
Wherein my letters, praying on his side,
Because I knew the man, were slighted off.

BRUTUS. You wrong'd yourself to write in such a case.

CASSIUS. In such a time as this it is not meet
That every nice offense should bear his comment.

BRUTUS. Let me tell you, Cassius, you yourself
Are much condemn'd to have an itching palm;
To sell and mart your offices for gold
To undeservers.

CASSIUS. I an itching palm!
You know that you are Brutus that speak this,
Or, by the gods, this speech were else your last.

BRUTUS. The name of Cassius honours this corruption,
And chastisement doth therefore hide his head.

CASSIUS. Chastisement!

BRUTUS. Remember March, the ides of March remember:
Did not great Julius bleed for justice' sake?
What villain touch'd his body, that did stab,
And not for justice? What! shall one of us,
That struck the foremost man of all this world
But for supporting robbers, shall we now
Contaminate our fingers with base bribes,
And sell the mighty space of our large honours
For so much trash as may be grasped thus?
I had rather be a dog, and bay the moon,
Than such a Roman.

CASSIUS. Brutus, bait not me;
I'll not endure it: you forget yourself,
To hedge me in. I am a soldier, I,
Older in practice, abler than yourself
To make conditions.

BRUTUS. Go to; you are not, Cassius.

CASSIUS. I am.

BRUTUS. I say you are not.

CASSIUS. Urge me no more, I shall forget myself;
Have mind upon your health; tempt me no further.

BRUTUS. Away, slight man!

CASSIUS. Is 't possible?

BRUTUS. Hear me, for I will speak.

Must I give way and room to your rash choler?
Shall I be frighted when a madman stares?
  CASSIUS. O ye gods! ye gods! Must I endure all this?
  BRUTUS. All this! ay, more: fret till your proud heart break;
Go show your slaves how choleric you are,
And make your bondmen tremble. Must I budge?
Must I observe you? Must I stand and crouch
Under your testy humour? By the gods,
You shall digest the venom of your spleen,
Though it do split you; for, from this day forth,
I'll use you for my mirth, yea, for my laughter,
When you are waspish.
  CASSIUS.   Is it come to this?
  BRUTUS. You say you are a better soldier:
Let it appear so; make your vaunting true,
And it shall please me well. For mine own part,
I shall be glad to learn of noble men.
  CASSIUS. You wrong me every way; you wrong me, Brutus;
I said an elder soldier, not a better:
Did I say, 'better'?
  BRUTUS.   If you did, I care not.
  CASSIUS. When Caesar liv'd, he durst not thus have mov'd me.
  BRUTUS. Peace, peace! you durst not so have tempted him.
  CASSIUS. I durst not!
  BRUTUS. No.
  CASSIUS. What! durst not tempt him!
  BRUTUS.   For your life you durst not.
  CASSIUS. Do not presume too much upon my love;
I may do that I shall be sorry for.
  BRUTUS. You have done that you should be sorry for.
There is no terror, Cassius, in your threats;
For I am arm'd so strong in honesty
That they pass by me as the idle wind,
Which I respect not. I did send to you
For certain sums of gold, which you denied me;
For I can raise no money by vile means:

By heaven, I had rather coin my heart,
And drop my blood for drachmas, than to wring
From the hard hands of peasants their vile trash
By any indirection. I did send
To you for gold to pay my legions,
Which you denied me: was that done like Cassius?
Should I have answer'd Caius Cassius so?
When Marcus Brutus grows so covetous,
To lock such rascal counters from his friends,
Be ready, gods with all your thunderbolts;
Dash him to pieces!

CASSIUS.   I denied you not.

BRUTUS. You did.

CASSIUS.   I did not: he was but a fool
That brought my answer back. Brutus hath riv'd my heart.
A friend should bear his friend's infirmities,
But Brutus makes mine greater than they are.

BRUTUS. I do not, till you practise them on me.

CASSIUS. You love me not.

BRUTUS.   I do not like your faults.

CASSIUS. A friendly eye could never see such faults.

BRUTUS. A flatterer's would not, though they do appear
As huge as high Olympus.

CASSIUS. Come, Antony, and young Octavius, come,
Revenge yourselves alone on Cassius,
For Cassius is aweary of the world;
Hated by one he loves; brav'd by his brother;
Check'd like a bondman; all his faults observ'd,
Set in a note-book, learn'd, and conn'd by rote,
To cast into my teeth. O! I could weep
My spirit from mine eyes. There is my dagger,
And here my naked breast; within, a heart
Dearer than Plutus' mine, richer than gold:
If that thou be'st a Roman, take it forth;
I, that denied thee gold, will give my heart:
Strike, as thou didst at Caesar; for, I know,

When thou didst hate him worst, thou lov'dst him better
Than ever thou lov'dst Cassius.

BRUTUS.   Sheathe your dagger:
Be angry when you will, it shall have scope;
Do what you will, dishonour shall be humour.
O Cassius! you are yoked with a lamb
That carries anger as the flint bears fire,
Who, much enforced, shows a hasty spark,
And straight is cold again.

CASSIUS.   Hath Cassius liv'd
To be but mirth and laughter to his Brutus,
When grief and blood ill-temper'd vexeth him?

BRUTUS. When I spoke that I was ill-temper'd too.

CASSIUS. Do you confess so much? Give me your hand.

BRUTUS. And my heart too.

CASSIUS.   O Brutus!

BRUTUS.   What's the matter?

CASSIUS. Have not you love enough to bear with me,
When that rash humour which my mother gave me
Makes me forgetful?

BRUTUS.   Yes, Cassius; and from henceforth
When you are over-earnest with your Brutus,
He'll think your mother chides, and leave you so.

[*Noise within.*

POET. [*Within.*] Let me go in to see the generals;
There is some grudge between 'em, 'tis not meet
They be alone.

LUCILIUS. [*Within.*] You shall not come to them.

POET. [*Within.*] Nothing but death shall stay me.

Enter POET, *followed by* LUCILIUS, TITINIUS, *and* LUCIUS.

CASSIUS. Now now! What's the matter?

POET. For shame, you generals! What do you mean?
Love, and be friends, as two such men should be;
For I have seen more years, I'm sure, than ye.

CASSIUS. Ha, ha! how vilely doth this cynic rime!

BRUTUS. Get you hence, sirrah; saucy fellow, hence!

CASSIUS. Bear with him, Brutus, 'tis his fashion.

BRUTUS. I'll know his humour, when he knows his time.
What should the wars do with these jigging fools?
Companion, hence!

CASSIUS.   Away, away! be gone.   [Exit POET.

BRUTUS. Lucilius and Titinius, bid the commanders
Prepare to lodge their companies to-night.

CASSIUS. And come yourselves, and bring Messala with you
Immediately to us.   [Exeunt LUCILIUS and TITINIUS.

BRUTUS.   Lucius, a bowl of wine!   [Exit LUCIUS.

CASSIUS. I did not think you could have been so angry.

BRUTUS. O Cassius! I am sick of many griefs.

CASSIUS. Of your philosophy you make no use
If you give place to accidental evils.

BRUTUS. No man bears sorrow better: Portia is dead.

CASSIUS. Ha! Portia!

BRUTUS. She is dead.

CASSIUS. How 'scap'd I killing when I cross'd you so?
O insupportable and touching loss!
Upon what sickness?

BRUTUS.   Impatient of my absence,
And grief that young Octavius with Mark Antony
Have made themselves so strong;—for with her death
That tidings came:—with this she fell distract,
And, her attendants absent, swallow'd fire.

CASSIUS. And died so?

BRUTUS.   Even so.

CASSIUS.   O ye immortal gods!

Enter LUCIUS, *with wine and tapers.*

BRUTUS. Speak no more of her. Give me a bowl of wine.
In this I bury all unkindness, Cassius.   [Drinks.

CASSIUS. My heart is thirsty for that noble pledge.
Fill, Lucius, till the wine o'erswell the cup;

I cannot drink too much of Brutus' love.　　　　*[Drinks.*
BRUTUS. Come in, Titinius.　　　　*[Exit* LUCIUS.

Re-enter TITINIUS, *with* MESSALA.

　　　　　　　Welcome, good Messala.
Now sit we close about this taper here,
And call in question our necessities.
　CASSIUS. Portia, art thou gone?
　BRUTUS.　　　　　　No more, I pray you.
Messala, I have here received letters,
That young Octavius and Mark Antony
Come down upon us with a mighty power,
Bending their expedition towards Philippi.
　MESSALA. Myself have letters of the self-same tenour.
　BRUTUS. With what addition?
　MESSALA. That by proscription and bills of outlawry,
Octavius, Antony, and Lepidus
Have put to death an hundred senators.
　BRUTUS. Therein our letters do not well agree;
Mine speak of seventy senators that died
By their proscriptions, Cicero being one.
　CASSIUS. Cicero one!
　MESSALA.　　　　　Cicero is dead,
And by that order of proscription.
Had you your letters from your wife, my lord?
　BRUTUS. No, Messala.
　MESSALA. Nor nothing in your letters writ of her?
　BRUTUS. Nothing, Messala.
　MESSALA.　　　　　That, methinks, is strange.
　BRUTUS. Why ask you? Hear you aught of her in yours?
　MESSALA. No, my lord.
　BRUTUS. Now, as you are a Roman, tell me true.
　MESSALA. Then like a Roman bear the truth I tell:
For certain she is dead, and by strange manner.
　BRUTUS. Why, farewell, Portia. We must die, Messala:

With meditating that she must die once,
I have the patience to endure it now.
  MESSALA. Even so great men great losses should endure.
  CASSIUS. I have as much of this in art as you,
But yet my nature could not bear it so.
  BRUTUS. Well, to our work alive. What do you think
Of marching to Philippi presently?
  CASSIUS. I do not think it good.
  BRUTUS.   Your reason?
  CASSIUS.   This is it:
'Tis better that the enemy seek us:
So shall he waste his means, weary his soldiers,
Doing himself offence; whilst we, lying still,
Are full of rest, defence, and nimbleness.
  BRUTUS. Good reasons must, of force, give place to better,
The people 'twixt Philippi and this ground
Do stand but in a forc'd affection;
For they have grudg'd us contribution:
The enemy, marching along by them,
By them shall make a fuller number up,
Come on refresh'd, new-added, and encourag'd;
From which advantage shall we cut him off,
If at Philippi we do face him there,
These people at our back.
  CASSIUS.   Hear me, good brother.
  BRUTUS. Under your pardon. You must note beside,
That we have tried the utmost of our friends,
Our legions are brim-full, our cause is ripe:
The enemy increaseth every day;
We, at the height, are ready to decline.
There is a tide in the affairs of men,
Which, taken at the flood, leads on to fortune;
Omitted, all the voyage of their life
Is bound in shallows and in miseries.
On such a full sea are we now afloat;

"O mighty Caesar! Dost thou lie so low?
Are all thy conquests, glories, triumphs, spoils,
Shrunk to this little measure?"   *Act 3, Scene I*

And we must take the current when it serves,
Or lose our ventures.

CASSIUS.   Then, with your will, go on;
We'll along ourselves, and meet them at Philippi.

BRUTUS. The deep of night is crept upon our talk,
And nature must obey necessity,
Which we will niggard with a little rest.
There is no more to say?

CASSIUS.   No more. Good-night:
Early to-morrow will we rise, and hence.

BRUTUS. Lucius!

Re-enter LUCIUS.

          My gown.   [*Exit* LUCIUS.
          Farewell, good Messala.
Good-night, Titinius. Noble, noble Cassius,
Good-night, and good repose.

CASSIUS.   O my dear brother!
This was an ill beginning of the night:
Never come such division 'tween our souls!
Let it not, Brutus.

BRUTUS.   Every thing is well.

CASSIUS. Good-night, my lord.

BRUTUS.   Good-night, good brother.

TITINIUS. ⎫
MESSALA. ⎬ Good-night, Lord Brutus.

BRUTUS.   Farewell, every one.
          [*Exeunt* CASSIUS, TITINIUS, *and* MESSALA.

Re-enter LUCIUS, *with the gown.*

Give me the gown. Where is thy instrument?

LUCIUS. Here in the tent.

BRUTUS.   What! thou speak'st drowsily
Poor knave, I blame thee not; thou art o'er-watch'd.

Call Claudius and some other of my men;
I'll have them sleep on cushions in my tent.

LUCIUS. Varro! and Claudius!

Enter VARRO *and* CLAUDIUS.

VARRO. Calls my lord?

BRUTUS. I pray you, sirs, lie in my tent and sleep:
It may be I shall raise you by and by
On business to my brother Cassius.

VARRO. So please you, we will stand and watch your pleasure.

BRUTUS. I will not have it so; lie down, good sirs;
It may be I shall otherwise bethink me.
Look, Lucius, here's the book I sought for so;
I put it in the pocket of my gown.

[VARRO *and* CLAUDIUS *lie down.*

LUCIUS. I was sure your lordship did not give it me.

BRUTUS. Bear with me, good boy, I am much forgetful.
Canst thou hold up thy heavy eyes awhile,
And touch thy instrument a strain or two?

LUCIUS. Ay, my lord, an 't please you.

BRUTUS.   It does, my boy:
I trouble thee too much, but thou art willing.

LUCIUS. It is my duty, sir.

BRUTUS. I should not urge thy duty past thy might;
I know young bloods look for a time of rest.

LUCIUS. I have slept, my lord, already.

BRUTUS. It was well done, and thou shalt sleep again;
I will not hold thee long: if I do live,
I will be good to thee.   [*Music, and a Song.*
This is a sleepy tune: O murderous slumber!
Lay'st thou thy leaden mace upon my boy,
That plays thee music? Gentle knave, good-night;
I will not do thee so much wrong to wake thee.
If thou dost nod, thou break'st thy instrument;
I'll take it from thee; and, good boy, good-night.

Let me see, let me see; is not the leaf turn'd down
Where I left reading? Here it is, I think.

 Enter the Ghost of CAESAR.

How ill this taper burns! Ha! who comes here?
I think it is the weakness of mine eyes
That shapes this monstrous apparition.
It comes upon me. Art thou any thing?
Art thou some god, some angel, or some devil,
That mak'st my blood cold and my hair to stare?
Speak to me what thou art.
 GHOST. Thy evil spirit, Brutus.
 BRUTUS.   Why com'st thou?
 GHOST. To tell thee thou shalt see me at Philippi.
 BRUTUS. Well; then I shall see thee again?
 GHOST.   Ay, at Philippi.
 BRUTUS. Why, I will see thee at Philippi then.
          [Ghost vanishes.
Now I have taken heart thou vanishest:
Ill spirit, I would hold more talk with thee.
Boy, Lucius! Varro! Claudius! Sirs, awake!
Claudius!
 LUCIUS. The strings, my lord, are false.
 BRUTUS. He thinks he still is at his instrument.
Lucius, awake!
 LUCIUS. My lord!
 BRUTUS. Didst thou dream, Lucius, that thou so criedst out?
 LUCIUS. My lord, I do not know that I did cry.
 BRUTUS. Yes, that thou didst. Didst thou see any thing?
 LUCIUS. Nothing, my lord.
 BRUTUS. Sleep again, Lucius. Sirrah, Claudius!
Fellow thou! awake!
 VARRO. My lord!
 CLAUDIUS. My lord!
 BRUTUS. Why did you so cry out, sirs, in your sleep?

VARRO.
CLAUDIUS. } Did we, my lord?

BRUTUS. Ay: saw you any thing?

VARRO. No, my lord, I saw nothing.

CLAUDIUS. Nor I, my lord.

BRUTUS. Go, and commend me to my brother Cassius.
Bid him set on his powers betimes before,
And we will follow.

VARRO.
CLAUDIUS. } It shall be done, my lord.

[*Exeunt.*

Act 5

Scene I. The Plains of Philippi

Enter OCTAVIUS, ANTONY, *and their Army.*

OCTAVIUS. Now, Antony, our hopes are answered:
You said the enemy would not come down,
But keep the hills and upper regions;
It proves not so; their battles are at hand;
They mean to warn us at Philippi here,
Answering before we do demand of them.
ANTONY. Tut! I am in their bosoms, and I know
Wherefore they do it: they could be content
To visit other places; and come down
With fearful bravery, thinking by this face
To fasten in our thoughts that they have courage;
But 'tis not so.

Enter a MESSENGER.

MESSENGER. Prepare, you generals:
The enemy comes on in gallant show;
Their bloody sign of battle is hung out,
And something to be done immediately.
ANTONY. Octavius, lead your battle softly on,
Upon the left hand of the even field.
OCTAVIUS. Upon the right hand I; keep thou the left.
ANTONY. Why do you cross me in this exigent?
OCTAVIUS. I do not cross you; but I will do so. [*March.*

81

Drum.   Enter BRUTUS, CASSIUS, *and their Army;* LUCILIUS,
TITINIUS, MESSALA, *and Others.*

BRUTUS. They stand, and would have parley.

CASSIUS. Stand fast, Titinius: we must out and talk.

OCTAVIUS. Mark Antony, shall we give sign of battle?

ANTONY. No, Caesar, we will answer on their charge.
Make forth; the generals would have some words.

OCTAVIUS. Stir not until the signal.

BRUTUS. Words before blows: is it so, countrymen?

OCTAVIUS. Not that we love words better, as you do.

BRUTUS. Good words are better than bad strokes, Octavius.

ANTONY. In your bad strokes, Brutus, you give good words:
Witness the hole you made in Caesar's heart,
Crying, 'Long live! hail, Caesar!'

CASSIUS.   Antony,
The posture of your blows are yet unknown;
But for your words, they rob the Hybla bees,
And leave them honeyless.

ANTONY.   Not stingless too?

BRUTUS. O! yes, and soundless too;
For you have stol'n their buzzing, Antony,
And very wisely threat before you sting.

ANTONY. Villains! you did not so when your vile daggers
Hack'd one another in the sides of Caesar:
You show'd your teeth like apes, and fawn'd like hounds,
And bow'd like bondmen, kissing Caesar's feet;
Whilst damned Casca, like a cur, behind
Struck Caesar on the neck. O you flatterers!

CASSIUS. Flatterers! Now, Brutus, thank yourself:
This tongue had not offended so to-day,
If Cassius might have rul'd.

OCTAVIUS. Come, come, the cause: if arguing make us sweat,
The proof of it will turn to redder drops.
Look;
I draw a sword against conspirators;

When think you that the sword goes up again?
Never, till Caesar's three-and-thirty wounds
Be well aveng'd; or till another Caesar
Have added slaughter to the sword of traitors.
    BRUTUS. Caesar, thou canst not die by traitor's hands,
Unless thou bring'st them with thee.
    OCTAVIUS.   So I hope;
I was not born to die on Brutus' sword.
    BRUTUS. O! if thou wert the noblest of thy strain,
Young man, thou couldst not die more honourable.
    CASSIUS. A peevish schoolboy, worthless of such honour,
Join'd with a masquer and a reveller.
    ANTONY. Old Cassius still!
    OCTAVIUS.   Come, Antony; away!
Defiance, traitors, hurl we in your teeth.
If you dare fight to-day, come to the field;
If not, when you have stomachs.
          [Exeunt OCTAVIUS, ANTONY, *and their Army.*
    CASSIUS. Why now, blow wind, swell billow, and swim bark!
The storm is up, and all is on the hazard.
    BRUTUS. Ho!
Lucilius! hark, a word with you.
    LUCILIUS.   My lord?
                  *[*BRUTUS *and* LUCILIUS *talk apart.*
    CASSIUS. Messala!
    MESSALA.   What says my general?
    CASSIUS.   Messala,
This is my birth-day; as this very day
Was Cassius born. Give me thy hand, Messala:
Be thou my witness that against my will,
As Pompey was, am I compell'd to set
Upon one battle all our liberties.
You know that I held Epicurus strong,
And his opinion; now I change my mind,
And partly credit things that do presage.
Coming from Sardis, on our former ensign

Two mighty eagles fell, and there they perch'd,
Gorging and feeding from our soldiers' hands;
Who to Philippi here consorted us:
This morning are they fled away and gone,
And in their stead do ravens, crows, and kites
Fly o'er our heads, and downward look on us,
As we were sickly prey: their shadows seem
A canopy most fatal, under which
Our army lies, ready to give up the ghost.

MESSALA. Believe not so.

CASSIUS.   I but believe it partly,
For I am fresh of spirit and resolv'd
To meet all perils very constantly.

BRUTUS. Even so, Lucilius.

CASSIUS.   Now, most noble Brutus,
The gods to-day stand friendly, that we may,
Lovers in peace, lead on our days to age!
But since the affairs of men rest still incertain,
Let's reason with the worst that may befall.
If we do lose this battle, then is this
The very last time we shall speak together:
What are you, then, determined to do?

BRUTUS. Even by the rule of that philosophy
By which I did blame Cato for the death
Which he did give himself; I know not how,
But I do find it cowardly and vile,
For fear of what might fall, so to prevent
The time of life: arming myself with patience,
To stay the providence of some high powers
That govern us below.

CASSIUS.   Then, if we lose this battle,
You are contented to be led in triumph
Thorough the streets of Rome?

BRUTUS. No, Cassius, no: think not, thou noble Roman,
That ever Brutus will go bound to Rome;
He bears too great a mind: but this same day

Must end that work the ides of March begun;
And whether we shall meet again I know not.
Therefore our everlasting farewell take:
For ever, and for ever, farewell, Cassius!
If we do meet again, why, we shall smile;
If not, why then, this parting was well made.
CASSIUS. For ever, and for ever, farewell, Brutus!
If we do meet again, we'll smile indeed;
If not, 'tis true this parting was well made.
BRUTUS. Why, then, lead on. O! that a man might know
The end of this day's business, ere it come;
But it sufficeth that the day will end,
And then the end is known. Come, ho! away!   [*Exeunt.*

Scene II.   The Same. The Field of Battle

Alarum. Enter BRUTUS *and* MESSALA.

BRUTUS. Ride, ride, Messala, ride, and give these bills
Unto the legions on the other side.   [*Loud alarum.*
Let them set on at once, for I perceive
But cold demeanour in Octavius' wing,
And sudden push gives them the overthrow.
Ride, ride, Messala: let them all come down.   [*Exeunt.*

Scene III.   Another Part of the Field

Alarum. Enter CASSIUS *and* TITINIUS.

CASSIUS. O! look, Titinius, look, the villains fly:
Myself have to mine own turn'd enemy;
This ensign here of mine was turning back;
I slew the coward, and did take it from him.
TITINIUS. O Cassius! Brutus gave the word too early;
Who, having some advantage on Octavius,

Took it too eagerly: his soldiers fell to spoil,
Whilst we by Antony are all enclos'd.

Enter PINDARUS.

PINDARUS. Fly further off, my lord, fly further off;
Mark Antony is in your tents, my lord:
Fly, therefore, noble Cassius, fly far off.
CASSIUS. This hill is far enough. Look, look, Titinius;
Are those my tents where I perceive the fire?
TITINIUS. They are, my lord.
CASSIUS.   Titinius, if thou lov'st me,
Mount thou my horse, and hide thy spurs in him,
Till he have brought thee up to yonder troops
And here again; that I may rest assur'd
Whether yond troops are friend or enemy.
TITINIUS. I will be here again, even with a thought.   [*Exit.*
CASSIUS. Go, Pindarus, get higher on that hill;
My sight was ever thick; regard Titinius,
And tell me what thou not'st about the field.

                                        [PINDARUS *ascends the hill.*
This day I breathed first; time is come round,
And where I did begin, there shall I end;
My life is run his compass. Sirrah, what news?
PINDARUS. [*Above.*] O my lord!
CASSIUS. What news?
PINDARUS. Titinius is enclosed round about
With horsemen, that make to him on the spur;
Yet he spurs on: now they are almost on him;
Now, Titinius! now some light; O! he lights too:
He's ta'en; [*Shout.*] and, hark! they shout for joy.
CASSIUS. Come down; behold no more.
O, coward that I am, to live so long,
To see my best friend ta'en before my face!

     PINDARUS *descends.*

Come hither, sirrah:

In Parthia did I take thee prisoner;
And then I swore thee, saving of thy life,
That whatsoever I did bid thee do,
Thou shouldst attempt it. Come now, keep thine oath;
Now be a freeman; and with this good sword,
That ran through Caesar's bowels, search this bosom.
Stand not to answer; here, take thou the hilts;
And, when my face is cover'd, as 'tis now,
Guide thou the sword. Caesar, thou are reveng'd,
Even with the sword that kill'd thee.   [*Dies.*

PINDARUS. So, I am free; yet would not so have been,
Durst I have done my will. O Cassius,
Far from this country Pindarus shall run,
Where never Roman shall take note of him.   [*Exit.*

Re-enter TITINIUS *with* MESSALA.

MESSALA. It is but change, Titinius; for Octavius
Is overthrown by noble Brutus' power,
As Cassius' legions are by Antony.
TITINIUS. These tidings will well comfort Cassius.
MESSALA. Where did you leave him?
TITINIUS.   All disconsolate,
With Pindarus his bondman, on this hill.
MESSALA. Is not that he that lies upon the ground?
TITINIUS. He lies not like the living. O my heart!
MESSALA. Is not that he?
TITINIUS.   No, this was he, Messala,
But Cassius is no more. O setting sun!
As in thy red rays thou dost sink to-night,
So in his red blood Cassius' day is set;
The sun of Rome is set. Our day is gone;
Clouds, dews, and dangers come; our deeds are done.
Mistrust of my success hath done this deed.
MESSALA. Mistrust of good success hath done this deed.
O hateful error, melancholy's child!
Why dost thou show to the apt thoughts of men

The things that are not? O error! soon conceiv'd,
Thou never com'st unto a happy birth,
But kill'st the mother that engender'd thee.

    TITINIUS. What, Pindarus! Where art thou, Pindarus?

    MESSALA. See him, Titinius, whilst I go to meet
The noble Brutus, thrusting this report
Into his ears; I may say, thrusting it;
For piercing steel and darts envenomed
Shall be as welcome to the ears of Brutus
As tidings of this sight.

    TITINIUS.   Hie you, Messala,
And I will seek for Pindarus the while.

                                  [Exit MESSALA.

Why didst thou send me forth, brave Cassius?
Did I not meet thy friends? and did not they
Put on my brows this wreath of victory,
And bid me give it thee? Didst thou not hear their shouts?
Alas! thou hast misconstru'd every thing.
But, hold thee, take this garland on thy brow;
Thy Brutus bid me give it thee, and I
Will do his bidding. Brutus, come apace,
And see how I regarded Caius Cassius.
By your leave, gods: this is a Roman's part:
Come, Cassius' sword, and find Titinius' heart.   *[Kills himself.*

    Alarum. Re-enter MESSALA, *with* BRUTUS, *Young* CATO,
STRATO, VOLUMNIUS, *and* LUCILIUS.

    BRUTUS. Where, where, Messala, doth his body lie?

    MESSALA. Lo, yonder: and Titinius mourning it.

    BRUTUS. Titinius' face is upward.

    CATO.   He is slain.

    BRUTUS. O Julius Caesar! thou art mighty yet!
Thy spirit walks abroad, and turns our swords
In our own proper entrails.   *[Low alarums.*

    CATO.   Brave Titinius!
Look whe'r he have not crown'd dead Cassius!

BRUTUS. Are yet two Romans living such as these?
The last of all the Romans, fare thee well!
It is impossible that ever Rome
Should breed thy fellow. Friends, I owe more tears
To this dead man than you shall see me pay.—
I shall find time, Cassius, I shall find time.—
Come therefore, and to Thasos send his body:
His funerals shall not be in our camp,
Lest it discomfort us. Lucilius, come;
And come, young Cato;—let us to the field.
Labeo and Flavius, set our battles on:—
'Tis three o'clock; and, Romans, yet ere night
We shall try fortune in a second fight.   [*Exeunt.*

Scene IV.   *Another Part of the Field*

Alarum. Enter fighting, SOLDIERS *of both armies; then*
BRUTUS, *Young* CATO, LUCILIUS, *and Others.*

BRUTUS. Yet, countrymen, O! yet hold up your heads!
CATO. What bastard doth not? Who will go with me?
I will proclaim my name about the field:
I am the son of Marcus Cato, ho!
A foe to tyrants, and my country's friend;
I am the son of Marcus Cato, ho!
BRUTUS. And I am Brutus, Marcus Brutus, I;
Brutus, my country's friend; know me for Brutus!
     [*Exit, charging the enemy.* CATO *is overpowered, and falls.*
LUCILIUS. O young and noble Cato, art thou down?
Why, now thou diest as bravely as Titinius,
And mayst be honour'd being Cato's son.
FIRST SOLDIER. Yield, or thou diest.
LUCILIUS.   Only I yield to die:
There is so much that thou wilt kill me straight.
                                        [*Offering money.*
Kill Brutus, and be honour'd in his death.

FIRST SOLDIER. We must not. A noble prisoner!
SECOND SOLDIER. Room, ho! Tell Antony, Brutus is ta'en.
FIRST SOLDIER. I'll tell the news: here comes the general.

Enter ANTONY.

Brutus is ta'en, my lord.
ANTONY. Where is he?
LUCILIUS. Safe, Antony; Brutus is safe enough:
I dare assure thee that no enemy
Shall ever take alive the noble Brutus:
The gods defend him from so great a shame!
When you do find him, or alive or dead,
He will be found like Brutus, like himself.
ANTONY. This is not Brutus, friend; but, I assure you,
A prize no less in worth. Keep this man safe,
Give him all kindness: I had rather have
Such men my friends than enemies. Go on,
And see whe'r Brutus be alive or dead;
And bring us word unto Octavius' tent,
How every thing is chanc'd.   *[Exeunt.*

Scene V. *Another Part of the Field*

Enter BRUTUS, DARDANIUS, CLITUS, *and* VOLUMNIUS.

BRUTUS. Come, poor remains of friends, rest on this rock.
CLITUS. Statilius show'd the torch-light; but, my lord,
He came not back: he is or ta'en or slain.
BRUTUS. Sit thee down, Clitus: slaying is the word;
It is a deed in fashion. Hark thee, Clitus.   *[Whispers.*
CLITUS. What, I, my lord? No, not for all the world.
BRUTUS. Peace, then! no words.
CLITUS.   I'll rather kill myself.
BRUTUS. Hark thee, Dardanius.   *[Whispers.*
DARDANIUS.   Shall I do such a deed?
CLITUS. O, Dardanius!

DARDANIUS. O, Clitus!

CLITUS. What ill request did Brutus make to thee?

DARDANIUS. To kill him, Clitus. Look, he meditates.

CLITUS. Now is that noble vessel full of grief,

That it runs over even at his eyes.

BRUTUS. Come hither, good Volumnius: list a word.

VOLUMNIUS. What says my lord?

BRUTUS.   Why this, Volumnius:

The ghost of Caesar hath appear'd to me

Two several times by night; at Sardis once,

And this last night here in Philippi fields.

I know my hour is come.

VOLUMNIUS.   Not so, my lord.

BRUTUS. Nay, I am sure it is, Volumnius.

Thou seest the world, Volumnius, how it goes;

Our enemies have beat us to the pit:

It is more worthy to leap in ourselves,

Than tarry till they push us. Good Volumnius,

Thou know'st that we two went to school together;

Even for that our love of old, I prithee,

Hold thou my sword-hilts, whilst I run on it.

VOLUMNIUS. That's not an office for a friend, my lord.

                                    [Alarum still.

CLITUS. Fly, fly, my lord! there is no tarrying here.

BRUTUS. Farewell to you; and you; and you, Volumnius.

Strato, thou hast been all this while asleep;

Farewell to thee too, Strato. Countrymen,

My heart doth joy that yet, in all my life,

I found no man but he was true to me.

I shall have glory by this losing day,

More than Octavius and Mark Antony

By this vile conquest shall attain unto.

So fare you well at once; for Brutus' tongue

Hath almost ended his life's history:

Night hangs upon mine eyes; my bones would rest,

That have but labour'd to attain this hour.

[*Alarum. Cry within*, 'Fly, fly, fly!'

CLITUS. Fly, my lord, fly.

BRUTUS.   Hence! I will follow.

[*Exeunt* CLITUS, DARDANIUS, *and* VOLUMNIUS.

I prithee, Strato, stay thou by thy lord:
Thou art a fellow of a good respect;
Thy life hath had some smatch of honour in it:
Hold then my sword, and turn away thy face,
While I do run upon it. Wilt thou, Strato?

STRATO. Give me your hand first: fare you well, my lord.

BRUTUS. Farewell, good Strato.—[*He runs on his sword.*]
Caesar, now be still;

I kill'd not thee with half so good a will.   [*Dies.*

Alarum. Retreat. Enter OCTAVIUS, ANTONY, MESSALA, LUCIL-
IUS, *and Army.*

OCTAVIUS. What man is that?

MESSALA. My master's man. Strato, where is thy master?

STRATO. Free from the bondage you are in, Messala;
The conquerors can but make a fire of him;
For Brutus only overcame himself,
And no man else hath honour by his death.

LUCILIUS. So Brutus should be found. I thank thee, Brutus,
That thou hast prov'd Lucilius' saying true.

OCTAVIUS. All that serv'd Brutus, I will entertain them.
Fellow, wilt thou bestow thy time with me?

STRATO. Ay, if Messala will prefer me to you.

OCTAVIUS. Do so, good Messala.

MESSALA. How died my master, Strato?

STRATO. I held the sword, and he did run on it.

MESSALA. Octavius, then take him to follow thee,
That did the latest service to my master.

ANTONY. This was the noblest Roman of them all;
All the conspirators save only he
Did that they did in envy of great Caesar;

He only, in a general honest thought
And common good to all, made one of them.
His life was gentle, and the elements
So mix'd in him that Nature might stand up
And say to all the world, 'This was a man!'
     OCTAVIUS. According to his virtue let us use him,
With all respect and rites of burial.
Within my tent his bones to-night shall lie,
Most like a soldier, order'd honourably.
So, call the field to rest; and let's away,
To part the glories of this happy day.   [*Exeunt.*

Hamlet

PRINCE OF DENMARK

INTRODUCTION

Written. 1601–1602.

Published, in an imperfect form, 1603; more perfectly, 1604.

Source of the Plot. A play upon the subject of Hamlet, now lost, seems to have been popular in London during the last decades of the sixteenth century. Some think that it was an early work of Shakespeare's. No evidence supports this theory. He probably knew the play, and may have acted in it.

The story is told by Saxo Grammaticus in his *Historia Danica.* Francis de Belleforest printed a version of it in his *Histoires Tragiques.* An English translation from de Belleforest, called the *Hystorie of Hamblet,* was published (or perhaps reprinted) in London in 1608. Shakespeare seems to have known both de Belleforest and the *Hystorie.*

The Fable. Claudius, brother to the King of Denmark, conniving with Gertrude the Queen, poisons his brother, and seizes the throne. Soon afterwards he marries Gertrude. At this point the play begins.

Hamlet, son of the murdered king, sick at heart at his mother's hasty re-marriage, and troubled by his love for Ophelia, returns to Denmark. The ghost of his father reveals the manner of the murder to him, and makes him swear to be revenged. The revelation so affects him that the murderers begin to fear him. He cannot bring himself to kill Claudius. In a play he shows them that he knows their guilt.

While speaking with his mother, he discovers and kills a spy hidden behind the arras. The spy is Polonius, father of Laertes and of Ophelia.

Claudius causes Hamlet to sail for England, on the pretext

97

HAMLET

at the killing of Polonius has brought him into danger from the populace. He plans that Hamlet shall be killed on his arrival. Hamlet discovers the treacherous purpose and returns unhurt to Denmark.

During Hamlet's absence at sea, Laertes learns how Polonius was killed and swears to be revenged on Hamlet. Hamlet's return gives him his opportunity.

Claudius suggests that the revenge be taken at a fencing-bout. Laertes shall fence with Hamlet, using a poisoned foil. If this fails, Hamlet shall be given poisoned wine.

In a scuffle during the fencing-bout the fencers change foils. Gertrude, by mistake, drinks the poisoned wine and dies. Laertes, hurt by the poisoned foil, dies. Hamlet, also hurt by the poisoned foil, kills Claudius and dies too.

Hamlet is the most baffling of the great plays, because it is about baffling: that is the theme: Hamlet is baffled because, being wise, he finds the wise course difficult to decide upon.

A murder has been done, blood calls for vengeance: something from outside life urges Hamlet to take vengeance, but his wisdom does not admit vengeance, it seeks justice, and cannot see its way to justice; however necessary justice may be. Hamlet's indecision, or inaction, baffles that power outside life that urges him to take vengeance. The play is a confusion or welter of promptings to kill and seekings for a righter course than killing.

All through the play there is the uneasiness of something trying to get done, something from outside life trying to get into life, but baffled always because the instrument chosen is, himself, a little outside life, as the wise must be. This baffling of the purpose of the dead leads to a baffling of the living, and, at last, to something like an arrest of life, a deadlock, in which each act, however violent, makes the obscuring of life's purpose greater.

The powers outside life send a poor ghost to Hamlet to prompt him to an act of justice. After baffled hours, often interrupted by cock-crow, he gives his message. Hamlet is charged with the double task of executing judgment and showing mercy. It is a charge given to many people (generally common people) in the system of the plays. It is given to two other men in this play. It is nothing more than the fulfilling of the kingly office, so bloodily seized by Claudius before the opening of the play. At this point, it may be well to consider the society in which the kingly office is to be exercised.

The society is created with Shakespeare's fullest power. It is not an image of the world in little, like the world of the late historical plays. It is an image of the world as intellect is made to feel it. It is a society governed by the enemies of intellect, by the sensual and the worldly, by deadly sinners and the philosophers of bread and cheese. The King is a drunken, incestuous murderer, who fears intellect. The Queen is a false woman, who cannot understand and has betrayed intellect. Polonius is a counsellor who suspects intellect. Ophelia is a doll without intellect. Laertes is a boor who destroys intellect. The courtiers are parasites who flourish on the decay of intellect. Fortinbras, bright and noble, marching to the drum to win a dunghill, gives a colour to the folly. The only friends of the wise man are Horatio, the school-fellow, and the leader of a cry of players.

The task set by the dead is a simple one, but to a delicate mind any violent act involves not only a large personal sacrifice of ideal, but a tearing-up by the roots of half the order of the world. Wisdom is founded upon justice; but justice, to the wise man, is more a scrupulous quality in the mind than the doing of expedient acts upon sinners. Hamlet is neither "weak" nor "unpractical," as so many call him. What he hesitates to do may be necessary, or even just, as the world goes, but it is a defilement of personal ideals, difficult for a wise mind to justify. It is so great a defilement, and a world so composed is so great a defilement, that death seems preferable to action and existence alike.

The play at this point presents a double image of action baffled by wisdom. Hamlet baffles the dealing of the justice of

Fate, and also the death plotted for him by his uncle. His weapon, in both cases, is his justice, his precise scrupulousness of mind, the niceness of mental balance which gives to all that he says the double-edge of wisdom. It is the faculty, translated into the finer terms of thought, which the ghost seeks to make real with bloodshed. Justice, in her grosser as in her finer form, is concerned with the finding of the truth. The first half of the play, though it exposes and develops the fable, is a dual image of a search for truth, of a seeking for certainty that would justify a violent act. The King is probing Hamlet's mind with gross human probes, to find out if he be mad. Hamlet is searching the King's mind with the finest of intellectual probes, to find out if he be guilty. The probe used by him, the fragment of a play within a play, is the work of a man with a knowledge of the impotence of intellect:

> Our will and fates do so contrary run
> That our devices still are overthrown . . .

and a faith in the omnipotence of intellect:

> Our thoughts are ours, their ends none of our own . . .

To this man, five minutes after the lines have exposed the guilty man, comes a chance to kill his uncle. Hamlet "might do it pat" while he is at prayers. The knowledge that the sword will not reach the real man, since damnation comes from within, not from without, arrests his hand. Fate offers an instant for the doing of her purpose. Hamlet puts the instant by, with his baffling slowness, made up of mercy and wisdom. Fate, or the something outside life which demands the King's blood, so that life may go back to her channel, is foiled. The action cannot bring itself to be. A wise human purpose is, for the moment, stronger than the eternal purpose of Nature, the roughly just.

It is a part of this play's ironic teaching that life must not be baffled; but that, when she has been wrenched from her course, she must either be wrenched back to it or kept violently in the channel to which she has been forced.

In *Macbeth,* a not dissimilar play, the life violently altered is kept in the strange channel by a succession of violent acts. In *Hamlet,* when Hamlet's merciful wisdom has decided that the life violently altered shall not be wrenched back, his destroying wisdom decides that she shall not be kept in the strange channel. The King, just in his way, seeks to find out if Hamlet be sane. If Hamlet be sane, he must die. His death will secure the King's position. By his death life will be kept in the strange channel. Polonius, the King's agent, learns that Hamlet is sane and something more. Fate demands violence this way if she may not have it in the other. She offers an instant for the doing of her purpose. Hamlet puts the instant by with his baffling swiftness, which strikes on the instant, when the Queen's honour and his own life depend on it. The first bout in this play of the baffling of action falls to Hamlet. The second bout, in which the King's purpose is again baffled, by the sending of the two courtiers to their death in England, also falls to Hamlet. The bloody purpose from outside life and the bloody purpose from within life are both baffled and kept from being by the two extremes so perfectly balanced in the wise nature.

Extremes in the Shakespearean system are tragical things. In Shakespeare, the pathway of excess leads, not as with Blake, to the palace of wisdom, but to destruction. The two extremes in Hamlet, of slowness and swiftness, set up in life the counter forces which destroy extremes, so that life, the common thing, may continue to be common. The mercy of Hamlet leaves the King free to plot his death. The swiftness of Hamlet gives to the King a hand and sword to work his will.

In other plays, the working of extremes to the punishment dealt by life to all excess is simple and direct. In this play, nothing is simple and direct. Fate's direct workings are baffled by a mind too complex to be active on the common planes. The baffling of Fate's purpose leads to a condition in life like the "slack water" between tides. Laertes, when his father is killed, raises the town and comes raving to the presence to stab the killer. He is baffled by the King's wisdom. Ophelia, "incapable of her own distress," goes mad and drowns herself. The play seems to hesitate and stand still while the energies spilled in the baffling of Fate work and simmer and grow strong, till they combine with Fate in the preparation of an end that shall not be baffled. Even so, "the end men looked for cometh not." The end comes to both actions at once in the squalor of a chance-medley. Fate has her will at last. Life, who was so long baffled, only hesitated. She destroys the man who wrenched her from her course, and the man who would neither wrench her back nor let her stay, and the women who loved these men, and the men who loved them. Revenge and chance together restore life to her course, by a destruction of the lives too beastly, and of the lives too hasty, and of the lives too foolish, and of the life too wise, to be all together on earth at the same time.

It is difficult to praise the poetry of *Hamlet*. Nearly all the play is as familiar by often quotation as the New Testament. The great, wise, and wonderful beauty of the play is a part of the English mind for ever. It is difficult to live for a day anywhere in England without hearing or reading a part of Hamlet. Lines that are little quoted are the lines to quote here—

> The bird of dawning singeth all night long . . .

> The glow-worm shows the matin to be near . . .

> this fell sergeant, death,
> Is strict in his arrest . . .

> O proud death!
> What feast is toward in thine eternal cell,
> That thou so many princes at a shot
> So bloodily hast struck?

The last speech, great as the speech at the end of Timon, and noble, like that, with a music beyond the art of voices, is constructed on a similar metrical basis.

> Let four captains
> Bear Hamlet, like a soldier, to the stage;

For he was likely, had he been put on,
To have prov'd most royally: and, for his passage,
The soldiers' music and the rites of war
Speak loudly for him.
Take up the bodies: such a sight as this
Becomes the field, but here shows much amiss.
Go, bid the soldiers shoot.

There can be no doubt that an early play of *Hamlet* existed and was well known. It may well have been by Kyd or some playwright of the same manner. It is likely that in this early play "the croaking raven did bellow for revenge" and very likely went on bellowing till he got it. How far this early play helped Shakespeare, by encouraging him to do better or provoking him to do differently, cannot be known, but it is probable that in this early play, as in Shakespeare's play, the minds and methods of Claudius and Hamlet were in conflict.

We have three versions of Shakespeare's *Hamlet*. The first of these, called the First Quarto, is the essential Shakespeare play cut to the bare bones for stage performance, and printed from some imperfect record perhaps taken surreptitiously, in shorthand, during a performance. The maker of the record took down Polonius's name as CORAMBIS.

It is likely that this First Quarto was, in the main, with slight additions and omissions, the text usually played by Shakespeare's company.

As I have said, it was cut to the bare bones for performance, by the fatal scissors of the company.

In what is called the Second Quarto, we have another, much fuller, version of Shakespeare's play, preserving some of the cuts.

In the First Folio, we have a third, still fuller version. Players today usually make their acting versions from all three versions, as best suits their immediate design or personal talent. The First Quarto version preserves the essential play.

His friends testify, and the plays show, that Shakespeare wrote easily from an abundance of intellectual power and light seldom given to man. Often, the fable must have been luminous within him from the instant that he began to write: poetry came from him not as a gum that oozed, but as a sun that dawned. There are certain acts, or half plays, that must have been written at a sitting: he was always a poet of power.

In *Hamlet,* one sometimes feels that the subtlety of the concept, the hesitancy of the judging mind, so questioned the power, as to make it uncertain and to baffle the light it brought.

DRAMATIS PERSONÆ

CLAUDIUS, King of Denmark
HAMLET, Son to the late, and Nephew to the present, King
FORTINBRAS, Prince of Norway
HORATIO, Friend to Hamlet
POLONIUS, Principal Secretary of State
LAERTES, his Son
VOLTIMAND }
CORNELIUS } Ambassadors to Norway
ROSENCRANTZ }
GUILDENSTERN } formerly Fellow Students with Hamlet
OSRIC, a Fop
A GENTLEMAN
A PRIEST
MARCELLUS }
BERNARDO } Officers
FRANCISCO, a Soldier
REYNALDO, Servant to Polonius
A CAPTAIN
ENGLISH AMBASSADORS
PLAYERS. TWO CLOWNS, GRAVE-DIGGERS
GERTRUDE, Queen of Denmark and Mother to Hamlet
OPHELIA, Daughter to Polonius
LORDS, LADIES, OFFICERS, SOLDIERS, SAILORS, MESSENGERS, AND
    ATTENDANTS
GHOST of Hamlet's Father

SCENE. *Elsinore*

Act 1

Scene I.   Elsinore. A Platform before the Castle

FRANCISCO *at his post. Enter to him* BERNARDO.

BERNARDO. Who's there?

FRANCISCO. Nay, answer me. Stand and unfold yourself.

BERNARDO. Long live the king!

FRANCISCO. Bernardo?

BERNARDO. He.

FRANCISCO. You come most carefully upon your hour.

BERNARDO. 'Tis now struck twelve; get thee to bed, Francisco.

FRANCISCO. For this relief much thanks; 'tis bitter cold,
And I am sick at heart.

BERNARDO. Have you had quiet guard?

FRANCISCO.   Not a mouse stirring.

BERNARDO. Well, good-night.
If you do meet Horatio and Marcellus,
The rivals of my watch, bid them make haste.

FRANCISCO. I think I hear them. Stand, ho! Who is there?

Enter HORATIO *and* MARCELLUS.

HORATIO. Friends to this ground.

MARCELLUS.   And liegemen to the Dane.

FRANCISCO. Give you good-night.

MARCELLUS.   O! farewell, honest soldier:
Who hath reliev'd you?

106

FRANCISCO. Bernardo has my place.
Give you good-night. [*Exit.*
MARCELLUS. Holla! Bernardo!
BERNARDO. Say,
What! is Horatio there?
HORATIO. A piece of him.
BERNARDO. Welcome, Horatio; welcome, good Marcellus.
HORATIO. What! has this thing appear'd again to-night?
BERNARDO. I have seen nothing.
MARCELLUS. Horatio says 'tis but our fantasy,
And will not let belief take hold of him
Touching this dreaded sight twice seen of us:
Therefore I have entreated him along
With us to watch the minutes of this night;
That if again this apparition come,
He may approve our eyes and speak to it.
HORATIO. Tush, tush! 'twill not appear.
BERNARDO. Sit down awhile,
And let us once again assail your ears,
That are so fortified against our story,
What we two nights have seen.
HORATIO. Well, sit we down,
And let us hear Bernardo speak of this.
BERNARDO. Last night of all,
When yond same star that's westward from the pole
Had made his course to illume that part of heaven
Where now it burns, Marcellus and myself,
The bell then beating one,—

Enter GHOST.

MARCELLUS. Peace! break thee off; look, where it comes again!
BERNARDO. In the same figure like the king that's dead.
MARCELLUS. Thou art a scholar; speak to it, Horatio.
BERNARDO. Looks it not like the king? mark it, Horatio.
HORATIO. Most like: it harrows me with fear and wonder.

BERNARDO. It would be spoke to.

MARCELLUS. Question it, Horatio.

HORATIO. What art thou that usurp'st this time of night,
Together with that fair and war-like form
In which the majesty of buried Denmark
Did sometimes march? by heaven I charge thee, speak!

MARCELLUS. It is offended.

BERNARDO. See! it stalks away.

HORATIO. Stay! speak, speak! I charge thee, speak!

[*Exit* GHOST.

MARCELLUS. 'Tis gone, and will not answer.

BERNARDO. How now, Horatio! you tremble and look pale:
Is not this something more than fantasy?
What think you on 't?

HORATIO. Before my God, I might not this believe
Without the sensible and true avouch
Of mine own eyes.

MARCELLUS. Is it not like the king?

HORATIO. As thou art to thyself:
Such was the very armour he had on
When he the ambitious Norway combated;
So frown'd he once, when in an angry parle
He smote the sledded Polacks on the ice.
'Tis strange.

MARCELLUS. Thus twice before, and jump at this dead hour,
With martial stalk hath he gone by our watch.

HORATIO. In what particular thought to work I know not;
But in the gross and scope of my opinion,
This bodes some strange eruption to our state.

MARCELLUS. Good now, sit down, and tell me, he that knows,
Why this same strict and most observant watch
So nightly toils the subject of the land,
And why such daily cast of brazen cannon,
And foreign mart for implements of war,
Why such impress of shipwrights, whose sore task
Does not divide the Sunday from the week,

The "Flower" portrait of Shakespeare in the
Royal Shakespeare Theatre, Stratford-on-Avon

What might be toward, that this sweaty haste
Doth make the night joint-labourer with the day:
Who is't that can inform me?

HORATIO.   That can I;
At least, the whisper goes so. Our last king,
Whose image even but now appear'd to us,
Was, as you know, by Fortinbras of Norway,
Thereto prick'd on by a most emulate pride,
Dar'd to the combat; in which our valiant Hamlet—
For so this side of our known world esteem'd him—
Did slay this Fortinbras; who, by a seal'd compact,
Well ratified by law and heraldry,
Did forfeit with his life all those his lands
Which he stood seiz'd of, to the conqueror;
Against the which, a moiety competent
Was gagéd by our king; which had return'd
To the inheritance of Fortinbras,
Had he been vanquisher; as, by the same co-mart,
And carriage of the article design'd,
His fell to Hamlet. Now, sir, young Fortinbras,
Of unimprovéd mettle hot and full,
Hath in the skirts of Norway here and there
Shark'd up a list of lawless resolutes
For food and diet to some enterprise
That hath a stomach in 't; which is no other—
As it doth well appear unto our state—
But to recover of us, by strong hand
And terms compulsative, those foresaid lands
So by his father lost. And this, I take it,
Is the main motive of our preparations,
The source of this our watch and the chief head
Of this post-haste and romage in the land.

BERNARDO. I think it be no other but e'en so;
Well may it sort that this portentous figure
Comes arméd through our watch, so like the king
That was and is the question of these wars.

HORATIO. A mote it is to trouble the mind's eye.
In the most high and palmy state of Rome,
A little ere the mightiest Julius fell,
The graves stood tenantless, and the sheeted dead
Did squeak and gibber in the Roman streets;
As stars with trains of fire and dews of blood,
Disasters in the sun; and the moist star
Upon whose influence Neptune's empire stands
Was sick almost to doomsday with eclipse;
And even the like precurse of fierce events,
As harbingers preceding still the fates
And prologue to the omen coming on,
Have heaven and earth together demonstrated
Unto our climatures and countrymen.

     Re-enter GHOST.

But, soft! behold! lo! where it comes again.
I'll cross it, though it blast me. Stay, illusion!
If thou hast any sound, or use of voice,
Speak to me:
If there be any good thing to be done,
That may to thee do ease and grace to me,
Speak to me:
If thou art privy to thy country's fate,
Which happily foreknowing may avoid,
O! speak!
Or if thou hast uphoarded in thy life
Extorted treasure in the womb of earth,
For which, they say, you spirits oft walk in death,
Speak of it: stay, and speak! [*Cock crows.*] Stop it, Marcellus.

  MARCELLUS. Shall I strike at it with my partisan?

  HORATIO. Do, if it will not stand.

  BERNARDO.   'Tis here!

  HORATIO.   'Tis here!

                                 [*Exit* GHOST.

  MARCELLUS. 'Tis gone!
We do it wrong, being so majestical,

To offer it the show of violence;
For it is, as the air, invulnerable,
And our vain blows malicious mockery.

BERNARDO. It was about to speak when the cock crew.

HORATIO. And then it started like a guilty thing
Upon a fearful summons. I have heard,
The cock, that is the trumpet to the morn,
Doth with his lofty and shrill-sounding throat
Awake the god of day; and at his warning,
Whether in sea or fire, in earth or air,
Th' extravagant and erring spirit hies
To his confine; and of the truth herein
This present object made probation.

MARCELLUS. It faded on the crowing of the cock.
Some say that ever 'gainst that season comes
Wherein our Saviour's birth is celebrated,
The bird of dawning singeth all night long;
And then, they say, no spirit dare stir abroad;
The nights are wholesome; then no planets strike,
No fairy takes, nor witch hath power to charm,
So hallow'd and so gracious is that time.

HORATIO. So have I heard and do in part believe it.
But look, the morn in russet mantle clad
Walks o'er the dew of yon high eastern hill;
Break we our watch up; and by my advice
Let us impart what we have seen to-night
Unto young Hamlet; for, upon my life,
This spirit, dumb to us, will speak to him.
Do you consent we shall acquaint him with it,
As needful in our loves, fitting our duty?

MARCELLUS. Let's do 't, I pray; and I this morning know
Where we shall find him most conveniently. [*Exeunt.*

Scene II.   The Council Chamber

Enter CLAUDIUS, *King of Denmark,* GERTRUDE, *the Queen,* COUNCILLORS, POLONIUS *and his son* LAERTES, VOLTIMAND *and* CORNELIUS, HAMLET *and* ATTENDANTS.

KING. Though yet of Hamlet our dear brother's death
The memory be green, and that it us befitted
To bear our hearts in grief, and our whole kingdom
To be contracted in one brow of woe,
Yet so far hath discretion fought with nature
That we with wisest sorrow think on him,
Together with remembrance of ourselves.
Therefore our sometime sister, now our queen,
Th' imperial jointress to this war-like state,
Have we, as 'twere with a defeated joy,
With one auspicious and one dropping eye,
With mirth in funeral and with dirge in marriage,
In equal scale weighing delight and dole,
Taken to wife: nor have we herein barr'd
Your better wisdoms, which have freely gone
With this affair along: for all, our thanks.
Now follows, that you know, young Fortinbras,
Holding a weak supposal of our worth,
Or thinking by our late dear brother's death
Our state to be disjoint and out of frame,
Colleaguéd with the dream of his advantage,
He hath not fail'd to pester us with message,
Importing the surrender of those lands
Lost by his father, with all bands of law,
To our most valiant brother. So much for him.
Now for ourself and for this time of meeting.
Thus much the business is: we have here writ
To Norway, uncle of young Fortinbras,
Who, impotent and bed-rid, scarcely hears
Of this his nephew's purpose, to suppress

His further gait herein; in that the levies,
The lists and full proportions, are all made
Out of his subject; and we here dispatch
You, good Cornelius, and you, Voltimand,
For bearers of this greeting to old Norway,
Giving to you no further personal power
To business with the king more than the scope
Of these delated articles allow.
Farewell and let your haste commend your duty.

CORNELIUS. ⎱
VOLTIMAND. ⎰ In that and all things will we show our duty.

KING. We doubt it nothing: heartily farewell.

          [Exeunt VOLTIMAND *and* CORNELIUS.
And now, Laertes, what's the news with you?
You told us of some suit; what is't, Laertes?
You cannot speak of reason to the Dane,
And lose your voice; what wouldst thou beg, Laertes,
That shall not be my offer, not thy asking?
The head is not more native to the heart,
The hand more instrumental to the mouth,
Than is the throne of Denmark to thy father.
What wouldst thou have, Laertes?

LAERTES.   Dread my lord,
Your leave and favour to return to France;
From whence though willingly I came to Denmark,
To show my duty in your coronation,
Yet now, I must confess, that duty done,
My thoughts and wishes bend again toward France
And bow them to your gracious leave and pardon.

KING. Have you your father's leave? What says Polonius?

POLONIUS. He hath, my lord, wrung from me my slow leave
By laboursome petition, and at last
Upon his will I seal'd my hard consent:
I do beseech you, give him leave to go.

KING. Take thy fair hour, Laertes; time be thine,
And thy best graces spend it at thy will.

But now, my cousin Hamlet, and my son,—

HAMLET. [*Aside.*] A little more than kin, and less than kind.

KING. How is it that the clouds still hang on you?

HAMLET. Not so, my lord; I am too much i' the sun.

QUEEN. Good Hamlet, cast thy nighted colour off,
And let thine eye look like a friend on Denmark.
Do not for ever with thy vailéd lids
Seek for thy noble father in the dust:
Thou know'st 'tis common; all that live must die,
Passing through nature to eternity.

HAMLET. Ay, madam, it is common.

QUEEN.   If it be,
Why seems it so particular with thee?

HAMLET. Seems, madam! Nay, it is; I know not 'seems.'
'Tis not alone my inky cloak, good mother,
Nor customary suits of solemn black,
Nor windy suspiration of forc'd breath,
No, nor the fruitful river in the eye,
Nor the dejected haviour of the visage,
Together with all forms, modes, shows of grief,
That can denote me truly; these indeed seem,
For they are actions that a man might play:
But I have that within which passeth show;
These but the trappings and the suits of woe.

KING. 'Tis sweet and commendable in your nature, Hamlet,
To give these mourning duties to your father:
But, you must know, your father lost a father;
That father lost, lost his; and the survivor bound
In filial obligation for some term
To do obsequious sorrow; but to persever
In obstinate condolement is a course
Of impious stubbornness; 'tis unmanly grief:
It shows a will most incorrect to heaven,
A heart unfortified, a mind impatient,
An understanding simple and unschool'd:
For what we know must be and is as common

As any the most vulgar thing to sense,
Why should we in our peevish opposition
Take it to heart? Fie! 'tis a fault to heaven,
A fault against the dead, a fault to nature,
To reason most absurd, whose common theme
Is death of fathers, and who still hath cried,
From the first corse till he that died to-day,
'This must be so.' We pray you, throw to earth
This unprevailing woe, and think of us
As of a father; for let the world take note,
You are the most immediate to our throne;
And with no less nobility of love
Than that which dearest father bears his son
Do I impart toward you. For your intent
In going back to school in Wittenberg,
It is most retrograde to our desire;
And we beseech you, bend you to remain
Here, in the cheer and comfort of our eye,
Our chiefest courtier, cousin, and our son.
   QUEEN. Let not thy mother lose her prayers, Hamlet:
I pray thee, stay with us; go not to Wittenberg.
     HAMLET. I shall in all my best obey you, madam.
     KING. Why, 'tis a loving and a fair reply:
Be as ourself in Denmark. Madam, come;
This gentle and unforc'd accord of Hamlet
Sits smiling to my heart; in grace whereof,
No jocund health that Denmark drinks to-day,
But the great cannon to the clouds shall tell,
And the king's rouse the heavens shall bruit again,
Re-speaking earthly thunder. Come away.
               [*Exeunt all except* HAMLET.
     HAMLET. O! that this too too solid flesh would melt,
Thaw and resolve itself into a dew;
Or that the Everlasting had not fix'd
His canon 'gainst self-slaughter! O God! God!
How weary, stale, flat, and unprofitable

Seem to me all the uses of this world.
Fie on 't! Ah fie! 'tis an unweeded garden,
That grows to seed; things rank and gross in nature
Possess it merely. That it should come to this!
But two months dead: nay, not so much, not two:
So excellent a king; that was, to this,
Hyperion to a satyr; so loving to my mother
That he might not beteem the winds of heaven
Visit her face too roughly. Heaven and earth!
Must I remember? why, she would hang on him,
As if increase of appetite had grown
By what it fed on; and yet, within a month,
Let me not think on't: Frailty, thy name is woman!
A little month; or ere those shoes were old
With which she follow'd my poor father's body,
Like Niobe, all tears; why she, even she,—
O God! a beast, that wants discourse of reason,
Would have mourn'd longer,—married with mine uncle,
My father's brother, but no more like my father
Than I to Hercules: within a month,
Ere yet the salt of most unrighteous tears
Had left the flushing in her galléd eyes,
She married. O! most wicked speed, to post
With such dexterity to incestuous sheets.
It is not nor it cannot come to good;
But break, my heart, for I must hold my tongue!

Enter HORATIO, MARCELLUS, *and* BERNARDO.

HORATIO. Hail to your lordship!
HAMLET.   I am glad to see you well:
Horatio, or I do forget myself.
HORATIO. The same, my lord, and your poor servant ever.
HAMLET. Sir, my good friend; I'll change that name with you.
And what make you from Wittenberg, Horatio?
Marcellus?
MARCELLUS. My good lord,—

Kronborg Castle at Elsinore, Denmark, the setting for *Hamlet*

HAMLET. I am very glad to see you. [*To* BERNARDO.] Good
    even, sir.
But what, in faith, make you from Wittenberg?
    HORATIO. A truant disposition, good my lord.
    HAMLET. I would not hear your enemy say so,
Nor shall you do mine ear that violence,
To make it truster of your own report
Against yourself; I know you are no truant.
But what is your affair in Elsinore?
We'll teach you to drink deep ere you depart.
    HORATIO. My lord, I came to see your father's funeral.
    HAMLET. I pray thee, do not mock me, fellow-student;
I think it was to see my mother's wedding.
    HORATIO. Indeed, my lord, it follow'd hard upon.
    HAMLET. Thrift, thrift, Horatio! the funeral bak'd meats
Did coldly furnish forth the marriage tables.
Would I had met my dearest foe in heaven
Or ever I had seen that day, Horatio!
My father, methinks I see my father.
    HORATIO. O! where, my lord?
    HAMLET.   In my mind's eye, Horatio.
    HORATIO. I saw him once; he was a goodly king.
    HAMLET. He was a man, take him for all in all,
I shall not look upon his like again.
    HORATIO. My lord, I think I saw him yesternight.
    HAMLET. Saw who?
    HORATIO. My lord, the king your father.
    HAMLET.   The king, my father!
    HORATIO. Season your admiration for a while
With an attent ear, till I may deliver,
Upon the witness of these gentlemen,
This marvel to you.
    HAMLET.   For God's love, let me hear.
    HORATIO. Two nights together had these gentlemen,
Marcellus and Bernardo, on their watch,
In the dead vast and middle of the night,

Been thus encounter'd: a figure like your father,
Arméd at point exactly, cap-a-pe,
Appears before them, and with solemn march
Goes slow and stately by them: thrice he walk'd
By their oppress'd and fear-surpriséd eyes,
Within his truncheon's length; whilst they, distill'd
Almost to jelly with the act of fear,
Stand dumb and speak not to him. This to me
In dreadful secrecy impart they did,
And I with them the third night kept the watch;
Where, as they had deliver'd, both in time,
Form of the thing, each word made true and good,
The apparition comes. I knew your father;
These hands are not more like.

  HAMLET.   But where was this?
  MARCELLUS. My lord, upon the platform where we watch'd.
  HAMLET. Did you not speak to it?
  HORATIO.   My lord, I did;
But answer made it none; yet once methought
It lifted up it head and did address
Itself to motion, like as it would speak;
But even then the morning cock crew loud,
And at the sound it shrunk in haste away
And vanish'd from our sight.

  HAMLET.   'Tis very strange.
  HORATIO. As I do live, my honour'd lord, 'tis true;
And we did think it writ down in our duty
To let you know of it.

  HAMLET. Indeed, indeed, sirs, but this troubles me.
Hold you the watch to-night?

  MARCELLUS. ⎫
  BERNARDO. ⎭   We do, my lord.

  HAMLET. Arm'd, say you?
  MARCELLUS. ⎫
  BERNARDO. ⎭   Arm'd, my lord.

HAMLET. From top to toe?

MARCELLUS. ⎤
BERNARDO. ⎦ My lord, from head to foot.

HAMLET. Then saw you not his face?

HORATIO. O yes! my lord; he wore his beaver up.

HAMLET. What! look'd he frowningly?

HORATIO. A countenance more in sorrow than in anger.

HAMLET. Pale or red?

HORATIO. Nay, very pale.

HAMLET. And fix'd his eyes upon you?

HORATIO. Most constantly.

HAMLET. I would I had been there.

HORATIO. It would have much amaz'd you.

HAMLET. Very like, very like. Stay'd it long?

HORATIO. While one with moderate haste might tell a hundred.

MARCELLUS ⎤
BERNARDO. ⎦ Longer, longer.

HORATIO. Not when I saw it.

HAMLET. His beard was grizzled, no?

HORATIO. It was, as I have seen it in his life,
A sable silver'd.

HAMLET. I will watch to-night;
Perchance 'twill walk again.

HORATIO. I warrant it will.

HAMLET. If it assume my noble father's person,
I'll speak to it, though hell itself should gape
And bid me hold my peace. I pray you all,
If you have hitherto conceal'd this sight,
Let it be tenable in your silence still;
And whatsoever else shall hap to-night,
Give it an understanding, but no tongue:
I will requite your loves. So, fare you well.
Upon the platform, 'twixt eleven and twelve,
I'll visit you.

ALL.   Our duty to your honour.

HAMLET. Your loves, as mine to you. Farewell.

[*Exeunt* HORATIO, MARCELLUS, *and* BERNARDO.

My father's spirit (in arms!) all is not well;

I doubt some foul play: would the night were come!

Till then sit still, my soul: foul deeds will rise,

Though all the earth o'erwhelm them, to men's eyes.   [*Exit.*

Scene III.   A Room in Polonius' House

Enter LAERTES *and* OPHELIA.

LAERTES. My necessaries are embark'd; farewell:

And, sister, as the winds give benefit

And convoy is assistant, do not sleep,

But let me hear from you.

OPHELIA.   Do you doubt that?

LAERTES. For Hamlet, and the trifling of his favour,

Hold it a fashion and a toy in blood,

A violet in the youth of primy nature,

Forward, not permanent, sweet, not lasting,

The perfume and suppliance of a minute;

No more.

OPHELIA. No more but so?

LAERTES.   Think it no more:

For nature, crescent, does not grow alone

In thews and bulk; but, as this temple waxes,

The inward service of the mind and soul

Grows wide withal. Perhaps he loves you now,

And now no soil nor cautel doth besmirch

The virtue of his will; but you must fear,

His greatness weigh'd, his will is not his own,

For he himself is subject to his birth;

He may not, as unvalu'd persons do,

Carve for himself, for on his choice depends

The safety and the health of the whole state;

70

And therefore must his choice be circumscrib'd
Unto the voice and yielding of that body
Whereof he is the head. Then if he says he loves you,
It fits your wisdom so far to believe it
As he in his particular act and place
May give his saying deed; which is no further
Than the main voice of Denmark goes withal.
Then weigh what loss your honour may sustain,
If with too credent ear you list his songs,
Or lose your heart, or your chaste treasure open
To his unmaster'd importunity.
Fear it, Ophelia, fear it, my dear sister;
And keep you in the rear of your affection,
Out of the shot and danger of desire.
The chariest maid is prodigal enough
If she unmask her beauty to the moon;
Virtue herself 'scapes not calumnious strokes;
The canker galls the infants of the spring
Too oft before their buttons be disclos'd,
And in the morn and liquid dew of youth
Contagious blastments are most imminent.
Be wary then; best safety lies in fear:
Youth to itself rebels, though none else near.

    OPHELIA. I shall th' effect of this good lesson keep,
As watchman to my heart. But, good my brother,
Do not, as some ungracious pastors do,
Show me the steep and thorny way to heaven,
Whiles, like a puff'd and reckless libertine,
Himself the primrose path of dalliance treads,
And recks not his own rede.

    LAERTES.   O! fear me not.
I stay too long; but here my father comes.

    Enter POLONIUS.

A double blessing is a double grace;
Occasion smiles upon a second leave.

    POLONIUS. Yet here, Laertes! aboard, aboard, for shame!

The wind sits in the shoulder of your sail,
And you are stay'd for. There, my blessing with thee!
And these few precepts in thy memory
Look thou character. Give thy thoughts no tongue,
Nor any unproportion'd thought his act.
Be thou familiar, but by no means vulgar;
The friends thou hast, and their adoption tried,
Grapple them to thy soul with hoops of steel;
But do not dull thy palm with entertainment
Of each new-hatch'd, unfledg'd comrade. Beware
Of entrance to a quarrel, but, being in,
Bear 't that th' opposéd may beware of thee.
Give every man thine ear, but few thy voice;
Take each man's censure, but reserve thy judgment.
Costly thy habit as thy purse can buy,
But not express'd in fancy; rich, not gaudy;
For the apparel oft proclaims the man,
And they in France of the best rank and station
Are most select and generous, chief in that.
Neither a borrower, nor a lender be;
For loan oft loses both itself and friend,
And borrowing dulls the edge of husbandry.
This above all: to thine own self be true,
And it must follow, as the night the day,
Thou canst not then be false to any man.
Farewell; my blessing season this in thee!
    LAERTES. Most humbly do I take my leave, my lord.
    POLONIUS. The time invites you; go, your servants tend.
    LAERTES. Farewell, Ophelia; and remember well
What I have said to you.
    OPHELIA.   'Tis in my memory lock'd,
And you yourself shall keep the key of it.
    LAERTES. Farewell.   *[Exit.*
    POLONIUS. What is 't, Ophelia, he hath said to you?
    OPHELIA. So please you, something touching the Lord Hamlet.
    POLONIUS. Marry, well bethought:

'Tis told me, he hath very oft of late
Given private time to you; and you yourself
Have of your audience been most free and bounteous.
If it be so,—as so 'tis put on me,
And that in way of caution,—I must tell you,
You do not understand yourself so clearly
As it behoves my daughter and your honour.
What is between you? give me up the truth.

OPHELIA. He hath, my lord, of late made many tenders
Of his affection to me.

POLONIUS. Affection! pooh! you speak like a green girl,
Unsifted in such perilous circumstance.
Do you believe his tenders, as you call them?

OPHELIA. I do not know, my lord, what I should think.

POLONIUS. Marry, I'll teach you: think yourself a baby,
That you have ta'en these tenders for true pay,
Which are not sterling. Tender yourself more dearly;
Or,—not to crack the wind of the poor phrase,
Running it thus,—you'll tender me a fool.

OPHELIA. My lord, he hath importun'd me with love
In honourable fashion.

POLONIUS. Ay, fashion you may call it: go to, go to.

OPHELIA. And hath given countenance to his speech, my lord,
With almost all the holy vows of heaven.

POLONIUS. Ay, springes to catch woodcocks. I do know,
When the blood burns, how prodigal the soul
Lends the tongue vows: these blazes, daughter,
Giving more light than heat, extinct in both,
Even in their promise, as it is a-making,
You must not take for fire. From this time
Be somewhat scanter of your maiden presence;
Set your entreatments at a higher rate
Than a command to parley. For Lord Hamlet,
Believe so much in him, that he is young,
And with a larger tether may he walk
Than may be given you: in few, Ophelia,

Do not believe his vows, for they are brokers,
Not of that dye which their investments show,
But mere implorators of unholy suits,
Breathing like sanctified and pious bonds,
The better to beguile. This is for all:
I would not, in plain terms, from this time forth,
Have you so slander any moment's leisure,
As to give words or talk with the Lord Hamlet.
Look to 't, I charge you; come your ways.

OPHELIA. I shall obey, my lord.   [*Exeunt.*

Scene IV.   The Platform

Enter HAMLET, HORATIO, *and* MARCELLUS.

HAMLET. The air bites shrewdly; it is very cold.

HORATIO. It is a nipping and an eager air.

HAMLET. What hour now?

HORATIO.   I think it lacks of twelve.

MARCELLUS. No, it is struck.

HORATIO. Indeed? I heard it not: then it draws near the season
Wherein the spirit held his wont to walk.

[*A flourish of trumpets, and ordnance shot off, within.*
What does this mean, my lord?

HAMLET. The king doth wake to-night and takes his rouse,
Keeps wassail and the swaggering up-spring reels;
And, as he drains his draughts of Rhenish down,
The kettle-drum and trumpet thus bray out
The triumph of his pledge.

HORATIO.   Is it a custom?

HAMLET. Ay, marry, is 't:
But to my mind,—though I am native here
And to the manner born,—it is a custom
More honour'd in the breach than the observance.
This heavy-headed revel east and west
Makes us traduc'd and tax'd of other nations;

They clepe us drunkards, and with swinish phrase
Soil our addition; and indeed it takes
From our achievements, though perform'd at height,
The pith and marrow of our attribute.
So, oft it chances in particular men,
That for some vicious mole of nature in them,
As, in their birth,—wherein they are not guilty,
Since nature cannot choose his origin,—
By the o'ergrowth of some complexion,
Oft breaking down the pales and forts of reason,
Or by some habit that too much o'er-leavens
The form of plausive maners; that these men,
Carrying, I say, the stamp of one defect,
Being nature's livery, or fortune's star,
His virtues else, be they as pure as grace,
As infinite as man may undergo,
Shall in the general censure take corruption
From that particular fault: the dram of evil
Doth all the noble substance often dout,
To his own scandal.

    Enter GHOST.

HORATIO.   Look, my lord, it comes.
HAMLET. Angels and ministers of grace defend us!
Be thou a spirit of health or goblin damn'd,
Bring with thee airs from heaven or blasts from hell,
Be thy intents wicked or charitable,
Thou com'st in such a questionable shape
That I will speak to thee: I'll call thee Hamlet,
King, father; royal Dane, O! answer me:
Let me not burst in ignorance; but tell
Why thy canoniz'd bones, hearsèd in death,
Have burst their cerements; why the sepulchre,
Wherein we saw thee quietly inurn'd,
Hath op'd his ponderous and marble jaws,
To cast thee up again. What may this mean,

That thou, dead corse, again in complete steel
Revisits thus the glimpses of the moon,
Making night hideous; and we fools of nature
So horridly to shake our disposition
With thoughts beyond the reaches of our souls?
Say, why is this? wherefore? what should we do?

[*The* GHOST *beckons* HAMLET.

HORATIO. It beckons you to go away with it,
As if it some impartment did desire
To you alone.

MARCELLUS. Look, with what courteous action
It waves you to a more removéd ground:
But do not go with it.

HORATIO. No, by no means.

HAMLET. It will not speak; then, will I follow it.

HORATIO. Do not, my lord.

HAMLET. Why, what should be the fear?
I do not set my life at a pin's fee;
And for my soul, what can it do to that,
Being a thing immortal as itself?
It waves me forth again; I'll follow it.

HORATIO. What if it tempt you toward the flood, my lord,
Or to the dreadful summit of the cliff
That beetles o'er his base into the sea,
And there assume some other horrible form,
Which might deprive your sovereignty of reason
And draw you into madness? think of it;
The very place puts toys of desperation,
Without more motive, into every brain
That looks so many fathoms to the sea
And hears it roar beneath.

HAMLET. It waves me still. Go on, I'll follow thee.

MARCELLUS. You shall not go, my lord.

HAMLET. Hold off your hands!

HORATIO. Be rul'd; you shall not go.

HAMLET. My fate cries out,

And makes each petty artery in this body
As hardy as the Nemean lion's nerve. [GHOST *beckons.*
Still am I call'd. Unhand me, gentlemen,

[*Breaking from them.*
By heaven! I'll make a ghost of him that lets me:
I say, away! Go on, I'll follow thee.

[*Exeunt* GHOST *and* HAMLET.
HORATIO. He waxes desperate with imagination.
MARCELLUS. Let's follow; 'tis not fit thus to obey him.
HORATIO. Have after. To what issue will this come?
MARCELLUS. Something is rotten in the state of Denmark.
HORATIO. Heaven will direct it.
MARCELLUS.   Nay, let's follow him.

[*Exeunt.*

Scene V. *Another Part of the Platform*

Enter GHOST *and* HAMLET.

HAMLET. Whither wilt thou lead me? speak; I'll go no further.
GHOST. Mark me.
HAMLET.   I will.
GHOST.   My hour is almost come,
When I to sulphurous and tormenting flames
Must render up myself.
HAMLET.   Alas! poor ghost.
GHOST. Pity me not, but lend thy serious hearing
To what I shall unfold.
HAMLET.   Speak; I am bound to hear.
GHOST. So art thou to revenge, when thou shalt hear.
HAMLET. What?
GHOST. I am thy father's spirit;
Doom'd for a certain term to walk the night,
And for the day confin'd to fast in fires,
Till the foul crimes done in my days of nature
Are burnt and purg'd away. But that I am forbid

To tell the secrets of my prison-house,
I could a tale unfold whose lightest word
Would harrow up thy soul, freeze thy young blood,
Make thy two eyes like stars start from their spheres,
Thy knotted and combinéd locks to part,
And each particular hair to stand an end,
Like quills upon the fretful porpentine:
But this eternal blazon must not be
To ears of flesh and bood. List, list, O list!
If thou didst ever thy dear father love—

HAMLET. O God!

GHOST. Revenge his foul and most unnatural murder.

HAMLET. Murder!

GHOST. Murder most foul, as in the best it is;
But this most foul, strange, and unnatural.

HAMLET. Haste me to know 't, that I, with wings as swift
As meditation or the thoughts of love,
May sweep to my revenge.

GHOST.   I find thee apt,
And duller shouldst thou be than the fat weed
That rots itself in ease on Lethe wharf,
Wouldst thou not stir in this. Now, Hamlet, hear:
'Tis given out, that sleeping in mine orchard,
A serpent stung me; so the whole ear of Denmark
Is by a forgéd process of my death
Rankly abus'd; but know, thou noble youth,
The serpent that did sting thy father's life
Now wears his crown.

HAMLET.   O my prophetic soul!
My uncle?

GHOST. Ay, that incestuous, that adulterate beast,
With witchcraft of his wit, with traitorous gifts,—
O wicked wit and gifts, that have the power
So to seduce!—won to his shameful lust
The will of my most seeming-virtuous queen.

O Hamlet! what a falling-off was there;
From me, whose love was of that dignity
That it went hand in hand even with the vow
I made to her in marriage; and to decline
Upon a wretch whose natural gifts were poor
To those of mine!
But virtue, as it never will be mov'd,
Though lewdness court it in a shape of heaven,
So lust, though to a radiant angel link'd,
Will sate itself in a celestial bed,
And prey on garbage.
But, soft! methinks I scent the morning air;
Brief let me be. Sleeping within mine orchard,
My custom always of the afternoon,
Upon my secure hour thy uncle stole,
With juice of cursed hebona in a vial,
And in the porches of mine ears did pour
The leperous distilment; whose effect
Holds such an enmity with blood of man
That swift as quicksilver it courses through
The natural gates and alleys of the body,
And with a sudden vigour it doth posset
And curd, like eager droppings into milk,
The thin and wholesome blood: so did it mine;
And a most instant tetter bark'd about,
Most lazar-like, with vile and loathsome crust,
All my smooth body.
Thus was I, sleeping, by a brother's hand,
Of life, of crown, of queen, at once dispatch'd;
Cut off even in the blossoms of my sin,
Unhousel'd, disappointed, unanel'd,
No reckoning made, but sent to my account
With all my imperfections on my head:
O, horrible! O, horrible! most horrible!
If thou hast nature in thee, bear it not;

Let not the royal bed of Denmark be
A couch for luxury and damned incest.
But, howsoever thou pursu'st this act,
Taint not thy mind, nor let thy soul contrive
Against thy mother aught; leave her to heaven,
And to those thorns that in her bosom lodge,
To prick and sting her. Fare thee well at once!
The glow-worm shows the matin to be near,
And 'gins to pale his uneffectual fire;
Adieu, adieu! Hamlet, remember me.   [*Exit.*

    HAMLET. O all you host of heaven! O earth! What else?
And shall I couple hell? O fie! Hold, hold, my heart!
And you, my sinews, grow not instant old,
But bear me stiffly up! Remember thee!
Ay, thou poor ghost, while memory holds a seat
In this distracted globe. Remember thee!
Yea, from the table of my memory
I'll wipe away all trivial fond records,
All saws of books, all forms, all pressures past
That youth and observation copied there;
And thy commandment all alone shall live
Within the book and volume of my brain,
Unmix'd with baser matter: yes, by heaven!
O most pernicious woman!
O villain, villain, smiling, damnéd villain!
My tables,—meet it is I set it down,
That one may smile, and smile, and be a villain;
At least I'm sure it may be so in Denmark: [*Writing.*
So, uncle, there you are. Now to my word;
It is, 'Adieu, adieu! remember me.'
I have sworn't.

    HORATIO. [*Within.*] My lord, my lord!
    MARCELLUS. [*Within.*]   Lord Hamlet!
    HORATIO. [*Within.*]   Heaven secure him!
    MARCELLUS. [*Within.*] So be it!
    HORATIO. [*Within.*] Hillo, ho, ho, my lord!

HAMLET. Hillo, ho, ho, boy! come, bird, come.

Enter HORATIO *and* MARCELLUS.

MARCELLUS. How is't, my noble lord?

HORATIO. What news, my lord?

HAMLET. O! wonderful.

HORATIO. Good my lord, tell it.

HAMLET. No; you will reveal it.

HORATIO. Not I, my lord, by heaven!

MARCELLUS. Nor I, my lord.

HAMLET. How say you then, would heart of man once think it?
But you'll be secret?

HORATIO. ⎫
MARCELLUS. ⎭ Ay, by heaven, my lord.

HAMLET. There's ne'er a villain dwelling in all Denmark
But he's an arrant knave.

HORATIO. There needs no ghost, my lord, come from the grave.
To tell us this.

HAMLET. Why, right; you are i' the right;
And so without more circumstance at all,
I hold it fit that we shake hands and part;
You, as your business and desire shall point you,—
For every man hath business and desire,
Such as it is,—and, for mine own poor part,
Look you, I'll go pray.

HORATIO. These are but wild and whirling words, my lord.

HAMLET. I am sorry they offend you, heartily;
Yes, faith, heartily.

HORATIO. There's no offence, my lord.

HAMLET. Yes, by Saint Patrick, but there is, Horatio,
And much offence, too. Touching this vision here,
It is an honest ghost, that let me tell you;
For your desire to know what is between us,
O'ermaster 't as you may. And now, good friends,
As you are friends, scholars, and soldiers,
Give me one poor request.

HORATIO. What is 't, my lord? we will.

HAMLET. Never make known what you have seen to-night.

HORATIO.
MARCELLUS. } My lord, we will not.

HAMLET.   Nay, but swear 't.

HORATIO.   In faith,
My lord, not I.

MARCELLUS. Nor I, my lord, in faith.

HAMLET. Upon my sword.

MARCELLUS.   We have sworn, my lord, already.

HAMLET. Indeed, upon my sword, indeed.

GHOST. [*Beneath.*] Swear.

HAMLET. Ha, ha, boy! sayst thou so? art thou there, true-
penny?
Come on,—you hear this fellow in the cellarage,—
Consent to swear.

HORATIO.   Propose the oath, my lord.

HAMLET. Never to speak of this that you have seen,
Swear by my sword.

GHOST. [*Beneath.*] Swear.

HAMLET. *Hic et ubique?* then we'll shift our ground.
Come hither, gentlemen,
And lay your hands again upon my sword:
Never to speak of this that you have heard,
Swear by my sword.

GHOST. [*Beneath.*] Swear.

HAMLET. Well said, old mole! canst work i' the earth so fast?
A worthy pioner! once more remove, good friends.

HORATIO. O day and night, but this is wondrous strange!

HAMLET. And therefore as a stranger give it welcome.
There are more things in heaven and earth, Horatio,
Than are dreamt of in your philosophy.
But come;
Here, as before, never, so help you mercy,
How strange or odd soe'er I bear myself,
As I perchance hereafter shall think meet

"There's rosemary, that's for remembrance; pray, love, remember: and there is pansies, that's for thoughts."

Act 4, Scene V

Jean Simmons as Ophelia in Laurence Olivier's production of *Hamlet*.

To put an antic disposition on,
That you, at such times seeing me, never shall,
With arms encumber'd thus, or this head-shake,
Or by pronouncing of some doubtful phrase,
As, 'Well, well, we know,' or, 'We could, an if we would;'
Or, 'If we list to speak,' or, 'There be, an if they might;'
Or such ambiguous giving out, to note
That you know aught of me: this not to do,
So grace and mercy at your most need help you,
Swear.

  GHOST. [*Beneath.*] Swear.   [*They swear.*

  HAMLET. Rest, rest, perturbéd spirit! So, gentlemen,
With all my love I do commend me to you:
And what so poor a man as Hamlet is
May do, to express his love and friending to you,
God willing, shall not lack. Let us go in together;
And still your fingers on your lips, I pray.
The time is out of joint; O curséd spite,
That ever I was born to set it right!
Nay, come, let's go together.   [*Exeunt.*

Act 2

Scene I. A Room in Polonius' House

Enter POLONIUS *and* REYNALDO.

POLONIUS. Give him this money and these notes, Reynaldo.

REYNALDO. I will, my lord.

POLONIUS. You shall do marvellous wisely, good Reynaldo,
Before you visit him, to make inquiry
Of his behaviour.

REYNALDO.   My lord, I did intend it.

POLONIUS. Marry, well said, very well said. Look you, sir,
Inquire me first what Danskers are in Paris;
And how, and who, what means, and where they keep,
What company, at what expense; and finding
By this encompassment and drift of question
That they do know my son, come you more nearer
Than your particular demands will touch it:
Take you, as 'twere, some distant knowledge of him;
As thus, 'I know his father, and his friends,
And, in part, him;' do you mark this, Reynaldo?

REYNALDO. Ay, very well, my lord.

POLONIUS. 'And, in part, him; but,' you may say, 'not well:
But if 't be he I mean, he's very wild,
Addicted so and so;' and there put on him
What forgeries you please; marry, none so rank
As may dishonour him; take heed of that;
But, sir, such wanton, wild, and usual slips
As are companions noted and most known

134

To youth and liberty.

REYNALDO.   As gaming, my lord?

POLONIUS. Ay, or drinking, fencing, swearing, quarrelling,
Drabbing; you may go so far.

REYNALDO. My lord, that would dishonour him.

POLONIUS. Faith, no; as you may season it in the charge.
You must not put another scandal on him,
That he is open to incontinency;
That's not my meaning; but breathe his faults so quaintly
That they may seem the taints of liberty,
The flash and outbreak of a fiery mind,
A savageness in unreclaiméd blood,
Of general assault.

REYNALDO.   But, my good lord,—

POLONIUS. Wherefore should you do this?

REYNALDO.   Ay, my lord,
I would know that.

POLONIUS.   Marry, sir, here's my drift;
And I believe it is a fetch of warrant:
You laying these slight sullies on my son,
As 'twere a thing a little soil'd i' the working,
Mark you,
Your party in converse, him you would sound,
Having ever seen in the prenominate crimes
The youth you breathe of guilty, be assur'd,
He closes with you in this consequence;
'Good sir,' or so; or 'friend,' or 'gentleman,'
According to the phrase or the addition
Of man and country.

REYNALDO.   Very good, my lord.

POLONIUS. And then, sir, does he this,—he does,—what was I
about to say? By the mass I was about to say something: where
did I leave?

REYNALDO. At 'closes in the consequence.'
At 'friend or so,' and 'gentleman.'

POLONIUS. At 'closes in the consequence,' ay, marry;

He closes with you thus: 'I know the gentleman;
I saw him yesterday, or t' other day,
Or then, or then; with such, or such; and, as you say,
There was a' gaming; there o'ertook in 's rouse;
There falling out at tennis;' or perchance,
'I saw him enter such a house of sale,'
Videlicet, a brothel, or so forth.
See you now;
Your bait of falsehood takes this carp of truth;
And thus do we of wisdom and of reach,
With windlasses, and with assays of bias,
By indirections find directions out:
So by my former lecture and advice
Shall you my son. You have me, have you not?
 REYNALDO. My lord, I have.
 POLONIUS.   God be wi' you; fare you well.
 REYNALDO. Good my lord!
 POLONIUS. Observe his inclination in yourself.
 REYNALDO. I shall, my lord.
 POLONIUS. And let him ply his music.
 REYNALDO.   Well, my lord.
 POLONIUS. Farewell!   [*Exit* REYNALDO.

 Enter OPHELIA.

       How now, Ophelia! what's the matter?
 OPHELIA. O! my lord, my lord, I have been so affrighted!
 POLONIUS With what, in the name of God?
 OPHELIA. My lord, as I was sewing in my closet,
Lord Hamlet, with his doublet all unbrac'd;
No hat upon his head; his stockings foul'd,
Ungarter'd, and down-gyvéd to his ancle;
Pale as his shirt; his knees knocking each other;
And with a look so piteous in purport
As if he had been looséd out of hell
To speak of horrors, he comes before me.
 POLONIUS. Mad for thy love?

OPHELIA. My lord, I do not know;
But truly I do fear it.
POLONIUS. What said he?
OPHELIA. He took me by the wrist and held me hard,
Then goes he to the length of all his arm,
And with his other hand thus o'er his brow,
He falls to such perusal of my face
As he would draw it. Long stay'd he so;
At last, a little shaking of mine arm,
And thrice his head thus waving up and down,
He rais'd a sigh so piteous and profound
That it did seem to shatter all his bulk
And end his being. That done, he lets me go,
And with his head over his shoulder turn'd,
He seem'd to find his way without his eyes;
For out o' doors he went without their help,
And to the last bended their light on me.
POLONIUS. Come, go with me; I will go seek the king.
This is the very ecstasy of love,
Whose violent property fordoes itself
And leads the will to desperate undertakings
As oft as any passion under heaven
That does afflict our natures. I am sorry.
What! have you given him any hard words of late?
OPHELIA. No, my good lord; but, as you did command,
I did repel his letters and denied
His access to me.
POLONIUS. That hath made him mad.
I am sorry that with better heed and judgment
I had not quoted him; I fear'd he did but trifle,
And meant to wrack thee; but, beshrew my jealousy!
By heaven, it is as proper to our age
To cast beyond ourselves in our opinions
As it is common for the younger sort
To lack discretion. Come, go we to the king:
This must be known; which, being kept close, might move

More grief to hide than hate to utter love.
Come.   [*Exeunt.*

Scene II.   *A Room in the Castle*

Enter KING, QUEEN, ROSENCRANTZ, GUILDENSTERN, *and* AT-
TENDANTS.

KING. Welcome, dear Rosencrantz and Guildenstern!
Moreover that we much did long to see you,
The need we have to use you did provoke
Our hasty sending. Something have you heard
Of Hamlet's transformation; so call it,
Sith nor the exterior nor the inward man
Resembles that it was. What it should be
More than his father's death, that thus hath put him
So much from the understanding of himself,
I cannot dream of: I entreat you both,
That, being of so young days brought up with him,
And sith so neighbour'd to his youth and humour,
That you vouchsafe your rest here in our court
Some little time; so by your companies
To draw him on to pleasures, and to gather,
So much as from occasion you may glean,
Whe'r aught to us unknown afflicts him thus,
That open'd lies within our remedy.
  QUEEN. Good gentlemen, he hath much talk'd of you;
And sure I am two men there are not living
To whom he more adheres. If it will please you
To show us so much gentry and good will
As to expend your time with us awhile,
For the supply and profit of our hope,
Your visitation shall receive such thanks
As fits a king's remembrance.
  ROSENCRANTZ.   Both your majesties

Might, by the sovereign power you have of us,
Put your dread pleasures more into command
Than to entreaty.

GUILDENSTERN. But we both obey,
And here give up ourselves in the full bent,
To lay our service freely at your feet,
To be commanded.

KING. Thanks, Rosencrantz and gentle Guildenstern.

QUEEN. Thanks, Guildenstern and gentle Rosencrantz;
And I beseech you instantly to visit
My too much changéd son. Go, some of you,
And bring these gentlemen where Hamlet is.

GUILDENSTERN. Heavens make our presence and our practices
Pleasant and helpful to him!

QUEEN.   Ay, amen!

[*Exeunt* ROSENCRANTZ, GUILDENSTERN, *and some*
ATTENDANTS.

Enter POLONIUS.

POLONIUS. The ambassadors from Norway, my good lord,
Are joyfully return'd.

KING. Thou still hast been the father of good news.

POLONIUS. Have I, my lord? Assure you, my good liege,
I hold my duty, as I hold my soul,
Both to my God and to my gracious king;
And I do think—or else this brain of mine
Hunts not the trail of policy so sure
As it hath us'd to do—that I have found
The very cause of Hamlet's lunacy.

KING. O! speak of that; that do I long to hear.

POLONIUS. Give first admittance to the ambassadors;
My news shall be the fruit to that great feast.

KING. Thyself do grace to them, and bring them in.

[*Exit* POLONIUS.

He tells me, my dear Gertrude, he hath found

The head and source of all your son's distemper.

QUEEN. I doubt it is no other but the main;

His father's death, and our o'erhasty marriage.

KING. Well, we shall sift him.

Re-enter POLONIUS, *with* VOLTIMAND *and* CORNELIUS.

Welcome, my good friends!

Say, Voltimand, what from our brother Norway?

VOLTIMAND. Most fair return of greetings and desires.

Upon our first, he sent out to suppress

His nephew's levies, which to him appear'd

To be a preparation 'gainst the Polack;

But, better look'd into, he truly found

It was against your highness: whereat griev'd,

That so his sickness, age, and impotence

Was falsely borne in hand, sends out arrests

On Fortinbras; which he, in brief, obeys,

Receives rebuke from Norway, and, in fine,

Makes vow before his uncle never more

To give the assay of arms against your majesty.

Whereon old Norway, overcome with joy,

Gives him three thousand crowns in annual fee,

And his commission to employ those soldiers,

So levied as before, against the Polack;

With an entreaty, herein further shown,   [*Giving a paper.*

That it might please you to give quiet pass

Through your dominions for this enterprise,

On such regards of safety and allowance

As therein are set down.

KING.   It likes us well;

And at our more consider'd time we'll read,

Answer, and think upon this business:

Meantime we thank you for your well-took labour.

Go to your rest; at night we'll feast together:

Most welcome home.   [*Exeunt* VOLTIMAND *and* CORNELIUS.

POLONIUS.   This business is well ended.

"The treacherous instrument is in thy hand, Unbated and envenom'd."
Act 5, Scene II

Laertes (Sidney Mather) wounds Hamlet; then in scuffling, they change rapiers, and Hamlet (John Barrymore) wounds Laertes.

My liege, and madam, to expostulate
What majesty should be, what duty is,
Why day is day, night night, and time is time,
Were nothing but to waste night, day, and time.
Therefore, since brevity is the soul of wit,
And tediousness the limbs and outward flourishes,
I will be brief. Your noble son is mad:
Mad call I it; for, to define true madness,
What is 't but to be nothing else but mad?
But let that go.
    QUEEN.   More matter, with less art.
    POLONIUS. Madam, I swear I use no art at all.
That he is mad, 'tis true; 'tis true 'tis pity;
And pity 'tis 'tis true: a foolish figure;
But farewell it, for I will use no art.
Mad let us grant him, then; and now remains
That we find out the cause of this effect,
Or rather say, the cause of this defect,
For this effect defective comes by cause;
Thus it remains, and the remainder thus.
Perpend.
I have a daughter, have while she is mine;
Who, in her duty and obedience, mark,
Hath given me this: now, gather, and surmise.
To the celestial, and my soul's idol, the most beautified
    Ophelia.—
That's an ill phrase, a vile phrase; 'beautified' is a vile phrase;
but you shall hear. Thus:
In her excellent white bosom, these, &c.—
    QUEEN. Came this from Hamlet to her?
    POLONIUS. Good madam, stay awhile; I will be faithful.
            Doubt thou the stars are fire;
              Doubt that the sun doth move;
            Doubt truth to be a liar;
               But never doubt I love.
O dear Ophelia! I am ill at these numbers: I have not art

to reckon my groans; but that I love thee best, O most best!
believe it. Adieu.

> *Thine evermore, most dear lady, whilst this*
> *machine is to him,*
>> *Hamlet.*

This in obedience hath my daughter shown me;
And more above, hath his solicitings,
As they fell out by time, by means, and place,
All given to mine ear.

  KING.   But how hath she
Receiv'd his love?

  POLONIUS. What do you think of me?

  KING. As a man faithful and honourable.

  POLONIUS. I would fain prove so. But what might you think,
When I had seen this hot love on the wing,—
As I perceiv'd it (I must tell you that)
Before my daughter told me,—what might you,
Or my dear majesty, your queen here, think,
If I had play'd the desk or table-book,
Or given my heart a winking, mute and dumb,
Or look'd upon this love with idle sight;
What might you think? No, I went round to work,
And my young mistress thus I did bespeak:
'Lord Hamlet is a prince, out of thy star;
This must not be:' and then I prescripts gave her,
That she should lock herself from his resort,
Admit no messengers, receive no tokens.
Which done, she took the fruits of my advice;
And he, repulséd,—a short tale to make,—
Fell into a sadness, then into a fast,
Thence to a watch, thence into a weakness,
Thence to a lightness; and by this declension
Into the madness weherin now he raves,
And all we mourn for.

  KING.   Do you think 'tis this?

QUEEN. It may be, very like.

POLONIUS. Hath there been such a time,—I'd fain know that,—
That I have positively said, ' 'Tis so,'
When it prov'd otherwise?

KING.   Not that I know.

POLONIUS. Take this from this, if this be otherwise:
                    [*Pointing to his head and shoulder.*
If circumstances lead me, I will find
Where truth is hid, though it were hid indeed
Within the centre.

KING.   How may we try it further?

POLONIUS. You know sometimes he walks four hours together
Here in the lobby.

QUEEN.   So he does indeed.

POLONIUS. At such a time I'll loose my daughter to him;
Be you and I behind an arras then;
Mark the encounter; if he love her not,
And be not from his reason fallen thereon,
Let me be no assistant for a state,
But keep a farm, and carters.

KING.   We will try it.

QUEEN. But look, where sadly the poor wretch comes reading.

POLONIUS. Away! I do beseech you, both away.
I'll board him presently.
                    [*Exeunt* KING, QUEEN, *and* ATTENDANTS.

    Enter HAMLET, *reading.*

                    O! give me leave.
How does my good Lord Hamlet?

HAMLET. Well, God a-mercy.

POLONIUS. Do you know me, my lord?

HAMLET. Excellent well; you are a fishmonger.

POLONIUS. Not I, my lord.

HAMLET. Then I would you were so honest a man.

POLONIUS. Honest, my lord!

HAMLET. Ay, sir; to be honest, as this world goes, is to be one man picked out of ten thousand.

POLONIUS. That's very true, my lord.

HAMLET. For if the sun breed maggots in a dead dog, being a good kissing carrion,—Have you a daughter?

POLONIUS. I have, my lord.

HAMLET. Let her not walk i' the sun: conception is a blessing; but as your daughter may conceive, friend, look to 't.

POLONIUS. [Aside.] How say you by that? Still harping on my daughter: yet he knew me not at first; he said I was a fishmonger: he is far gone, far gone: and truly in my youth I suffered much extremity for love; very near this. I'll speak to him again. What do you read, my lord?

HAMLET. Words, words, words.

POLONIUS. What is the matter, my lord?

HAMLET. Between who?

POLONIUS. I mean the matter that you read, my lord.

HAMLET. Slanders, sir: for the satirical rogue says here that old men have grey beards, that their faces are wrinkled, their eyes purging thick amber and plum-tree gum, and that they have a plentiful lack of wit, together with most weak hams: all which, sir, though I most powerfully and potently believe, yet I hold it not honesty to have it thus set down; for yourself, sir, shall grow old as I am, if, like a crab, you could go backward.

POLONIUS. [Aside.] Though this be madness, yet there is method in 't. Will you walk out of the air, my lord?

HAMLET. Into my grave?

POLONIUS. Indeed, that is out o' the air. [Aside.] How pregnant sometimes his replies are! a happiness that often madness hits on, which reason and sanity could not so prosperously be delivered of. I will leave him, and suddenly contrive the means of meeting between him and my daughter. My honourable lord, I will most humbly take my leave of you.

HAMLET. You cannot, sir, take from me any thing that I will more willingly part withal; except my life, except my life, except my life.

POLONIUS. Fare you well, my lord.   [*Going.*
HAMLET. These tedious old fools!

Enter ROSENCRANTZ *and* GUILDENSTERN.

POLONIUS. You go to seek the Lord Hamlet; there he is.
ROSENCRANTZ. [*To* POLONIUS.] God save you, sir!
                                        [*Exit* POLONIUS.
GUILDENSTERN. Mine honoured lord!
ROSENCRANTZ. My most dear lord!
HAMLET. My excellent good friends! How dost thou, Guilden-
stern? Ah, Rosencrantz! Good lads, how do ye both?
ROSENCRANTZ. As the indifferent children of the earth.
GUILDENSTERN. Happy in that we are not over-happy; On For-
tune's cap we are not the very button.
HAMLET. Nor the soles of her shoe?
ROSENCRANTZ. Neither, my lord.
HAMLET. Then you live about her waist, or in the middle of
her favours?
GUILDENSTERN. Faith, her privates we.
HAMLET. In the secret parts of Fortune? O! most true; she is
a strumpet. What news?
ROSENCRANTZ. None, my lord, but that the world's grown
honest.
HAMLET. Then is doomsday near; but your news is not true.
Let me question more in particular: what have you, my good
friends, deserved at the hands of Fortune, that she sends you to
prison hither?
GUILDENSTERN. Prison, my lord!
HAMLET. Denmark's a prison.
ROSENCRANTZ. Then is the world one.
HAMLET. A goodly one; in which there are many confines,
wards, and dungeons, Denmark being one o' the worst.
ROSENCRANTZ. We think not so, my lord.
HAMLET. Why, then, 'tis none to you; for there is nothing
either good or bad, but thinking makes it so: to me it is a prison.

ROSENCRANTZ. Why, then your ambition makes it one; 'tis too narrow for your mind.

HAMLET. O God! I could be bounded in a nutshell, and count myself a king of infinite space, were it not that I have bad dreams.

GUILDENSTERN. Which dreams, indeed, are ambition, for the very substance of the ambitious is merely the shadow of a dream.

HAMLET. A dream itself is but a shadow.

ROSENCRANTZ. Truly, and I hold ambition of so airy and light a quality that it is but a shadow's shadow.

HAMLET. Then are our beggars bodies, and our monarchs and outstretched heroes the beggars' shadows. Shall we to the court? for, by my fay, I cannot reason.

ROSENCRANTZ. ⎫
GUILDENSTERN. ⎭ We'll wait upon you.

HAMLET. No such matter; I will not sort you with the rest of my servants, for, to speak to you like an honest man, I am most dreadfully attended. But, in the beaten way of friendship, what make you at Elsinore?

ROSENCRANTZ. To visit you, my lord; no other occasion.

HAMLET. Beggar that I am, I am even poor in thanks; but I thank you: and sure, dear friends, my thanks are too dear a halfpenny. Were you not sent for? Is it your own inclining? Is it a free visitation? Come, come, deal justly with me: come, come; nay, speak.

GUILDENSTERN. What should we say, my lord?

HAMLET. Why anything, but to the purpose. You were sent for; and there is a kind of confession in your looks which your modesties have not craft enough to colour: I know the good king and queen have sent for you.

ROSENCRANTZ. To what end, my lord?

HAMLET. That you must teach me. But let me conjure you, by the rights of our fellowship, by the consonancy of our youth, by the obligation of our ever-preserved love, and by what more dear a better proposer could charge you withal, be even and direct with me, whether you were sent for or no!

ROSENCRANTZ. [*Aside to* GUILDENSTERN.] What say you?

HAMLET. [*Aside.*] Nay, then, I have an eye of you. If you love me, hold not off.

GUILDENSTERN. My lord, we were sent for.

HAMLET. I will tell you why; so shall my anticipation prevent your discovery, and your secrecy to the king and queen moult no feather. I have of late,—but wherefore I know not,—lost all my mirth, forgone all custom of exercises; and indeed it goes so heavily with my disposition that this goodly frame, the earth, seems to me a sterile promontory; this most excellent canopy, the air, look you, this brave o'erhanging firmament, this majestical roof fretted with golden fire, why, it appears no other thing to me but a foul and pestilent congregation of vapours. What a piece of work is a man! How noble in reason! how infinite in faculty! in form, in moving, how express and admirable! in action how like an angel! in apprehension how like a god! the beauty of the world! the paragon of animals! And yet, to me, what is this quintessence of dust? man delights not me; no, nor woman neither, though, by your smiling, you seem to say so.

ROSENCRANTZ. My lord, there was no such stuff in my thoughts.

HAMLET. Why did you laugh then, when I said, 'man delights not me?'

ROSENCRANTZ. To think, my lord, if you delight not in man, what lenten entertainment the players shall receive from you: we coted them on the way; and hither are they coming to offer you service.

HAMLET. He that plays the King shall be welcome; his majesty shall have tribute of me; the adventurous Knight shall use his foil and target; the Lover shall not sigh gratis; the Humorous Man shall end his part in peace; the Clown shall make those laugh whose lungs are tickle o' the sere; and the Lady shall say her mind freely, or the blank verse shall halt for 't. What players are they?

ROSENCRANTZ. Even those you were wont to take delight in, the tragedians of the city.

HAMLET. How chances it they travel? their residence, both in reputation and profit, was better both ways.

ROSENCRANTZ. I think their inhibition comes by the means of the late innovation.

HAMLET. Do they hold the same estimation they did when I was in the city? Are they so followed?

ROSENCRANTZ. No, indeed they are not.

HAMLET. How comes it? Do they grow rusty?

ROSENCRANTZ. Nay, their endeavour keeps in the wonted pace: but there is, sir, an aery of children, little eyases, that cry out on the top of question, and are most tyranically clapped for't: these are now the fashion, and so berattle the common stages,—so they call them,—that many wearing rapiers are afraid of goose-quills, and dare scarce come thither.

HAMLET. What! are they children? who maintains 'em? how are they escoted? Will they pursue the quality no longer than they can sing? will they not say afterwards, if they should grow themselves to common players,—as it is most like, if their means are not better,—their writers do them wrong, to make them exclaim against their own succession?

ROSENCRANTZ. Faith, there has been much to-do on both sides: and the nation holds it no sin to tarre them to controversy: there was, for a while, no money bid for argument, unless the Poet and the Player went to cuffs in the question.

HAMLET. Is it possible?

GUILDENSTERN. O! there has been much throwing about of brains.

HAMLET. Do the boys carry it away?

ROSENCRANTZ. Ay, that they do, my lord; Hercules and his load too.

HAMLET. It is not very strange; for my uncle is King of Denmark, and those that would make mows at him while my father lived, give twenty, forty, fifty, a hundred ducats a-piece for his picture in little. 'Sblood, there is something in this more than natural, if philosophy could find it out.

[*Flourish of trumpets within.*

GUILDENSTERN. There are the players.

HAMLET. Gentlemen, you are welcome to Elsinore. Your hands, come then; the appurtenance of welcome is fashion and ceremony: let me comply with you in this garb, lest my extent to the players—which, I tell you, must show fairly outward—should more appear like entertainment than yours. You are welcome; but my uncle-father and aunt-mother are deceived.

GUILDENSTERN. In what, my dear lord?

HAMLET. I am but mad north-north-west: when the wind is southerly I know a hawk from a handsaw.

Enter POLONIUS.

POLONIUS. Well be with you, gentlemen!

HAMLET. Hark you, Guildenstern; and you too; at each ear a hearer: that great baby you see there is not yet out of his swaddling-clouts.

ROSENCRANTZ. Happily he's the second time come to them; for they say an old man is twice a child.

HAMLET. I will prophesy he comes to tell me of the players; mark it. You say right, sir; o' Monday morning; 'twas so indeed.

POLONIUS. My lord, I have news to tell you.

HAMLET. My lord, I have news to tell you. When Roscius was an actor in Rome,—

POLONIUS. The actors are come hither, my lord.

HAMLET. Buz, buz!

POLONIUS. Upon my honour,—

HAMLET. Then came each actor on his ass,—

POLONIUS. The best actors in the world, either for tragedy, comedy, history, pastoral, pastoral-comical, historical-pastoral, tragical-historical, tragical-comical-historical-pastoral, scene individable, or poem unlimited: Seneca cannot be too heavy, nor Plautus too light. For the law of writ and the liberty, these are the only men.

HAMLET. O Jephthah, judge of Israel, what a treasure hadst thou!

POLONIUS. What a treasure had he, my lord?

HAMLET. Why

> *One fair daughter and no more,*
> *The which he lovéd passing well.*

POLONIUS. [*Aside.*] Still on my daughter.

HAMLET. Am I not i' the right, old Jephthah?

POLONIUS. If you call me Jephthah, my lord, I have a daughter that I love passing well.

HAMLET. Nay, that follows not.

POLONIUS. What follows, then, my lord?

HAMLET. Why,

> *As by lot, God wot.*

And then, you know,

> *It came to pass, as most like it was.—*

The first row of the pious chanson will show you more; for look where my abridgment comes.

Enter four or five PLAYERS.

You are welcome, masters; welcome, all. I am glad to see thee well: welcome, good friends. O, my old friend! Why, thy face is valanced since I saw thee last: comest thou to beard me in Denmark? What! my young lady and mistress! By 'r lady, your ladyship is nearer heaven than when I saw you last, by the altitude of a chopine. Pray God, your voice, like a piece of uncurrent gold, be not cracked within the ring. Masters, you are all welcome. We'll e'en to 't like French falconers, fly at anything we see: we'll have a speech straight. Come, give us a taste of your quality; come, a passionate speech.

FIRST PLAYER. What speech, my good lord?

HAMLET. I heard thee speak me a speech once, but it was never acted; or, if it was, not above once; for the play, I remember, pleased not the million; 'twas caviare to the general: but it was—as I received it, and others, whose judgments in such matters cried in the top of mine—an excellent play, well digested in the scenes, set down with as much modesty as cunning. I remember one said there were no sallets in the lines to make the matter savoury, nor no matter in the phrase that might indict the author of affectation; but called it an honest method, as

wholesome as sweet, and by very much more handsome than
fine. One speech in it I chiefly loved; 'twas Æneas' tale to Dido;
and thereabout of it especially, where he speaks of Priam's
slaughter. If it live in your memory, begin at this line: let me
see, let me see:—

The rugged Pyrrhus, like the Hyrcanian beast,—

'tis not so, it begins with Pyrrhus:—

The rugged Pyrrhus, he, whose sable arm,
Black as his purpose, did the night resemble
When he lay couchéd in the ominous horse,
Hath now this dread and black complexion smear'd
With heraldry more dismal; head to foot
Now is he total gules; horridly trick'd
With blood of fathers, mothers, daughters, sons,
Bak'd and impasted with the parching streets,
That lend a tyrannous and damnéd light
To their vile murders: roasted in wrath and fire,
And thus o'er-sizéd with coagulate gore,
With eyes like carbuncles, the hellish Pyrrhus
Old grandsire Priam seeks.
So proceed you.

POLONIUS. 'Fore God, my lord, well spoken; with good accent
and good discretion.

FIRST PLAYER.   *Anon, he finds him*
Striking too short at Greeks; his antique sword,
Rebellious to his arm, lies where it falls,
Repugnant to command. Unequal match'd,
Pyrrhus at Priam drives; in rage strikes wide;
But with the whiff and wind of his fell sword
The unnerved father falls. Then senseless Ilium,
Seeming to feel this blow, with flaming top
Stoops to his base, and with a hideous crash
Takes prisoner Pyrrhus' ear: for lo! his sword,
Which was declining on the milky head
Of reverend Priam, seem'd i' the air to stick:
So, as a painted tyrant, Pyrrhus stood,

And like a neutral to his will and matter,
Did nothing.
But, as we often see, against some storm,
A silence in the heavens, the rack stand still,
The bold winds speechless and the orb below
As hush as death, anon the dreadful thunder
Doth rend the region; so, after Pyrrhus' pause,
Aroused vengeance sets him new a-work;
And never did the Cyclops' hammers fall
On Mars's armour, forg'd for proof eterne,
With less remorse than Pyrrhus' bleeding sword
Now falls on Priam.
Out, out, thou strumpet, Fortune! All you gods,
In general synod, take away her power;
Break all the spokes and fellies from her wheel,
And bowl the round nave down the hill of heaven,
As low as to the fiends!

POLONIUS. This is too long.

HAMLET. It shall to the barber's, with your beard. Prithee,
say on; he's for a jig or a tale of bawdry, or he sleeps. Say on;
come to Hecuba.

FIRST PLAYER. *But who, O! who had seen the mobled queen—*

HAMLET. 'The mobled queen?'—

POLONIUS. That's good; 'mobled queen' is good.

FIRST PLAYER. *Run barefoot up and down, threat'ning the*
flames
With bisson rheum; a clout upon that head
Where late the diadem stood; and, for a robe,
About her lank and all o'er-teeméd loins,
A blanket, in the alarm of fear caught up;
Who this had seen, with tongue in venom steep'd,
'Gainst Fortune's state would treason have pronounc'd:
But if the gods themselves did see her then,
When she saw Pyrrhus make malicious sport
In mincing with his sword her husband's limbs,
The instant burst of clamour that she made—

Unless things mortal move them not at all—
Would have made milch the burning eyes of heaven,
And passion in the gods.

POLONIUS. Look! wh'er he has not turned his colour and has tears in 's eyes. Prithee, no more.

HAMLET. 'Tis well; I'll have thee speak out the rest soon. Good my lord, will you see the players well bestowed? Do you hear, let them be well used; for they are the abstracts and brief chronicles of the time: after your death you were better have a bad epitaph than their ill report while you live.

POLONIUS. My lord, I will use them according to their desert.

HAMLET. God's bodikins, man, much better; use every man after his desert, and who shall 'scape whipping? Use them after your own honour and dignity: the less they deserve, the more merit is in your bounty. Take them in.

POLONIUS. Come, sirs.

HAMLET. Follow him, friends: we'll hear a play to-morrow. [*Exit* POLONIUS, *with all the* PLAYERS *but the* FIRST.] Dost thou hear me, old friend; can you play The Murder of Gonzago?

FIRST PLAYER. Ay, my lord.

HAMLET. We'll ha 't to-morrow night. You could, for a need, study a speech of some dozen or sixteen lines, which I would set down and insert in 't, could you not?

FIRST PLAYER. Ay, my lord.

HAMLET. Very well. Follow that lord; and look you mock him not. [*Exit* FIRST PLAYER.] [*To* ROSENCRANTZ *and* GUILDENSTERN.] My good friends, I'll leave you till night; you are welcome to Elsinore.

ROSENCRANTZ. Good my lord!

[*Exeunt* ROSENCRANTZ *and* GUILDENSTERN.

HAMLET. Ay, so, God be wi' ye! Now I am alone.
O! what a rogue and peasant slave am I:
Is it not monstrous that this player here,
But in a fiction, in a dream of passion,
Could force his soul so to his own conceit
That from her working all his visage wann'd,

Tears in his eyes, distraction in 's aspect,
A broken voice, and his whole function suiting
With forms to his conceit? and all for nothing!
For Hecuba!
What's Hecuba to him or he to Hecuba
That he should weep for her? What would he do
Had he the motive and the cue for passion
That I have? He would drown the stage with tears,
And cleave the general ear with horrid speech,
Make mad the guilty and appal the free,
Confound the ignorant, and amaze indeed
The very faculties of eyes and ears.
Yet I,
A dull and muddy-mettled rascal, peak,
Like John-a-dreams, unpregnant of my cause,
And can say nothing; no, not for a king,
Upon whose property and most dear life
A damn'd defeat was made. Am I a coward?
Who calls me villain? breaks my pate across?
Plucks off my beard and blows it in my face?
Tweaks me by the nose? gives me the lie i' the throat,
As deep as to the lungs? Who does me this?
Ha!
Swounds, I should take it, for it cannot be
But I am pigeon-liver'd, and lack gall
To make oppression bitter, or ere this
I should have fatted all the region kites
With this slave's offal. Bloody, bawdy villain!
Remorseless, treacherous, lecherous, kindless villain!
O! vengeance!
Why, what an ass am I! This is most brave
That I, the son of a dear father murder'd,
Prompted to my revenge by heaven and hell,
Must, like a whore, unpack my heart with words,
And fall a-cursing, like a very drab,
A scullion! Fie upon 't! foh!

About, my brain; hum, I have heard,
That guilty creatures sitting at a play
Have by the very cunning of the scene
Been struck so to the soul that presently
They have proclaim'd their malefactions;
For murder, though it have no tongue, will speak
With most miraculous organ. I'll have these players
Play something like the murder of my father
Before mine uncle; I'll observe his looks;
I'll tent him to the quick: if he but blench
I know my course. The spirit that I have seen
May be the devil: and the devil hath power
To assume a pleasing shape; yea, and perhaps
Out of my weakness and my melancholy—
As he is very potent with such spirits—
Abuses me to damn me. I'll have grounds
More relative than this: the play's the thing
Wherein I'll catch the conscience of the king.   [*Exit.*

Act 3

Scene I. A Room in the Castle

Enter KING, QUEEN, POLONIUS, OPHELIA, ROSENCRANTZ, *and* GUILDENSTERN.

KING. And can you, by no drift of conference,
Get from him why he puts on this confusion,
Grating so harshly all his days of quiet
With turbulent and dangerous lunacy?

ROSENCRANTZ. He does confess he feels himself distracted;
But from what cause he will by no means speak.

GUILDENSTERN. Nor do we find him forward to be sounded,
But, with a crafty madness, keeps aloof,
When we would bring him on to some confession
Of his true state.

QUEEN.   Did he receive you well?

ROSENCRANTZ. Most like a gentleman.

GUILDENSTERN. But with much forcing of his disposition.

ROSENCRANTZ. Niggard of question, but of our demands
Most free in his reply.

QUEEN.   Did you assay him
To any pastime?

ROSENCRANTZ. Madam, it so fell out that certain players
We o'er-raught on the way; of these we told him,
And there did seem in him a kind of joy
To hear of it: they are here about the court,
And, as I think, they have already order
This night to play before him.

156

POLONIUS.   'Tis most true;
And he beseech'd me to entreat your majesties
To hear and see the matter.
KING. With all my heart; and it doth much content me
To hear him so inclin'd.
Good gentlemen, give him a further edge,
And drive his purpose on to these delights.
ROSENCRANTZ. We shall, my lord.
                         [*Exeunt* ROSENCRANTZ *and* GUILDENSTERN.
KING.   Sweet Gertrude, leave us too;
For we have closely sent for Hamlet hither,
That he, as 'twere by accident, may here
Affront Ophelia.
Her father and myself, lawful espials,
Will so bestow ourselves, that, seeing, unseen,
We may of their encounter frankly judge,
And gather by him, as he is behav'd,
If 't be the affliction of his love or no
That thus he suffers for.
QUEEN.   I shall obey you.
And for your part, Ophelia, I do wish
That your good beauties be the happy cause
Of Hamlet's wildness; so shall I hope your virtues
Will bring him to his wonted way again,
To both your honours.
OPHELIA.   Madam, I wish it may.   [*Exit* QUEEN.
POLONIUS. Ophelia, walk you here. Gracious, so please you,
We will bestow ourselves. [*To* OPHELIA.] Read on this book;
That show of such an exercise may colour
Your loneliness. We are oft to blame in this,
'Tis too much prov'd, that with devotion's visage
And pious action we do sugar o'er
The Devil himself.
KING. [*Aside.*]   O! 'tis too true;
How smart a lash that speech doth give my conscience!
The harlot's cheek, beautied with plastering art,

Is not more ugly to the thing that helps it
Than is my deed to my most painted word:
O heavy burden!

POLONIUS.   I hear him coming; let's withdraw, my lord.

[Exeunt KING *and* POLONIUS.

Enter HAMLET.

HAMLET. To be, or not to be: that is the question:
Whether 'tis nobler in the mind to suffer
The slings and arrows of outrageous fortune,
Or to take arms against a sea of troubles,
And by opposing end them? To die: to sleep;
No more; and, by a sleep to say we end
The heart-ache and the thousand natural shocks
That flesh is heir to, 'tis a consummation
Devoutly to be wish'd. To die, to sleep;
To sleep: perchance to dream: ay, there's the rub;
For in that sleep of death what dreams may come
When we have shuffled off this mortal coil,
Must give us pause. There's the respect
That makes calamity of so long life;
For who would bear the whips and scorns of time,
The oppressor's wrong, the proud man's contumely,
The pangs of dispriz'd love, the law's delay,
The insolence of office, and the spurns
That patient merit of the unworthy takes,
When he himself might his quietus make
With a bare bodkin? who would fardels bear,
To grunt and sweat under a weary life,
But that the dread of something after death,
The undiscover'd country from whose bourn
No traveller returns, puzzles the will,
And makes us rather bear those ills we have
Than fly to others that we know not of?
Thus conscience does make cowards of us all;
And thus the native hue of resolution
Is sicklied o'er with the pale cast of thought,

And enterprises of great pitch and moment
With this regard their currents turn awry,
And lose the name of action. Soft you now!
The fair Ophelia! Nymph, in thy orisons
Be all my sins remember'd.

OPHELIA.   Good my lord,
How does your honour for this many a day?

HAMLET. I humbly thank you; well, well, well.

OPHELIA. My lord, I have remembrances of yours,
That I have longéd long to re-deliver;
I pray you, now receive them.

HAMLET.   No, not I;
I never gave you aught.

OPHELIA. My honour'd lord, you know right well you did;
And, with them, words of so sweet breath compos'd
As made the things more rich: their perfume lost,
Take these again; for to the noble mind
Rich gifts wax poor when givers prove unkind.
There, my lord.

HAMLET. Ha, ha! are you honest?

OPHELIA. My lord!

HAMLET. Are you fair?

OPHELIA. What means your lordship?

HAMLET. That if you be honest and fair, your honesty should admit no discourse to your beauty.

OPHELIA. Could beauty, my lord, have better commerce than with honesty?

HAMLET. Ay, truly; for the power of beauty will sooner transform honesty from what it is to a bawd than the force of honesty can translate beauty into his likeness: this was sometimes a paradox, but now the time gives it proof. I did love you once.

OPHELIA. Indeed, my lord, you made me believe so.

HAMLET. You should not have believed me; for virtue cannot so inoculate our old stock but we shall relish of it: I loved you not.

OPHELIA. I was the more deceived.

HAMLET. Get thee to a nunnery: why wouldst thou be a breeder of sinners? I am myself indifferent honest; but yet I could accuse me of such things that it were better my mother had not borne me. I am very proud, revengeful, ambitious; with more offences at my beck than I have thoughts to put them in, imagination to give them shape, or time to act them in. What should such fellows as I do crawling between heaven and earth? We are arrant knaves, all; believe none of us. Go thy ways to a nunnery. Where's your father?

OPHELIA. At home, my lord.

HAMLET. Let the doors be shut upon him, that he may play the fool nowhere but in's own house. Farewell.

OPHELIA. O! help him, you sweet heavens!

HAMLET. If thou dost marry, I'll give thee this plague for thy dowry: be thou as chaste as ice, as pure as snow, thou shalt not escape calumny. Get thee to a nunnery, go; farewell. Or, if thou wilt needs marry, marry a fool; for wise men know well enough what monsters you make of them. To a nunnery, go; and quickly too. Farewell.

OPHELIA. O heavenly powers, restore him!

HAMLET. I have heard of your paintings too, well enough; God hath given you one face, and you make yourselves another: you jig, you amble, and you lisp, and nickname God's creatures, and make your wantonness your ignorance. Go to, I'll no more on't; it hath made me mad. I say, we will have no more marriages; those that are married already, all but one, shall live; the rest shall keep as they are. To a nunnery, go. [*Exit.*

OPHELIA. O! what a noble mind is here o'erthrown:
The courtier's, soldier's, scholar's, eye, tongue, sword;
The expectancy and rose of the fair state,
The glass of fashion and the mould of form,
The observ'd of all observers, quite, quite down!
And I, of ladies most deject and wretched,
That suck'd the honey of his music vows,
Now see that noble and most sovereign reason,
Like sweet bells jangled, out of tune and harsh;

That unmatch'd form and feature of blown youth
Blasted with ecstasy: O! woe is me,
To have seen what I have seen, see what I see!
    Re-enter KING *and* POLONIUS.
    KING. Love! his affections do not that way tend;
Nor what he spake, though it lack'd form a little,
Was not like madness. There's something in his soul
O'er which his melancholy sits on brood;
And, I do doubt, the hatch and the disclose
Will be some danger; which for to prevent,
I have in quick determination
Thus set it down: he shall with speed to England,
For the demand of our neglected tribute:
Haply the seas and countries different
With variable objects shall expel
This something-settled matter in his heart,
Whereon his brains still beating puts him thus
From fashion of himself. What think you on't?
    POLONIUS. It shall do well: but yet do I believe
The origin and commencement of his grief
Sprung from neglected love. How now, Ophelia!
You need not tell us what Lord Hamlet said;
We heard it all. My lord, do as you please;
But, if you hold it fit, after the play,
Let his queen mother all alone entreat him
To show his griefs: let her be round with him;
And I'll be plac'd, so please you, in the ear
Of all their conference. If she find him not,
To England send him, or confine him where
Your wisdom best shall think.
    KING.   It shall be so:
Madness in great ones must not unwatch'd go.   [*Exeunt.*

Scene II. A Hall in the Castle

Enter HAMLET *and certain* PLAYERS.

HAMLET. Speak the speech, I pray you, as I pronounced it to you, trippingly on the tongue; but if you mouth it, as many of your players do, I had as lief the town-crier spoke my lines. Nor do not saw the air too much with your hand, thus; but use all gently: for in the very torrent, tempest, and—as I may say— whirlwind of passion, you must acquire and beget a temperance, that may give it smoothness. O! it offends me to the soul to hear a robustious periwig-pated fellow tear a passion to tatters, to very rags, to split the ears of the groundlings, who for the most part are capable of nothing but inexplicable dumb-shows and noise: I would have such a fellow whipped for o'er-doing Termagant; it out-herods Herod: pray you, avoid it.

FIRST PLAYER. I warrant your honour.

HAMLET. Be not too tame neither, but let your own discretion be your tutor: suit the action to the word, the word to the action; with this special observance, that you o'erstep not the modesty of nature; for anything so overdone is from the purpose of playing, whose end, both at the first and now, was and is, to hold, as 'twere, the mirror up to nature; to show virtue her own feature, scorn her own image, and the very age and body of the time his form and pressure. Now, this overdone, or come tardy off, though it make the unskilful laugh, cannot but make the judicious grieve; the censure of which one must in your allowance o'erweigh a whole theatre of others. O! there be players that I have seen play, and heard others praise, and that highly, not to speak it profanely, that, neither having the accent of Christians nor the gait of Christian, pagan, nor man, have so strutted and bellowed that I have thought some of nature's journeymen had made men and not made them well, they imitated humanity so abominably.

FIRST PLAYER. I hope we have reformed that indifferently with us.

HAMLET. O! reform it altogether. And let those that play your clowns speak no more than is set down for them; for there be of them that will themselves laugh, to set on some quantity of barren spectators to laugh too, though in the mean time some necessary question of the play be then to be considered; that's villanous, and shows a most pitiful ambition in the fool that uses it. Go, make you ready. [*Exeunt* PLAYERS.

Enter POLONIUS, ROSENCRANTZ *and* GUILDENSTERN.

How now, my lord! will the king hear this piece of work?
POLONIUS. And the queen too, and that presently.
HAMLET. Bid the players make haste. [*Exit* POLONIUS.
Will you two help to hasten them?
ROSENCRANTZ.
GUILDENSTERN. } We will, my lord.

[*Exeunt* ROSENCRANTZ *and* GUILDENSTERN.
HAMLET. What, ho! Horatio!
Enter HORATIO.
HORATIO. Here, sweet lord, at your service.
HAMLET. Horatio, thou art e'en as just a man
As e'er my conversation cop'd withal.
HORATIO. O! my dear lord,—
HAMLET.   Nay, do not think I flatter;
For what advancement may I hope from thee,
That no revenue hast but thy good spirits
To feed and clothe thee? Why should the poor be flatter'd?
No; let the candied tongue lick absurd pomp,
And crook the pregnant hinges of the knee
Where thrift may follow fawning. Dost thou hear?
Since my dear soul was mistress of her choice
And could of men distinguish, her election
Hath seal'd thee for herself; for thou hast been
As one, in suffering all, that suffers nothing,
A man that fortune's buffets and rewards
Hast ta'en with equal thanks; and bless'd are those
Whose blood and judgment are so well co-mingled

That they are not a pipe for fortune's finger
To sound what stop she please. Give me that man
That is not passion's slave, and I will wear him
In my heart's core, ay, in my heart of heart,
As I do thee. Something too much of this.
There is a play to-night before the king;
One scene of it comes near the circumstance
Which I have told thee of my father's death:
I prithee, when thou seest that act afoot,
Even with the very comment of thy soul
Observe mine uncle; if his occulted guilt
Do not itself unkennel in one speech,
It is a damnéd ghost that we have seen,
And my imaginations are as foul
As Vulcan's stithy. Give him heedful note;
For I mine eyes will rivet to his face,
And after we will both our judgments join
In censure of his seeming.

    HORATIO.   Well, my lord:
If he steal aught the whilst this play is playing,
And 'scape detecting, I will pay the theft.

    HAMLET. They are coming to the play; I must be idle:
Get you a place.

    Danish march. A Flourish. Enter KING, QUEEN, POLONIUS,
OPHELIA, ROSENCRANTZ, GUILDENSTERN, *and Others.*

    KING. How fares our cousin Hamlet?

    HAMLET. Excellent, i' faith; of the chameleon's dish: I eat the
air, promise-crammed; you cannot feed capons so.

    KING. I have nothing with this answer, Hamlet; these words
are not mine.

    HAMLET. No, nor mine now. [*To* POLONIUS.] My lord, you
played once i' the university, you say?

    POLONIUS. That did I, my lord, and was accounted a good
actor.

    HAMLET. And what did you enact?

POLONIUS. I did enact Julius Caesar: I was killed i' the Capitol; Brutus killed me.

HAMLET. It was a brute part of him to kill so capital a calf there. Be the players ready?

ROSENCRANTZ. Ay, my lord; they stay upon your patience.

QUEEN. Come hither, my good Hamlet, sit by me.

HAMLET. No, good mother, here's metal more attractive.

POLONIUS. [*To the* KING.] O ho! do you mark that?

HAMLET. Lady, shall I lie in your lap?

[Lying down at OPHELIA'S *feet.*

OPHELIA. No, my lord.

HAMLET. I mean, my head upon your lap?

OPHELIA. Ay, my lord.

HAMLET. Do you think I meant country matters?

OPHELIA. I think nothing, my lord.

HAMLET. That's a fair thought to lie between maids' legs.

OPHELIA. What is, my lord?

HAMLET. Nothing.

OPHELIA. You are merry, my lord.

HAMLET. Who, I?

OPHELIA. Ay, my lord.

HAMLET. O God, your only jig-maker. What should a man do but be merry? for, look you, how cheerfully my mother looks, and my father died within's two hours.

OPHELIA. Nay, 'tis twice two months, my lord.

HAMLET. So long? Nay, then, let the devil wear black, for I'll have a suit of sables. O heavens! die two months ago, and not forgotten yet? Then there's hope a great man's memory may outlive his life half a year; but, by'r lady, he must build churches then, or else shall he suffer not thinking on, with the hobby-horse, whose epitaph is, 'For, O! for, O! the hobby-horse is forgot.'

Hautboys play. The dumb-show enters.

Enter a KING *and a* QUEEN, *very lovingly; the* QUEEN *embracing him, and he her. She kneels, and makes show of protes-*

*tation unto him. He takes her up, and declines his head
upon her neck; lays him down upon a bank of flowers: she,
seeing him asleep, leaves him. Anon comes in a fellow, takes
off his crown, kisses it, and pours poison in the* KING's *ears,
and exit. The* QUEEN *returns, finds the* KING *dead, and makes
passionate action. The* POISONER, *with some two or three*
MUTES, *comes in again, seeming to lament with her. The
dead body is carried away. The* POISONER *wooes the* QUEEN
*with gifts; she seems loath and unwilling awhile, but in the
end accepts his love.* [*Exeunt.*

OPHELIA. What means this, my lord?

HAMLET. Marry, this is miching mallecho; it means mischief.

OPHELIA. Belike this show imports the argument of the play.

Enter PROLOGUE.

HAMLET. We shall know by this fellow: the players cannot
keep counsel; they'll tell all.

OPHELIA. Will he tell us what this show meant?

HAMLET. Ay, or any show that you'll show him; be not you
ashamed to show, he'll not shame to tell you what it means.

OPHELIA. You are naught, you are naught. I'll mark the play.

PROLOGUE. *For us and for our tragedy,*
Here stooping to your clemency,
We beg your hearing patiently.

HAMLET. Is this a prologue, or the posy of a ring?

OPHELIA. 'Tis brief, my lord.

HAMLET. As woman's love.

Enter two PLAYERS, KING *and* QUEEN.

P. KING. *Full thirty times hath Phœbus' cart gone round*
Neptune's salt wash and Tellus' orbéd ground,
And thirty dozen moons with borrow'd sheen
About the world have times twelve thirties been,
Since love our hearts and Hymen did our hands
Unite commutual in most sacred bands.

P. QUEEN. *So many journeys may the sun and moon*
Make us again count o'er ere love be done!
But, woe is me! you are so sick of late,
So far from cheer and from your former state,
That I distrust you. Yet, though I distrust,
Discomfort you, my lord, it nothing must;
For women's fear and love holds quantity,
In neither aught, or in extremity.
Now, what my love is, proof hath made you know;
And as my love is siz'd, my fear is so.
Where love is great, the littlest doubts are fear;
Where little fears grow great, great love grows there.

P. KING. *Faith, I must leave thee, love, and shortly too;*
My operant powers their functions leave to do:
And thou shalt live in this fair world behind,
Honour'd, belov'd; and haply one as kind
For husband shalt thou—

P. QUEEN. *O! confound the rest;*
Such love must needs be treason in my breast:
In second husband let me be accurst;
None wed the second but who kill'd the first.

HAMLET. [*Aside.*] Wormwood, wormwood.

P. QUEEN. *The instances that second marriage move,*
Are base respects of thrift, but none of love;
A second time I kill my husband dead,
When second husband kisses me in bed.

P. KING. *I do believe you think what now you speak;*
But what we do determine oft we break.
Purpose is but the slave to memory,
Of violent birth, but poor validity;
Which now, like fruit unripe, sticks on the tree,
But fall unshaken when they mellow be.
Most necessary 'tis that we forget
To pay ourselves what to ourselves is debt;
What to ourselves in passion we propose,
The passion ending, doth the purpose lose.

The violence of either grief or joy
Their own enactures with themselves destroy;
Where joy most revels grief doth most lament,
Grief joys, joy grieves, on slender accident.
This world is not for aye, nor 'tis not strange,
That even our love should with our fortunes change;
For 'tis a question left us yet to prove
Whe'r love lead fortune or else fortune love.
The great man down, you mark his favourite flies;
The poor advanc'd makes friends of enemies.
And hitherto doth love on fortune tend,
For who not needs shall never lack a friend;
And who in want a hollow friend doth try
Directly seasons him his enemy.
But, orderly to end where I begun,
Our wills and fates do so contrary run
That our devices still are overthrown,
Our thoughts are ours, their ends none of our own:
So think thou wilt no second husband wed;
But die thy thoughts when thy first lord is dead.

P. QUEEN. *Nor earth to me give food, nor heaven light!*
Sport and repose lock from me day and night!
To desperation turn my trust and hope!
An anchor's cheer in prison be my scope!
Each opposite that blanks the face of joy
Meet what I would have well, and it destroy!
Both here and hence pursue me lasting strife,
If, once a widow, ever I be wife!

HAMLET. If she should break it now!

P. KING. *'Tis deeply sworn. Sweet, leave me here awhile;*
My spirits grow dull, and fain I would beguile
The tedious day with sleep.   [*Sleeps.*

P. QUEEN.   *Sleep rock thy brain;*
And never come mischance between us twain!   [*Exit.*

HAMLET. Madam, how like you this play?

QUEEN. The lady doth protest too much, methinks.

HAMLET. O! but she'll keep her word.

KING. Have you heard the argument? Is there no offence in 't?

HAMLET. No, no, they do but jest, poison in jest; no offence i' the world.

KING. What do you call the play?

HAMLET. The Mouse-trap. Marry, how? Tropically. This play is the image of a murder done in Vienna: Gonzago is the duke's name; his wife, Baptista. You shall see anon; 'tis a knavish piece of work: but what of that? your majesty and we that have free souls, it touches us not; let the galled jade wince, our withers are unwrung.

Enter PLAYER *as* LUCIANUS.

This is one Lucianus, nephew to the king.

OPHELIA. You are a good chorus, my lord.

HAMLET. I could interpret between you and your love, if I could see the puppets dallying.

OPHELIA. You are keen, my lord, you are keen.

HAMLET. It would cost you a groaning to take off my edge.

OPHELIA. Still better, and worse.

HAMLET. So you mis-take your husbands. Begin, murderer; pox, leave thy damnable faces, and begin. Come; the croaking raven doth bellow for revenge.

LUCIANUS. *Thoughts black, hands apt, drugs fit, and time agreeing;*
Confederate season, else no creature seeing;
Thou mixture rank, of midnight weeds collected,
With Hecate's ban thrice blasted, thrice infected,
Thy natural magic and dire property,
On wholesome life usurp immediately.

[*Pours the poison into the Sleeper's ears.*

HAMLET. He poisons him i' the garden for 's estate. His name's Gonzago; the story is extant, and writ in very choice Italian. You shall see anon how the murderer gets the love of Gonzago's wife.

OPHELIA. The king rises.

HAMLET. What! frighted with false fire?

QUEEN. How fares my lord?

POLONIUS. Give o'er the play.

KING. Give me some light: away!

ALL. Lights, lights, lights!

[Exeunt all except HAMLET *and* HORATIO.

HAMLET. Why, let the stricken deer go weep,
    The hart ungalled play;
    For some must watch, while some must sleep:
    So runs the world away.
Would not this, sir, and a forest of feathers, if the rest of my
fortunes turn Turk with me, with two Provincial roses on my
razed shoes, get me a fellowship in a cry of players, sir?

HORATIO. Half a share.

HAMLET. A whole one, I.
    For thou dost know, O Damon dear,
    This realm dismantled was
    Of Jove himself; and now reigns here
    A very, very—pajock.

HORATIO. You might have rhymed.

HAMLET. O good Horatio! I'll take the ghost's word for a
thousand pound. Didst perceive?

HORATIO. Very well, my lord.

HAMLET. Upon the talk of the poisoning?

HORATIO. I did very well note him.

Re-enter ROSENCRANTZ *and* GUILDENSTERN.

HAMLET. Ah, ha! Come, some music! come, the recorders!
    For if the king like not the comedy,
    Why then, belike he likes it not, perdy.
Come, some music!

GUILDENSTERN. Good my lord, vouchsafe me a word with you.

HAMLET. Sir, a whole history.

GUILDENSTERN. The king, sir,—

HAMLET. Ay, sir, what of him?

GUILDENSTERN. Is in his retirement marvellous distempered.

HAMLET. With drink, sir?

GUILDENSTERN. No, my lord, rather with choler.

HAMLET. Your wisdom should show itself more richer to signify this to his doctor; for, for me to put him to his purgation would perhaps plunge him into far more choler.

GUILDENSTERN. Good my lord, put your discourse into some frame, and start not so wildly from my affair.

HAMLET. I am tame, sir; pronounce.

GUILDENSTERN. The queen, your mother, in most great affliction of spirit, hath sent me to you.

HAMLET. You are welcome.

GUILDENSTERN. Nay, good my lord, this courtesy is not of the right breed. If it shall please you to make me a wholesome answer, I will do your mother's commandment; if not, your pardon and my return shall be the end of my business.

HAMLET. Sir, I cannot.

GUILDENSTERN. What, my lord?

HAMLET. Make you a wholesome answer; my wit's diseased; but, sir, such answer as I can make, you shall command; or, rather, as you say, my mother: therefore no more, but to the matter: my mother, you say,—

ROSENCRANTZ. Then, thus she says: your behaviour hath struck her into amazement and admiration.

HAMLET. O wonderful son, that can so astonish a mother! But is there no sequel at the heels of this mother's admiration? Impart.

ROSENCRANTZ. She desires to speak with you in her closet ere you go to bed.

HAMLET. We shall obey, were she ten times our mother. Have you any further trade with us?

ROSENCRANTZ. My lord, you once did love me.

HAMLET. So I do still, by these pickers and stealers.

ROSENCRANTZ. Good my lord, what is your cause of distemper? you do surely bar the door upon your own liberty, if you deny your griefs to your friend.

HAMLET. Sir, I lack advancement.

ROSENCRANTZ. How can that be when you have the voice of the king himself for your succession in Denmark?

HAMLET. Ay, sir, but 'While the grass grows,'—the proverb is something musty.

Enter PLAYERS, *with recorders.*

O! the recorders: let me see one. To withdraw with you: why do you go about to recover the wind of me, as if you would drive me into a toil?

GUILDENSTERN. O! my lord, if my duty be too bold, my love is too unmannerly.

HAMLET. I do not well understand that. Will you play upon this pipe?

GUILDENSTERN. My lord, I cannot.

HAMLET. I pray you.

GUILDENSTERN. Believe me, I cannot.

HAMLET. I do beseech you.

GUILDENSTERN. I know no touch of it, my lord.

HAMLET. 'Tis as easy as lying; govern these ventages with your finger and thumb, give it breath with your mouth, and it will discourse most eloquent music. Look you, these are the stops.

GUILDENSTERN. But these cannot I command to any utterance of harmony; I have not the skill.

HAMLET. Why, look you now, how unworthy a thing you make of me. You would play upon me; you would seem to know my stops; you would pluck out the heart of my mystery; you would sound me from my lowest note to the top of my compass; and there is much music, excellent voice, in this little organ, yet cannot you make it speak. 'Sblood, do you think I am easier to be played on than a pipe? Call me what instrument you will, though you can fret me, you cannot play upon me.

Enter POLONIUS.

God bless you, sir!

POLONIUS. My lord, the queen would speak with you, and presently.

The stage of the Globe Theatre where many of Shakespeare's plays were first performed, reconstructed in a model by Dr. John C. Adams.

HAMLET. Do you see yonder cloud that's almost in shape of a camel?

POLONIUS. By the mass, and 'tis like a camel, indeed.

HAMLET. Methinks it is like a weasel.

POLONIUS. It is backed like a weasel.

HAMLET. Or like a whale?

POLONIUS. Very like a whale.

HAMLET. Then I will come to my mother by and by. [*Aside.*] They fool me to the top of my bent. [*Aloud.*] I will come by and by.

POLONIUS. I will say so.   [*Exit.*

HAMLET. 'By and by' is easily said. Leave me, friends.
                              [*Exeunt all but* HAMLET.
'Tis now the very witching time of night,
When churchyards yawn and hell itself breathes out
Contagion to this world: now could I drink hot blood,
And do such bitter business as the day
Would quake to look on. Soft; now to my mother.
O heart! lose not thy nature; let not ever
The soul of Nero enter this firm bosom;
Let me be cruel, not unnatural;
I will speak daggers to her, but use none;
My tongue and soul in this be hypocrites;
How in my words soever she be shent,
To give them seals never, my soul, consent!   [*Exit.*

Scene III.   A Room in the Castle

Enter KING, ROSENCRANTZ, *and* GUILDENSTERN.

KING. I like him not, nor stands it safe with us
To let his madness range. Therefore prepare you;
I your commission will forthwith dispatch,
And he to England shall along with you.
The terms of our estate may not endure
Hazard so dangerous as doth hourly grow

Out of his lunacies.

GUILDENSTERN.   We will ourselves provide.
Most holy and religious fear it is
To keep those many many bodies safe
That live and feed upon your majesty.

ROSENCRANTZ. The single and peculiar life is bound
With all the strength and armour of the mind
To keep itself from noyance; but much more
That spirit upon whose weal depend and rest
The lives of many. The cease of majesty
Dies not alone, but, like a gulf doth draw
What's near it with it; it is a massy wheel,
Fix'd on the summit of the highest mount,
To whose huge spokes ten thousand lesser things
Are mortis'd and adjoin'd; which, when it falls,
Each small annexment, petty consequence,
Attends the boisterous ruin. Never alone
Did the king sigh, but with a general groan.

KING. Arm you, I pray you, to this speedy voyage;
For we will fetters put upon this fear,
Which now goes too free-footed.

ROSENCRANTZ. ⎱
GUILDENSTERN. ⎰ We will haste us.

[*Exeunt* ROSENCRANTZ *and* GUILDENSTERN.

Enter POLONIUS.

POLONIUS. My lord, he's going to his mother's closet:
Behind the arras I'll convey myself
To hear the process; I'll warrant she'll tax him home;
And, as you said, and wisely was it said,
'Tis meet that some more audience than a mother,
Since nature makes them partial, and should o'erhear
The speech of vantage. Fare you well, my liege:
I'll call upon you ere you go to bed
And tell you what I know.

KING. Thanks, dear my lord.

[*Exit* POLONIUS.

O! my offence is rank, it smells to heaven;
It hath the primal eldest curse upon 't;
A brother's murder! Pray can I not,
Though inclination be as sharp as will:
My stronger guilt defeats my strong intent;
And like a man to double business bound,
I stand in pause where I shall first begin,
And both neglect. What if this curséd hand
Were thicker than itself with brother's blood,
Is there not rain enough in the sweet heavens
To wash it white as snow? Whereto serves mercy
But to confront the visage of offence?
And what's in prayer but this two-fold force,
To be forestalléd, ere we come to fall,
Or pardon'd, being down? Then, I'll look up;
My fault is past. But, O! what form or prayer
Can serve my turn? 'Forgive me my foul murder?'
That cannot be since I am still possess'd
Of those effects for which I did the murder,
My crown, mine own ambition, and my queen.
May one be pardon'd and retain the offence?
In the corrupted currents of this world
Offence's gilded hand may shove by justice,
And oft 'tis seen the wicked prize itself
Buys out the law; but 'tis not so above;
There is no shuffling, there the action lies
In his true nature, and we ourselves compell'd
Even to the teeth and forehead of our faults
To give in evidence. What then? what rests?
Try what repentance can: what can it not?
Yet what can it, when one can not repent?
O wretched state! O bosom black as death!
O liméd soul, that struggling to be free

Art more engaged! Help, angels! make assay;
Bow, stubborn knees; and heart with strings of steel
Be soft as sinews of the new-born babe.
All may be well.   [*Retires and kneels.*

            Enter HAMLET.

HAMLET. Now might I do it pat, now he is praying;
And now I'll do 't: and so he goes to heaven;
And so am I reveng'd. That would be scann'd:
A villain kills my father; and for that,
I, his sole son, do this same villain send
To heaven.
Why, this is hire and salary, not revenge.
He took my father grossly, full of bread,
With all his crimes broad blown, as flush as May;
And how his audit stands who knows save heaven?
But in our circumstance and course of thought
'Tis heavy with him. And am I then reveng'd,
To take him in the purging of his soul,
When he is fit and season'd for his passage?
No.
Up, sword, and know thou a more horrid hent;
When he is drunk asleep, or in his rage,
Or in the incestuous pleasure of his bed,
At gaming, swearing, or about some act
That has no relish of salvation in 't;
Then trip him, that his heels may kick at heaven,
And that his soul may be as damn'd and black
As hell, whereto it goes. My mother stays:
This physic but prolongs thy sickly days.   [*Exit.*

        The KING *rises and advances.*

KING. My words fly up, my thoughts remain below:
Words without thoughts never to heaven go.   [*Exit.*

Scene IV. *The Queen's Apartment*

Enter QUEEN *and* POLONIUS.

POLONIUS. He will come straight. Look you lay home to him;
Tell him his pranks have been too broad to bear with,
And that your Grace hath screen'd and stood between
Much heat and him. I'll silence me e'en here.
Pray you, be round with him.
    HAMLET. [*Within.*] Mother, mother, mother!
    QUEEN.   I'll warrant you;
Fear me not. Withdraw, I hear him coming.
                      [POLONIUS *hides behind the arras.*
    Enter HAMLET.

HAMLET. Now, mother, what's the matter?
QUEEN. Hamlet, thou hast thy father much offended.
HAMLET. Mother, you have my father much offended.
QUEEN. Come, come, you answer with an idle tongue.
HAMLET. Go, go, you question with a wicked tongue.
QUEEN. Why, how now, Hamlet!
HAMLET.   What's the matter now?
QUEEN. Have you forgot me?
HAMLET.   No, by the rood, not so:
You are the queen, your husband's brother's wife;
And,—would it were not so!—you are my mother.
    QUEEN. Nay then, I'll set those to you that can speak.
    HAMLET. Come, come, and sit you down; you shall not budge;
You go not, till I set you up a glass
Where you may see the inmost part of you.
    QUEEN. What wilt thou do? thou wilt not murder me?
Help, help, ho!
    POLONIUS. [*Behind.*] What, ho! help! help! help!
    HAMLET. [*Draws.*] How now! a rat? Dead, for a ducat, dead!
                  [*Makes a pass through the arras.*

POLONIUS. [*Behind.*] O! I am slain.

QUEEN. O me! what hast thou done?

HAMLET. Nay, I know not: is it the king?

QUEEN. O! what a rash and bloody deed is this!

HAMLET. A bloody deed! almost as bad, good mother,
As kill a king, and marry with his brother.

QUEEN. As kill a king!

HAMLET.   Ay, lady, 'twas my word.

[*Lifts up the arras and discovers* POLONIUS.

[*To* POLONIUS.] Thou wretched, rash, intruding fool, farewell!
I took thee for thy better; take thy fortune;
Thou find'st to be too busy is some danger.
Leave wringing of your hands: peace! sit you down,
And let me wring your heart; for so I shall
If it be made of penetrable stuff,
If damnéd custom have not brass'd it so
That it is proof and bulwark against sense.

QUEEN. What have I done that thou dar'st wag thy tongue
In noise so rude against me?

HAMLET.   Such an act
That blurs the grace and blush of modesty,
Calls virtue hypocrite, takes off the rose
From the fair forehead of an innocent love
And sets a blister there, makes marriage vows
As false as dicers' oaths; O! such a deed
As from the body of contraction plucks
The very soul, and sweet religion makes
A rhapsody of words; heaven's face doth glow,
Yea, this solidity and compound mass,
With tristful visage, as against the doom,
Is thought-sick at the act.

QUEEN.   Ay me! what act,
That roars so loud and thunders in the index?

HAMLET. Look here, upon this picture, and on this;
The counterfeit presentment of two brothers.

See, what a grace was seated on this brow;
Hyperion's curls, the front of Jove himself,
An eye like Mars to threaten and command,
A station like the herald Mercury
New-lighted on a heaven-kissing hill,
A combination and a form indeed,
Where every god did seem to set his seal,
To give the world assurance of a man.
This was your husband: look you now, what follows.
Here is your husband; like a mildew'd ear,
Blasting his wholesome brother. Have you eyes?
Could you on this fair mountain leave to feed,
And batten on this moor? Ha! have you eyes?
You cannot call it love, for at your age
The hey-day in the blood is tame, it's humble,
And waits upon the judgment; and what judgment
Would step from this to this? Sense, sure, you have,
Else could you not have motion; but sure, that sense
Is apoplex'd; for madness would not err,
Nor sense to ecstasy was ne'er so thrall'd
But it reserv'd some quantity of choice.
To serve in such a difference. What devil was't
That thus hath cozen'd you at hoodman-blind?
Eyes without feeling, feeling without sight,
Ears without hands or eyes, smelling sans all,
Or but a sickly part of one true sense
Could not so mope.
O shame! where is thy blush? Rebellious hell,
If thou canst mutine in a matron's bones,
To flaming youth let virtue be as wax,
And melt in her own fire: proclaim no shame
When the compulsive ardour gives the charge,
Since frost itself as actively doth burn,
And reason panders will.
    QUEEN.   O Hamlet! speak no more;

Thou turn'st mine eyes into my very soul;
And there I see such black and grainéd spots
As will not leave their tinct.

    HAMLET.   Nay, but to live
In the rank sweat of an enseaméd bed,
Stew'd in corruption, honeying and making love
Over the nasty sty,—

    QUEEN.   O! speak to me no more;
These words like daggers enter in mine ears;
No more, sweet Hamlet!

    HAMLET.   A murderer, and a villain;
A slave that is not twentieth part the tithe
Of your precedent lord; a vice of kings;
A cut-purse of the empire and the rule,
That from a shelf the precious diadem stole,
And put it in his pocket!

    QUEEN.   No more!

    HAMLET. A king of shreds and patches,—

    Enter GHOST.

Save me and hover o'er me with your wings,
You heavenly guards! What would your gracious figure?

    QUEEN. Alas! he's mad!

    HAMLET. Do you not come your tardy son to chide,
That, laps'd in time and passion, lets go by
The important acting of your dread command?
O! say.

    GHOST. Do not forget: this visitation
Is but to whet thy almost blunted purpose.
But, look! amazement on thy mother sits;
O! step between her and her fighting soul;
Conceit in weakest bodies strongest works:
Speak to her, Hamlet.

    HAMLET.   How is it with you, lady?

QUEEN. Alas! how is 't with you,
That you do bend your eye on vacancy
And with the incorporal air do hold discourse?
Forth at your eyes your spirits wildly peep;
And, as the sleeping soldiers in the alarm,
Your bedded hair, like life in excrements,
Starts up and stands an end. O gentle son!
Upon the heat and flame of thy distemper
Sprinkle cool patience. Whereon do you look?

HAMLET. On him, on him! Look you, how pale he glares!
His form and cause conjoin'd, preaching to stones,
Would make them capable. Do not look upon me;
Lest with this piteous action you convert
My stern effects: then what I have to do
Will want true colour; tears perchance for blood.

QUEEN. To whom do you speak this?

HAMLET.   Do you see nothing there?

QUEEN. Nothing at all; yet all that is I see.

HAMLET. Nor did you nothing hear?

QUEEN.   No, nothing but ourselves.

HAMLET. Why, look you there! look, how it steals away;
My father, in his habit as he liv'd;
Look! where he goes, even now, out at the portal.   [*Exit* GHOST.

QUEEN. This is the very coinage of your brain:
This bodiless creation ecstasy
Is very cunning in.

HAMLET. Ecstasy!
My pulse, as yours, doth temperately keep time,
And makes as healthful music. It is not madness
That I have utter'd: bring me to the test,
And I the matter will re-word, which madness
Would gambol from. Mother, for love of grace,
Lay not that flattering unction to your soul,
That not your trespass but my madness speaks;
It will but skin and film the ulcerous place,

Whiles rank corruption, mining all within,
Infects unseen. Confess yourself to heaven;
Repent what's past; avoid what is to come;
And do not spread the compost on the weeds
To make them ranker. Forgive me this my virtue;
For in the fatness of these pursy times
Virtue itself of vice must pardon beg,
Yea, curb and woo for leave to do him good.

    QUEEN. O Hamlet! thou hast cleft my heart in twain.

    HAMLET. O! throw away the worser part of it,
And live the purer with the other half.
Good night; but go not to mine uncle's bed;
Assume a virtue, if you have it not.
That monster, custom, who all sense doth eat,
Of habits devil, is angel yet in this,
That to the use of actions fair and good
He likewise gives a frock or livery,
That aptly is put on. Refrain to-night;
And that shall lend a kind of easiness
To the next abstinence: the next more easy;
For use almost can change the stamp of nature,
And exorcise the devil or throw him out
With wondrous potency. Once more, good-night:
And when you are desirous to be bless'd,
I'll blessing beg of you. For this same lord,

                      [*Pointing to* POLONIUS.
I do repent: but heaven hath pleas'd it so,
To punish me with this, and this with me,
That I must be their scourage and minister.
I will bestow him, and will answer well
The death I gave him. So, again, good-night.
I must be cruel only to be kind:
Thus bad begins and worse remains behind.
One word more, good lady.

    QUEEN.   What shall I do?

HAMLET. Not this, by no means, that I bid you do:
Let the bloat king tempt you again to bed;
Pinch wanton on your cheek; call you his mouse;
And let him, for a pair of reechy kisses,
Or paddling in your neck with his damn'd fingers,
Make you to ravel all this matter out,
That I essentially am not in madness,
But mad in craft. 'Twere good you let him know;
For who that's but a queen, fair, sober, wise,
Would from a paddock, from a bat, a gib,
Such dear concernings hide? who would do so?
No, in despite of sense and secrecy,
Unpeg the basket on the house's top,
Let the birds fly, and, like the famous ape,
To try conclusions, in the basket creep,
And break your own neck down.

QUEEN. Be thou assur'd, if words be made of breath,
And breath of life, I have no life to breathe
What thou has said to me.

HAMLET. I must to England; you know that?

QUEEN.   Alack!
I had forgot: 'tis so concluded on.

HAMLET. There's letters seal'd; and my two schoolfellows,
Whom I will trust as I will adders fang'd,
They bear the mandate; they must sweep my way,
And marshal me to knavery. Let it work;
For 'tis the sport to have the enginer
Hoist with his own petar: and 't shall go hard
But I will delve one yard below their mines,
And blow them at the moon. O! 'tis most sweet,
When in one line two crafts directly meet.
This man shall set me packing;
I'll lug the guts into the neighbour room.
Mother, good-night. Indeed this counsellor
Is now most still, most secret, and most grave,

Who was in life a foolish prating knave.
Come, sir, to draw toward an end with you.
Good-night, mother.

[*Exeunt severally;* HAMLET *tugging in* POLONIUS.

Act 4

Scene I. A Room in the Castle

Enter KING, QUEEN, ROSENCRANTZ, *and* GUILDENSTERN.

KING. There's matter in these sighs, these profound heaves:
You must translate; 'tis fit we understand them.
Where is your son?
QUEEN. [*To* ROSENCRANTZ *and* GUILDENSTERN.] Bestow this
place on us a little while.

[*Exeunt* ROSENCRANTZ *and* GUILDENSTERN.
Ah, my good lord, what have I seen to-night.
KING. What, Gertrude? How does Hamlet?
QUEEN. Mad as the sea and wind, when both contend
Which is the mightier. In his lawless fit,
Behind the arras hearing something stir,
Whips out his rapier, cries, 'A rat! a rat!'
And, in his brainish apprehension, kills
The unseen good old man.
KING.   O heavy deed!
It had been so with us had we been there.
His liberty is full of threats to all;
To you yourself, to us, to every one.
Alas! how shall this bloody deed be answer'd?
It will be laid to us, whose providence
Should have kept short, restrain'd, and out of haunt,
This mad young man: but so much was our love,
We would not understand what was most fit,
But, like the owner of a foul disease,

185

To keep it from divulging, let it feed
Even on the pith of life. Where is he gone?
  QUEEN. To draw apart the body he hath kill'd;
O'er whom his very madness, like some ore
Among a mineral of metals base,
Shows itself pure: he weeps for what is done.
  KING. O Gertrude! come away.
The sun no sooner shall the mountains touch
But we will ship him hence; and this vile deed
We must, with all our majesty and skill,
Both countenance and excuse. Ho! Guildenstern!

Re-enter ROSENCRANTZ *and* GUILDENSTERN.

Friends both, go join you with some further aid:
Hamlet in madness hath Polonius slain,
And from his mother's closet hath he dragg'd him:
Go seek him out; speak fair, and bring the body
Into the chapel. I pray you, haste in this.
                         [Exeunt ROSENCRANTZ *and* GUILDENSTERN.
Come, Gertrude, we'll call up our wisest friends;
And let them know both what we mean to do,
And what's untimely done: so, haply, slander,
Whose whisper o'er the world's diameter,
As level as the cannon to his blank
Transports his poison'd shot, may miss our name,
And hit the woundless air. O! come away;
My soul is full of discord and dismay.   *[Exeunt.*

Scene II.   *Another Room in the Same*

  Enter HAMLET.

HAMLET. Safely stowed.
ROSENCRANTZ.
GUILDENSTERN. } *[Within.]* Hamlet! Lord Hamlet!

HAMLET. What noise? who calls on Hamlet?
O! here they come.

Enter ROSENCRANTZ *and* GUILDENSTERN.

ROSENCRANTZ. What have you done, my lord, with the dead
body?
HAMLET. Compounded it with dust, whereto 'tis kin.
ROSENCRANTZ. Tell us where 'tis, that we may take it thence
And bear it to the chapel.
HAMLET. Do not believe it.
ROSENCRANTZ. Believe what?
HAMLET. That I can keep your counsel and not mine own.
Besides, to be demanded of a sponge! what replication should be
made by the son of a king?
ROSENCRANTZ. Take you me for a sponge, my lord?
HAMLET. Ay, sir, that soaks up the king's countenance, his
rewards, his authorities. But such officers do the king best service
in the end: he keeps them, like an ape, in the corner of his jaw;
first mouthed, to be last swallowed: when he needs what you
have gleaned, it is but squeezing you, and, sponge, you shall be
dry again.
ROSENCRANTZ. I understand you not, my lord.
HAMLET. I am glad of it: a knavish speech sleeps in a foolish
ear.
ROSENCRANTZ. My lord, you must tell us where the body is,
and go with us to the king.
HAMLET. The body is with the king, but the king is not with
the body. The king is a thing—
GUILDENSTERN. A thing, my lord!
HAMLET. Of nothing: bring me to him. Hide fox, and all after.
                                                      [*Exeunt.*

Scene III. Another Room in the Same

Enter KING, *attended.*

KING. I have sent to seek him, and to find the body.
How dangerous is it that this man goes loose!
Yet must not we put the strong law on him:
He's lov'd of the distracted multitude,
Who like not in their judgment, but their eyes;
And where 'tis so, the offender's scourge is weigh'd,
But never the offence. To bear all smooth and even,
This sudden sending him away must seem
Deliberate pause: diseases desperate grown
By desperate appliance are reliev'd,
Or not at all.

Enter ROSENCRANTZ.

　　　　　　　How now! what hath befall'n?
ROSENCRANTZ. Where the dead body is bestow'd, my lord,
We cannot get from him.
KING.　　　　　　　But where is he?
ROSENCRANTZ. Without, my lord; guarded, to know your
　　pleasure.
KING. Bring him before us.
ROSENCRANTZ. Ho, Guildenstern! bring in my lord.

Enter HAMLET *and* GUILDENSTERN.

KING. Now, Hamlet, where's Polonius?
HAMLET. At supper.
KING. At supper! Where?
HAMLET. Not where he eats, but where he is eaten: a certain
convocation of politic worms are e'en at him. Your worm is your
only emperor for diet: we fat all creatures else to fat us, and
we fat ourselves for maggots: your fat king and your lean beggar

is but variable service; two dishes, but to one table: that's the
end.

KING. Alas, alas!

HAMLET. A man may fish with the worm that hath eat of a
king, and eat of the fish that hath fed of that worm.

KING. What dost thou mean by this?

HAMLET. Nothing, but to show you how a king may go a
progress through the guts of a beggar.

KING. Where is Polonius?

HAMLET. In heaven; send thither to see: if your messenger
find him not there, seek him i' the other place yourself. But,
indeed, if you find him not within this month, you shall nose
him as you go up the stairs into the lobby.

KING. [*To some* ATTENDANTS.] Go seek him there.

HAMLET. He will stay till you come.   [*Exeunt* ATTENDANTS.

KING. Hamlet, this deed, for thine especial safety,
Which we do tender, as we dearly grieve
For that which thou hast done, must send thee hence
With fiery quickness: therefore prepare thyself;
The bark is ready, and the wind at help,
The associates tend, and every thing is bent
For England.

HAMLET.   For England!

KING.   Ay, Hamlet.

HAMLET.   Good.

KING. So is it, if thou knew'st our purposes.

HAMLET. I see a cherub that sees them. But, come; for England! Farewell, dear mother.

KING. Thy loving father, Hamlet.

HAMLET. My mother: father and mother is man and wife, man
and wife is one flesh, and so, my mother. Come, for England!
                                                    [*Exit.*

KING. Follow him at foot; tempt him with speed aboard:
Delay it not, I'll have him hence to-night.
Away! for every thing is seal'd and done

That else leans on the affair: pray you, make haste.

[*Exeunt* ROSENCRANTZ *and* GUILDENSTERN.

And, England, if my love thou hold'st at aught,—
As my great power thereof may give thee sense,
Since yet thy cicatrice looks raw and red
After the Danish sword, and thy free awe
Pays homage to us,—thou mayst not coldly set
Our sovereign process, which imports at full,
By letters congruing to that effect,
The present death of Hamlet. Do it, England;
For like the hectic in my blood he rages,
And thou must cure me. Till I know 'tis done,
Howe'er my haps, my joys were ne'er begun.   [*Exit.*

Scene IV.   A Plain in Denmark

Enter FORTINBRAS, *a* CAPTAIN, *and* SOLDIERS, *marching.*

FORTINBRAS. Go, captain, from me greet the Danish king;
Tell him that, by his licence, Fortinbras
Claims the conveyance of a promis'd march
Over his kingdom. You know the rendezvous.
If that his majesty would aught with us,
We shall express our duty in his eye,
And let him know so.

CAPTAIN.   I will do 't, my lord.

FORTINBRAS. Go softly on.

[*Exeunt* FORTINBRAS *and* SOLDIERS.

Enter HAMLET, ROSENCRANTZ, GUILDENSTERN, &c.

HAMLET. Good sir, whose powers are these?

CAPTAIN. They are of Norway, sir.

HAMLET. How purpos'd, sir, I pray you?

CAPTAIN. Against some part of Poland.

HAMLET. Who commands them, sir?

CAPTAIN. The nephew to old Norway, Fortinbras.

HAMLET. Goes it against the main of Poland, sir,
Or for some frontier?

CAPTAIN. Truly to speak, and with no addition,
We go to gain a little patch of ground
That hath in it no profit but the name.
To pay five ducats, five, I would not farm it;
Nor will it yield to Norway or the Pole
A ranker rate, should it be sold in fee.

HAMLET. Why, then the Polack never will defend it.

CAPTAIN. Yes, 'tis already garrison'd.

HAMLET. Two thousand souls and twenty thousand ducats
Will not debate the question of this straw:
This is the imposthume of much wealth and peace,
That inward breaks, and shows no cause without
Why the man dies. I humbly thank you, sir.

CAPTAIN. God be wi' you, sir.   *[Exit.*

ROSENCRANTZ.   Will 't please you go, my lord?

HAMLET. I'll be with you straight. Go a little before.

                [Exeunt all except HAMLET.

How all occasions do inform against me,
And spur my dull revenge! What is a man,
If his chief good and market of his time
Be but to sleep and feed? a beast, no more.
Sure he that made us with such large discourse,
Looking before and after, gave us not
That capability and god-like reason
To fust in us unus'd. Now, whe'r it be
Bestial oblivion, or some craven scruple
Of thinking too precisely on the event,
A thought, which, quarter'd, hath but one part wisdom,
And ever three parts coward, I do not know
Why yet I live to say 'This thing's to do;'
Sith I have cause and will and strength and means
To do 't. Examples gross as earth exhort me:
Witness this army of such mass and charge
Led by a delicate and tender prince,

Whose spirit with divine ambition puff'd
Makes mouths at the invisible event,
Exposing what is mortal and unsure
To all that fortune, death and danger dare,
Even for an egg-shell. Rightly to be great
Is not to stir without great argument,
But greatly to find quarrel in a straw
When honour's at the stake. How stand I then,
That have a father kill'd, a mother stain'd,
Excitements of my reason and my blood,
And let all sleep, while, to my shame, I see
The imminent death of twenty thousand men,
That, for a fantasy and trick of fame,
Go to their graves like beds, fight for a plot
Whereon the numbers cannot try the cause,
Which is not tomb enough and continent
To hide the slain? O! from this time forth,
My thoughts be bloody, or be nothing worth!   [*Exit.*

Scene V.   Elsinore. A Room in the Castle

Enter QUEEN, HORATIO, *and a* GENTLEMAN.

QUEEN. I will not speak with her.
GENTLEMAN. She is importunate, indeed distract:
Her mood will needs be pitied.
QUEEN.   What would she have?
GENTLEMAN. She speaks much of her father; says she hears
There's tricks i' the world; and hems, and beats her heart;
Spurns enviously at straws; speaks things in doubt,
That carry but half sense: her speech is nothing,
Yet the unshapéd use of it doth move
The hearers to collection; they aim at it,
And botch the words up fit to their own thoughts;
Which, as her winks, and nods, and gestures yield them,
Indeed would make one think there might be thought,

Though nothing sure, yet much unhappily.

HORATIO. 'Twere good she were spoken with, for she may
strew
Dangerous conjectures in ill-breeding minds.

QUEEN. Let her come in.   [*Exit* GENTLEMAN.

To my sick soul, as sin's true nature is,
Each toy seems prologue to some great amiss:
So full of artless jealousy is guilt,
It spills itself in fearing to be spilt.

Re-enter GENTLEMAN, *with* OPHELIA.

OPHELIA Where is the beauteous majesty of Denmark?

QUEEN. How now, Ophelia!

OPHELIA.
          How should I your true love know
                    From another one?
          By his cockle hat and staff,
                    And his sandal shoon.

QUEEN. Alas! sweet lady, what imports this song?

OPHELIA. Say you? nay, pray you, mark.

          He is dead and gone, lady,
                    He is dead and gone;
          At his head a grass-green turf;
                    At his heels a stone.

O, ho!

QUEEN. Nay, but Ophelia,—

OPHELIA. Pray you, mark.

          White his shroud as the mountain snow,—

Enter KING.

QUEEN. Alas! look here, my lord.

OPHELIA.
          Larded all with sweet flowers;
          Which bewept to the grave did not go
                    With true-love showers.

KING. How do you, pretty lady?

OPHELIA. Well, God 'ild you! They say the owl was a baker's daughter. Lord! we know what we are, but know not what we may be. God be at your table!

KING. Conceit upon her father.

OPHELIA. Pray you, let's have no words of this; but when they ask you what it means, say you this:

> To-morrow is Saint Valentine's day,
>   All in the morning betime,
> And I a maid at your window,
>   To be your Valentine:
> Then up he rose, and donn'd his clothes,
>   And dupp'd the chamber door;
> Let in the maid, that out a maid
>   Never departed more.

KING. Pretty Ophelia!

OPHELIA. Indeed, la! without an oath, I'll make an end on 't:

> By Gis and by Saint Charity,
>   Alack, and fie for shame!
> Young men will do 't, if they come to 't;
>   By Cock they are to blame.
> Quoth she, before you tumbled me,
>   You promis'd me to wed:

(He answers.)

> So would I ha' done, by yonder sun,
>   An thou hadst not come to my bed.

KING. How long hath she been thus?

OPHELIA. I hope all will be well. We must be patient: but I cannot choose but weep, to think they should lay him i' the cold ground. My brother shall know of it: and so I thank you for your good counsel. Come, my coach! Good-night, ladies; good-night, sweet ladies; good-night, good-night.   [*Exit.*

KING. Follow her close; give her good watch, I pray you.

          [*Exit* HORATIO.

O! this is the poison of deep grief; it springs
All from her father's death. O Gertrude, Gertrude!
When sorrows come, they come not single spies,
But in battalions. First, her father slain;
Next, your son gone; but he most violent author
Of his own just remove: the people muddied,
Thick and unwholesome in their thoughts and whispers,
For good Polonius' death; and we have done but greenly,
In hugger-mugger to inter him: poor Ophelia
Divided from herself and her fair judgment,
Without the which we are pictures, or mere beasts:
Last, and as much containing as all these,
Her brother is in secret come from France,
Feeds on his wonder, keeps himself in clouds,
And wants not buzzers to infect his ear
With pestilent speeches of his father's death;
Wherein necessity, of matter beggar'd,
Will nothing stick our person to arraign
In ear and ear. O my dear Gertrude! this,
Like to a murdering-piece, in many places
Gives me superfluous death.   [*A noise within.*

  QUEEN.   Alack! what noise is this?

    Enter a GENTLEMAN.

  KING. Where are my Switzers? Let them guard the door.
What is the matter?
  GENTLEMAN.   Save yourself, my lord;
The ocean, overpeering of his list,
Eats not the flats with more impetuous haste
Than young Laertes, in a riotous head,
O'erbears your officers. The rabble call him lord;
And, as the world were now but to begin,
Antiquity forgot, custom not known,
The ratifiers and props of every word,
They cry, 'Choose we; Laertes shall be king!'

Caps, hands, and tongues, applaud it to the clouds,
'Laertes shall be king, Laertes king!'

QUEEN. How cheerfully on the false trail they cry!
O! this is counter, you false Danish dogs!

KING. The doors are broke.   [*Noise within.*

Enter LAERTES, *armed;* DANES *following.*

LAERTES. Where is the king? Sirs, stand you all without.

DANES. No, let's come in.

LAERTES.   I pray you, give me leave.

DANES. We will, we will.   [*They retire without the door.*

LAERTES. I thank you: keep the door. O thou vile king!
Give me my father.

QUEEN.   Calmly, good Laertes.

LAERTES. That drop of blood that's calm proclaims me bas-
  tard,
Cries cuckold to my father, brands the harlot
Even here, between the chaste unsmirchéd brows
Of my true mother.

KING.   What is the cause, Laertes,
That thy rebellion looks so giant-like?
Let him go, Gertrude; do not fear our person:
There's such divinity doth hedge a king,
That treason can but peep to what it would,
Acts little of his will. Tell me, Laertes,
Why thou art thus incens'd. Let him go, Gertrude.
Speak, man.

LAERTES. Where is my father?

KING.   Dead.

QUEEN.   But not by him.

KING. Let him demand his fill.

LAERTES. How came he dead? I'll not be juggled with.
To hell, allegiance! vows, to the blackest devil!
Conscience and grace, to the profoundest pit!
I dare damnation. To this point I stand,

That both the worlds I give to negligence,
Let come what comes; only I'll be reveng'd
Most thoroughly for my father.

    KING.   Who shall stay you?

    LAERTES. My will, not all the world:
And for my means, I'll husband them so well,
They shall go far with little.

    KING.   Good Laertes,
If you desire to know the certainty
Of your dear father's death, is 't writ in your revenge,
That, swoopstake, you will draw both friend and foe,
Winner and loser?

    LAERTES. None but his enemies.

    KING.   Will you know them then?

    LAERTES. To his good friends thus wide I'll ope my arms;
And like the kind life-rendering pelican,
Repast them with my blood.

    KING.   Why, now you speak
Like a good child and a true gentleman.
That I am guiltless of your father's death,
And am most sensibly in grief for it,
It shall as level to your judgment pierce
As day does to your eye.

    DANES.   [*Within.*] Let her come in.

    LAERTES. How now! what noise is that?

    Re-enter OPHELIA.

O heat, dry up my brains! tears seven times salt,
Burn out the sense and virtue of mine eye!
By heaven, thy madness shall be paid by weight,
Till our scale turn the beam. O rose of May!
Dear maid, kind sister, sweet Ophelia!
O heavens! is 't possible a young maid's wits
Should be as mortal as an old man's life?
Nature is fine in love, and where 'tis fine

It sends some precious instance of itself
After the thing it loves.

OPHELIA.

> They bore him barefac'd on the bier;
> Hey non nonny, nonny, hey nonny;
> And in his grave rain'd many a tear;

Fare you well, my dove!

LAERTES. Hadst thou thy wits, and didst persuade revenge,
It could not move thus.

OPHELIA.

> You must sing, a-down a-down,
> And you call him a-down-a.

O how the wheel becomes it! It is the false steward that stole his
master's daughter.

LAERTES. This nothing's more than matter.

OPHELIA. There's rosemary, that's for remembrance; pray,
love, remember: and there is pansies, that's for thoughts.

LAERTES. A document in madness, thoughts and remembrance
fitted.

OPHELIA. There's fennel for you, and columbines; there's rue
for you; and here's some for me; we may call it herb of grace o'
Sundays. O! you must wear your rue with a difference. There's a
daisy; I would give you some violets, but they withered all when
my father died. They say he made a good end,—

> For bonny sweet Robin is all my joy.

LAERTES. Thought and affliction, passion, hell itself,
She turns to favour and to prettiness.

OPHELIA.

> And will a' not come again?
> And will a' not come again?
> No, no, he is dead;
> Go to thy death-bed,
> He never will come again.
> His beard was as white as snow

All flaxen was his poll,
 He is gone, he is gone,
 And we cast away moan:
God ha' mercy on his soul!

And of all Christian souls I pray God. God be wi' ye!   [*Exit.*
 LAERTES. Do you see this, O God?
 KING. Laertes, I must commune with your grief,
Or you deny me right. Go but apart,
Make choice of whom your wisest friends you will,
And they shall hear and judge 'twixt you and me.
If by direct or by collateral hand
They find us touch'd, we will our kingdom give,
Our crown, our life, and all that we call ours,
To you in satisfaction; but if not,
Be you content to lend your patience to us,
And we shall jointly labour with your soul
To give it due content.
 LAERTES.   Let this be so:
His means of death, his obscure burial,
No trophy, sword, nor hatchment o'er his bones,
No noble rite nor formal ostentation,
Cry to be heard, as 'twere from heaven to earth,
That I must call 't in question.
 KING.   So you shall;
And where the offence is let the great axe fall.
I pray you go with me.   [*Exeunt.*

Scene VI. *Another Room in the Same*

Enter HORATIO *and a* SERVANT.

 HORATIO. What are they that would speak with me?
 SERVANT. Sailors, sir: they say, they have letters for you.
 HORATIO. Let them come in.   [*Exit* SERVANT.
I do not know from what part of the world
I should be greeted, if not from Lord Hamlet.

Enter SAILORS.

FIRST SAILOR. God bless you, sir.

HORATIO. Let him bless thee too.

SECOND SAILOR. He shall, sir, an 't please him. There's a letter for you, sir;—it comes from the ambassador that was bound for England;—if your name be Horatio, as I am let to know it is.

HORATIO. *Horatio, when thou shalt have overlooked this, give these fellows some means to the king: they have letters for him. Ere we were two days old at sea, a pirate of very war-like appointment gave us chase. Finding ourselves too slow of sail, we put on a compelled valour; in the grapple I boarded them: on the instant they got clear of our ship, so I alone became their prisoner. They have dealt with me like thieves of mercy, but they knew what they did; I am to do a good turn for them. Let the king have the letters I have sent; and repair thou to me with as much haste as thou wouldst fly death. I have words to speak in thine ear will make thee dumb, yet are they much too light for the bore of the matter. These good fellows will bring thee where I am. Rosencrantz and Guildenstern hold their course for England: of them I have much to tell thee. Farewell.*

He that thou knowest thine,

Hamlet.

Come, I will give you way for these your letters;
And do 't the speedier, that you may direct me
To him from whom you brought them.   [*Exeunt.*

Scene VII.   Another Room in the Same

Enter KING *and* LAERTES.

KING. Now must your conscience my acquittance seal,
And you must put me in your heart for friend,
Sith you have heard, and with a knowing ear,
That he which hath your noble father slain
Pursu'd my life.

LAERTES.   It well appears: but tell me

Why you proceeded not against these feats,
So crimeful and so capital in nature,
As by your safety, wisdom, all things else,
You mainly were stirr'd up.

    KING.   O! for two special reasons;
Which may to you, perhaps, seem much unsinew'd,
But yet to me they are strong. The queen his mother
Lives almost by his looks, and for myself,—
My virtue or my plague, be it either which,—
She's so conjunctive to my life and soul,
That, as the star moves not but in his sphere,
I could not but by her. The other motive,
Why to a public count I might not go,
Is the great love the general gender bear him;
Who, dipping all his faults in their affection,
Would, like the spring that turneth wood to stone,
Convert his gyves to graces; so that my arrows,
Too slightly timber'd for so loud a wind,
Would have reverted to my bow again,
And not where I had aim'd them.

    LAERTES. And so have I a noble father lost;
A sister driven into desperate terms,
Whose worth, if praises may go back again,
Stood challenger on mount of all the age
For her perfections. But my revenge will come.

    KING. Break not your sleeps for that; you must not think
That we are made of stuff so flat and dull
That we can let our beard be shook with danger
And think it pastime. You shortly shall hear more;
I lov'd your father, and we love ourself,
And that, I hope, will teach you to imagine.—

    Enter a MESSENGER.

How now! what news?

    MESSENGER.   Letters, my lord, from Hamlet:
This to your majesty; this to the queen.

KING. From Hamlet! Who brought them?

MESSENGER. Sailors, my lord, they say; I saw them not:
They were given me by Claudio, he receiv'd them
Of him that brought them.

KING.   Laertes, you shall hear them.
Leave us.   [*Exit* MESSENGER.

*High and mighty, you shall know I am set naked on your
kingdom. To-morrow shall I beg leave to see your kingly eyes;
when I shall, first asking your pardon thereunto, recount the
occasions of my sudden and more strange return.*

                                              Hamlet.

What should this mean? Are all the rest come back?
Or is it some abuse and no such thing?

LAERTES. Know you the hand?

KING.   'Tis Hamlet's character. 'Naked,'
And in a postscript here, he says, 'alone.'
Can you advise me?

LAERTES. I'm lost in it, my lord. But let him come!
It warms the very sickness in my heart,
That I shall live and tell him to his teeth,
'Thus diddest thou.'

KING.   If it be so, Laertes,
As how should it be so? how otherwise?
Will you be rul'd by me?

LAERTES.   Ay, my lord;
So you will not o'er-rule me to a peace.

KING. To thine own peace. If he be now return'd,
As checking at his voyage, and that he means
No more to undertake it, I will work him
To an exploit, now ripe in my device,
Under the which he shall not choose but fall;
And for his death no wind of blame shall breathe,
But even his mother shall uncharge the practice
And call it accident.

LAERTES.   My lord, I will be rul'd;
The rather, if you could devise it so

That I might be the organ.

KING.   It falls right.

You have been talk'd of since your travel much,
And that in Hamlet's hearing, for a quality
Wherein, they say, you shine; your sum of parts
Did not together pluck such envy from him
As did that one, and that, in my regard,
Of the unworthiest siege.

LAERTES.   What part is that, my lord?

KING. A very riband in the cap of youth,
Yet needful too; for youth no less becomes
The light and careless livery that it wears
Than settled age his sables and his weeds,
Importing health and graveness. Two months since
Here was a gentleman of Normandy:
I've seen myself, and serv'd against, the French,
And they can well on horseback; but this gallant
Had witchcraft in 't, he grew unto his seat,
And to such wondrous doing brought his horse,
As he had been incorps'd and demi-natur'd
With the brave beast; so far he topp'd my thought,
That I, in forgery of shapes and tricks,
Come short of what he did.

LAERTES.   A Norman was 't?

KING. A Norman.

LAERTES. Upon my life, Lamord.

KING.   The very same.

LAERTES. I know him well; he is the brooch indeed
And gem of all the nation.

KING. He made confession of you,
And gave you such a masterly report
For art and exercise in your defence,
And for your rapier most especially,
That he cried out, 'twould be a sight indeed
If one could match you; the scrimers of their nation,
He swore, had neither motion, guard, nor eye,

If you oppos'd them. Sir, this report of his
Did Hamlet so envenom with his envy
That he could nothing do but wish and beg
Your sudden coming o'er, to play with him.
Now, out of this,—

    LAERTES.   What out of this, my lord?

    KING. Laertes, was your father dear to you?
Or are you like the painting of a sorrow,
A face without a heart?

    LAERTES.   Why ask you this?

    KING. Not that I think you did not love your father,
But that I know love is begun by time,
And that I see, in passages of proof,
Time qualifies the spark and fire of it.
There lives within the very flame of love
A kind of wick or snuff that will abate it,
And nothing is at a like goodness still,
For goodness, growing to a plurisy,
Dies in his own too-much. That we would do,
We should do when we would, for this 'would' changes,
And hath abatements and delays as many
As there are tongues, are hands, are accidents;
And then this 'should' is like a spendthrift sigh,
That hurts by easing. But, to the quick o' the ulcer;
Hamlet comes back; what would you undertake
To show yourself your father's son in deed
More than in words?

    LAERTES.   To cut his throat i' the church.

    KING. No place indeed should murder sanctuarize;
Revenge should have no bounds. But, good Laertes,
Will you do this, keep close within your chamber.
Hamlet return'd shall know you are come home;
We'll put on those shall praise your excellence,
And set a double varnish on the fame
The Frenchman gave you, bring you, in fine, together,
And wager on your heads: he, being remiss,

The Shakespeare monument at Stratford-on-Avon

Most generous and free from all contriving,
Will not peruse the foils; so that, with ease
Or with a little shuffling, you may choose
A sword unbated, and, in a pass of practice
Requite him for your father.

    LAERTES.   I will do 't;
And, for that purpose, I'll anoint my sword.
I bought an unction of a mountebank,
So mortal that, but dip a knife in it,
Where it draws blood no cataplasm so rare,
Collected from all simples that have virtue
Under the moon, can save the thing from death
That is but scratch'd withal; I'll touch my point
With this contagion, that, if I gall him slightly,
It may be death.

    KING.   Let's further think of this;
Weigh what convenience both of time and means
May fit us to our shape. If this should fail,
And that our drift look through our bad performance
'Twere better not assay'd; therefore this project
Should have a back or second, that might hold,
If this should blast in proof. Soft! let me see;
We'll make a solemn wager on your cunnings:
I ha 't:
When in your motion you are hot and dry,—
As make your bouts more violent to that end,—
And that he calls for drink, I'll have prepar'd him
A chalice for the nonce, whereon but sipping,
If he by chance escape your venom'd stuck,
Our purpose may hold there. But stay! what noise?

    Enter QUEEN.

How now, sweet queen!

    QUEEN. One woe doth tread upon another's heel,
So fast they follow: your sister's drown'd, Laertes.

    LAERTES. Drown'd! O, where?

QUEEN. There is a willow grows aslant a brook,
That shows his hoar leaves in the glassy stream;
There with fantastic garlands did she come,
Of crow-flowers, nettles, daisies, and long purples,
That liberal shepherds give a grosser name,
But our cold maids do dead men's fingers call them:
There, on the pendent boughs her coronet weeds
Clambering to hang, an envious sliver broke,
When down her weedy trophies and herself
Fell in the weeping brook. Her clothes spread wide,
And, mermaid-like, awhile they bore her up;
Which time she chanted snatches of old lauds,
As one incapable of her own distress,
Or like a creature native and indu'd
Unto that element; but long it could not be
Till that her garments, heavy with their drink,
Pull'd the poor wretch from her melodious lay
To muddy death.
    LAERTES.   Alas! then, she is drown'd?
    QUEEN. Drown'd, drown'd.
    LAERTES. Too much of water hast thou, poor Ophelia,
And therefore I forbid my tears; but yet
It is our trick, nature her custom holds,
Let shame say what it will; when these are gone
The woman will be out. Adieu, my lord!
I have a speech of fire, that fain would blaze,
But that this folly douts it.   [*Exit.*
    KING.   Let's follow, Gertrude.
How much I had to do to calm his rage!
Now fear I this will give it start again;
Therefore let's follow.   [*Exeunt.*

Act 5

Scene I.   A Churchyard

Enter two CLOWNS, *with spades and mattock.*

FIRST CLOWN. Is she to be buried in Christian burial that wilfully seeks her own salvation?

SECOND CLOWN. I tell thee she is: and therefore make her grave straight: the crowner hath sat on her, and finds it Christian burial.

FIRST CLOWN. How can that be, unless she drowned herself in her own defence?

SECOND CLOWN. Why, 'tis found so.

FIRST CLOWN. It must be *se offendendo;* it cannot be else. For here lies the point: if I drown myself wittingly it argues an act; and an act hath three branches; it is, to act, to do, and to perform: argal, she drowned herself wittingly.

SECOND CLOWN. Nay, but hear you, goodman delver,—

FIRST CLOWN. Give me leave. Here lies the water; good: here stands the man; good: if the man go to this water, and drown himself, it is, will he, nill he, he goes; mark you that? but if the water come to him, and drown him, he drowns not himself: argal, he that is not guilty of his own death shortens not his own life.

SECOND CLOWN. But is this law?

FIRST CLOWN. Ay, marry, is't; crowner's quest law.

SECOND CLOWN. Will you ha' the truth on 't? If this had not been a gentlewoman she should have been buried out o' Christian burial.

FIRST CLOWN. Why, there thou sayest; and the more pity that great folk should have countenance in this world to drown or hang themselves more than their even Christian. Come, my spade. There is no ancient gentlemen but gardeners, ditchers, and grave-makers; they hold up Adam's profession.

SECOND CLOWN. Was he a gentleman?

FIRST CLOWN. A' was the first that ever bore arms.

SECOND CLOWN. Why, he had none.

FIRST CLOWN. What! art a heathen? How dost thou understand the Scripture? The Scripture says, Adam digged; could he dig without arms? I'll put another question to thee; if thou answerest me not to the purpose, confess theyself—

SECOND CLOWN. Go to.

FIRST CLOWN. What is he that builds stronger than either the mason, the shipwright, or the carpenter?

SECOND CLOWN. The gallows-maker; for that frame outlives a thousand tenants.

FIRST CLOWN. I like thy wit well, in good faith; the gallows does well, but how does it well? it does well to those that do ill; now thou dost ill to say the gallows is built stronger than the church: argal, the gallows may do well to thee. To't again; come.

SECOND CLOWN. Who builds stronger than a mason, a shipwright, or a carpenter?

FIRST CLOWN. Ay, tell me that, and unyoke.

SECOND CLOWN. Marry, now I can tell.

FIRST CLOWN. To 't.

SECOND CLOWN. Mass, I cannot tell.

Enter HAMLET *and* HORATIO *at a distance.*

FIRST CLOWN. Cudgel thy brains no more about it, for your dull ass will not mend his pace with beating; and, when you are asked this question next, say, 'a grave-maker:' the houses that he makes last till doomsday. Go, get thee to Yaughan; fetch me a stoup of liquor.   [*Exit* SECOND CLOWN.

FIRST CLOWN *digs, and sings.*

> In youth, when I did love, did love,
> Methought it was very sweet,
> To contract o' the time, for-a my behove,
> O! methought there was nothing meet.

HAMLET. Has this fellow no feeling of his business, that he sings at grave-making?

HORATIO. Custom hath made it in him a property of easiness.

HAMLET. 'Tis e'en so; the hand of little employment hath the daintier sense.

FIRST CLOWN.

> But age, with his stealing steps,
> Hath claw'd me in his clutch,
> And hath shipped me intil the land,
> As if I had never been such.

> *[Throws up a skull.*

HAMLET. That skull had a tongue in it, and could sing once; how the knave jowls it to the ground, as if it were Cain's jaw-bone, that did the first murder! This might be the pate of a politician, which this ass now o'er-reaches, one that would circumvent God, might it not?

HORATIO. It might, my lord.

HAMLET. Or of a courtier, which could say, 'Good morrow, sweet lord! How dost thou, good lord?' This might be my Lord Such-a-one, that praised my Lord Such-a-one's horse, when he meant to beg it, might it not?

HORATIO. Ay, my lord.

HAMLET. Why, e'en so, and now my Lady Worm's; chapless, and knocked about the mazzard with a sexton's spade. Here's fine revolution, an we had the trick to see 't. Did these bones cost no more the breeding but to play at loggats with 'em? mine ache to think on 't.

FIRST CLOWN.

> A pick-axe, and a spade, a spade,
> For and a shrouding sheet;

O! a pit of clay for to be made
For such a guest is meet.

[*Throws up another skull.*

HAMLET. There's another; why may not that be the skull of a lawyer? Where be his quiddities now, his quillets, his cases, his tenures, and his tricks? why does he suffer this rude knave now to knock him about the sconce with a dirty shovel, and will not tell him of his action of battery? Hum! This fellow might be in 's time a great buyer of land, with his statutes, his recognizances, his fines, his double vouchers, his recoveries; is this the fine of his fines, and the recovery of his recoveries, to have his fine pate full of fine dirt? will his vouchers vouch him no more of his purchases, and double ones too, than the length and breadth of a pair of indentures? The very conveyance of his lands will hardly lie in this box, and must the inheritor himself have no more, ha?

HORATIO. Not a jot more, my lord.

HAMLET. Is not parchment made of sheep-skins?

HORATIO. Ay, my lord, and of calf-skins too.

HAMLET. They are sheep and calves which seek out assurance in that. I will speak to this fellow. Whose grave's this, sir?

FIRST CLOWN. Mine, sir,

O! a pit of clay for to be made
For such a guest is meet.

HAMLET. I think it be thine, indeed; for thou liest in 't.

FIRST CLOWN. You lie out on 't, sir, and therefore it is not yours; for my part, I do not lie in 't, and yet it is mine.

HAMLET. Thou dost lie in 't, to be in 't and say it is thine: 'tis for the dead, not for the quick; therefore thou liest.

FIRST CLOWN. 'Tis a quick lie, sir; 'twill away again, from me to you.

HAMLET. What man dost thou dig it for?

FIRST CLOWN. For no man, sir.

HAMLET. What woman, then?

FIRST CLOWN. For none, neither.

HAMLET. Who is to be buried in 't?

FIRST CLOWN. One that was a woman, sir; but, rest her soul, she's dead.

HAMLET. How absolute the knave is! we must speak by the card, or equivocation will undo us. By the Lord, Horatio, these three years I have taken note of it; the age is grown so picked that the toe of the peasant comes so near the heel of the courtier, he galls his kibe. How long hast thou been a grave-maker?

FIRST CLOWN. Of all the days i' the year, I came to 't that day that our last King Hamlet overcame Fortinbras.

HAMLET. How long is that since?

FIRST CLOWN. Cannot you tell that? every fool can tell that; it was the very day that young Hamlet was born; he that is mad, and sent into England.

HAMLET. Ay, marry; why was he sent into England?

FIRST CLOWN. Why, because he was mad: he shall recover his wits there; or, if he do not, 'tis no great matter there.

HAMLET. Why?

FIRST CLOWN. 'Twill not be seen in him there; there the men are as mad as he.

HAMLET. How came he mad?

FIRST CLOWN. Very strangely, they say.

HAMLET. How strangely?

FIRST CLOWN. Faith, e'en with losing his wits.

HAMLET. Upon what ground?

FIRST CLOWN. Why, here in Denmark; I have been sexton here, man and boy, thirty years.

HAMLET. How long will a man lie i' the earth ere he rot?

FIRST CLOWN. Faith, if he be not rotten before he die,—as we have many pocky corses now-a-days, that will scarce hold the laying in,—he will last you some eight year or nine year; a tanner will last you nine year.

HAMLET. Why he more than another?

FIRST CLOWN. Why, sir, his hide is so tanned with his trade that he will keep out water a great while, and your water is a sore decayer of your whoreson dead body. Here's a skull now; this skull hath lain you i' the earth three-and-twenty years.

HAMLET. Whose was it?

FIRST CLOWN. A whoreson mad fellow's it was: whose do you think it was?

HAMLET. Nay, I know not.

FIRST CLOWN. A pestilence on him for a mad rogue! a' poured a flagon of Rhenish on my head once. This same skull, sir, was, sir, Yorick's skull, the king's jester.

HAMLET. This!

FIRST CLOWN. E'en that.

HAMLET. Let me see.—[*Takes the skull.*]—Alas! poor Yorick. I knew him, Horatio; a fellow of infinite jest, of most excellent fancy; he hath borne me on his back a thousand times; and now, how abhorred in my imagination it is! my gorge rises at it. Here hung those lips that I have kissed I know not how oft. Where be your gibes now? your gambols? your songs? your flashes of merriment, that were wont to set the table on a roar? Not one now, to mock your own grinning? quite chapfallen? Now get you to my lady's chamber, and tell her, let her paint an inch thick, to this favour she must come; make her laugh at that. Prithee, Horatio, tell me one thing.

HORATIO. What's that, my lord?

HAMLET. Dost thou think Alexander looked o' this fashion i' the earth?

HORATIO. E'en so.

HAMLET. And smelt so? pah!   [*Puts down the skull.*

HORATIO. E'en so, my lord.

HAMLET. To what base uses we may return, Horatio! Why may not imagination trace the noble dust of Alexander, till he find it stopping a bung-hole?

HORATIO. 'Twere to consider too curiously, to consider so.

HAMLET. No, faith, not a jot; but to follow him thither with modesty enough, and likelihood to lead it; as thus: Alexander died, Alexander was buried, Alexander returneth into dust; the dust is earth; of earth we make loam, and why of that loam, whereto he was converted, might they not stop a beer-barrel?

Imperious Cæsar, dead and turn'd to clay,

Might stop a hole to keep the wind away:
O! that that earth, which kept the world in awe,
Should patch a wall to expel the winter's flaw.
But soft! but soft! aside: here comes the king.

Enter KING, QUEEN, LAERTES, *and a coffin with* LORDS
ATTENDANT *and* PRIEST.

The queen, the courtiers: who is that they follow?
And with such maiméd rites? This doth betoken
The corse they follow did with desperate hand
Fordo its own life; 'twas of some estate.
Couch we awhile, and mark.   [*Retiring with* HORATIO.
    LAERTES What ceremony else?
    HAMLET.   That is Laertes,
A very noble youth: mark.
    LAERTES. What ceremony else?
    FIRST PRIEST. Her obsequies have been as far enlarg'd
As we have warrantise: her death was doubtful,
And, but that great command o'ersways the order,
She should in ground unsanctified have lodg'd
Till the last trumpet; for charitable prayers,
Shards, flints, and pebbles should be thrown on her;
Yet here she is allow'd her virgin crants,
Her maiden strewments, and the bringing home
Of bell and burial.
    LAERTES. Must there no more be done?
    FIRST PRIEST.   No more be done:
We should profane the service of the dead,
To sing sage requiem, and such rest to her
As to peace-parted souls.
    LAERTES.   Lay her i' th'earth;
And from her fair and unpolluted flesh
May violets spring! I tell thee, churlish priest,
A ministering angel shall my sister be,
When thou liest howling.

HAMLET. What! the fair Ophelia?

QUEEN. Sweets to the sweet: farewell! [*Scattering flowers.*
I hop'd thou shouldst have been my Hamlet's wife;
I thought thy bride-bed to have deck'd, sweet maid,
And not have strew'd thy grave.

LAERTES. O! treble woe
Fall ten times treble on that cursèd head
Whose wicked deed thy most ingenious sense
Depriv'd thee of. Hold off the earth awhile,
Till I have caught her once more in mine arms.

[*Leaps into the grave.*

Now pile your dust upon the quick and dead,
Till of this flat a mountain you have made,
To o'ertop old Pelion or the skyish head
Of blue Olympus.

HAMLET. [*Advancing.*] What is he whose grief
Bears such an emphasis? whose phrase of sorrow
Conjures the wandering stars, and makes them stand
Like wonder-wounded hearers? this is I,
Hamlet the Dane. [*Leaps into the grave.*

LAERTES. The devil take thy soul! [*Grapples with him.*

HAMLET. Thou pray'st not well.
I prithee, take thy fingers from my throat;
For though I am not splenetive and rash
Yet have I in me something dangerous,
Which let thy wisdom fear. Away thy hand!

KING. Pluck them asunder.

QUEEN. Hamlet! Hamlet!

ALL. Gentlemen,—

HORATIO. Good my lord, be quiet.

[*The* ATTENDANTS *part them, and
they come out of the grave.*

HAMLET. Why, I will fight with him upon this theme
Until my eyelids will no longer wag.

QUEEN. O my son! what theme?

HAMLET. I lov'd Ophelia: forty thousand brothers

Could not, with all their quantity of love,
Make up my sum. What wilt thou do for her?
  KING. O! he is mad, Laertes.
  QUEEN. For love of God, forbear him.
  HAMLET. 'Swounds, show me what thou'lt do:
Woo't weep? woo't fight? woo't fast? woo't tear thyself?
Woo't drink up eisel? eat a crocodile?
I'll do't. Dost thou come here to whine?
To outface me with leaping in her grave?
Be buried quick with her, and so will I:
And, if thou prate of mountains, let them throw
Millions of acres on us, till our ground,
Singeing his pate against the burning zone,
Make Ossa like a wart! Nay, an thou'lt mouth,
I'll rant as well as thou.
  QUEEN.   This is mere madness:
And thus a while the fit will work on him;
Anon as patient as the female dove,
When that her golden couplets are disclos'd,
His silence will sit drooping.
  HAMLET.   Hear you, sir;
What is the reason that you use me thus?
I lov'd you ever: but it is no matter;
Let Hercules himself do what he may,
The cat will mew and the dog will have his day.   [*Exit.*
  KING. I pray you, good Horatio, wait upon him.
                                        [*Exit* HORATIO.
[*To* LAERTES.] Strengthen your patience in our last night's
     speech;
We'll put the matter to the present push.
Good Gertrude, set some watch over your son.
This grave shall have a living monument:
An hour of quiet shortly shall we see;
Till then, in patience our proceeding be.   [*Exeunt.*

Scene II.   A Hall in the Castle

Enter HAMLET *and* HORATIO.

HAMLET. So much for this, sir: now shall you see the other;
You do remember all the circumstance?

HORATIO. Remember it, my lord?

HAMLET. Sir, in my heart there was a kind of fighting
That would not let me sleep; methought I lay
Worse than the mutines in the bilboes. Rashly,—
And prais'd be rashness for it, let us know,
Our indiscretion sometimes serves us well
When our deep plots do pall; and that should teach us
There's a divinity that shapes our ends,
Rough-hew them how we will.

HORATIO.   That is most certain.

HAMLET. Up from my cabin,
My sea-gown scarf'd about me, in the dark
Groped I to find out them, had my desire,
Finger'd their packet, and in fine withdrew
To mine own room again; making so bold—
My fears forgetting manners—to unseal
Their grand commission; where I found, Horatio,
O royal knavery! an exact command,
Larded with many several sorts of reasons
Importing Denmark's health, and England's too,
With, ho! such bugs and goblins in my life,
That, on the supervise, no leisure bated,
No, not to stay the grinding of the axe,
My head should be struck off.

HORATIO.   Is't possible?

HAMLET. Here's the commission: read it at more leisure.
But wilt thou hear me how I did proceed?

HORATIO. I beseech you.

HAMLET. Being thus be-netted round with villanies,—
Ere I could make a prologue to my brains

They had begun the play,—I sat me down,
Devis'd a new commission, wrote it fair;
I once did hold it, as our statists do,
A baseness to write fair, and labour'd much
How to forget that learning; but, sir, now
I did me yeoman's service. Wilt thou know
The effect of what I wrote?

HORATIO.   Ay, good my lord.

HAMLET. An earnest conjuration from the king,
As England was his faithful tributary,
As love between them like the palm should flourish,
As peace should still her wheaten garland wear,
And stand a comma 'tween their amities,
And many such-like 'As'es of great charge,
That, on the view and knowing of these contents,
Without debatement further, more or less,
He should the bearers put to sudden death,
Not shriving-time allow'd.

HORATIO.   How was this seal'd?

HAMLET. Why, even in that was heaven ordinant.
I had my father's signet in my purse,
Which was the model of that Danish seal;
Folded the writ up in form of the other,
Subscrib'd it, gave 't th' impression, plac'd it safely,
The changeling never known. Now, the next day
Was our sea-fight, and what to this was sequent
Thou know'st already.

HORATIO. So Guildenstern and Rosencrantz go to 't.

HAMLET. Why, man, they did make love to this employment;
They are not near my conscience; their defeat
Does by their own insinuation grow.
'Tis dangerous when the baser nature comes
Between the pass and fell-incenséd points
Of mighty opposites.

HORATIO.   Why, what a king is this!

HAMLET. Does it not, thinks't thee, stand me now upon—
He that hath kill'd my king and whor'd my mother,
Popp'd in between the election and my hopes,
Thrown out his angle for my proper life,
And with such cozenage—is 't not perfect conscience
To quit him with this arm? and is 't not to be damn'd
To let this canker of our nature come
In further evil?

HORATIO. It must be shortly known to him from England
What is the issue of the business there.

HAMLET. It will be short: the interim is mine;
And a man's life's no more than to say 'One.'
But I am very sorry, good Horatio,
That to Laertes I forgot myself;
For, by the image of my cause, I see
The portraiture of his: I'll court his favours:
But, sure, the bravery of his grief did put me
Into a towering passion.

HORATIO.   Peace! who comes here?

Enter OSRIC.

OSRIC. Your lordship is right welcome back to Denmark.

HAMLET. I humbly thank you, sir. [*Aside to* HORATIO.]
Dost know this water-fly?

HORATIO. [Aside to HAMLET.] No, my good lord.

HAMLET. [*Aside to* HORATIO.] Thy state is the more gracious; for 'tis a vice to know him. He hath much land, and fertile: let a beast be lord of beasts, and his crib shall stand at the king's mess: 'tis a chough; but, as I say, spacious in the possession of dirt.

OSRIC. Sweet lord, if your lordship were at leisure, I should impart a thing to you from his majesty.

HAMLET. I will receive it, sir, with all diligence of spirit. Put your bonnet to his right use; 'tis for the head.

OSRIC. I thank your lordship, 'tis very hot.

HAMLET. No, believe me, 'tis very cold; the wind is northerly.

OSRIC. It is indifferent cold, my lord, indeed.

HAMLET. But yet methinks it is very sultry and hot for my complexion.

OSRIC. Exceedingly, my lord; it is very sultry, as 'twere, I cannot tell how. But, my lord, his majesty bade me signify to you that he has laid a great wager on your head. Sir, this is the matter,—

HAMLET. I beseech you, remember—

[HAMLET *moves him to put on his hat.*

OSRIC. Nay, good my lord; for mine ease, in good faith. Sir, here is newly come to court Laertes; believe me, an absolute gentleman, full of most excellent differences, of very soft society and great showing; indeed, to speak feelingly of him, he is the card or calendar of gentry, for you shall find in him the continent of what part a gentleman would see.

HAMLET. Sir, his definement suffers no perdition in you; though, I know, to divide him inventorially would dizzy the arithmetic of memory, and yet but yaw neither, in respect of his quick sail. But, in the verity of extolment, I take him to be a soul of great article; and his infusion of such dearth and rareness, as, to make true diction of him, his semblable is his mirror; and who else would trace him, his umbrage, nothing more.

OSRIC. Your lordship speaks most infallibly of him.

HAMLET. The concernancy, sir? why do we wrap the gentleman in our more rawer breath?

OSRIC. Sir?

HORATIO. Is 't not possible to understand in another tongue? You will do 't, sir, really.

HAMLET. What imports the nomination of this gentleman?

OSRIC. Of Laertes?

HORATIO. His purse is empty already; all's golden words are spent.

HAMLET. Of him, sir.

OSRIC. I know you are not ignorant—

HAMLET. I would you did, sir; in faith, if you did, it would not much approve me. Well, sir.

OSRIC. You are not ignorant of what excellence Laertes is—

HAMLET. I dare not confess that, lest I should compare with him in excellence; but, to know a man well, were to know himself.

OSRIC. I mean, sir, for his weapon; but in the imputation laid on him by them in his meed, he's unfellowed.

HAMLET. What's his weapon?

OSRIC. Rapier and dagger.

HAMLET. That's two of his weapons; but, well.

OSRIC. The king, sir, hath wagered with him six Barbary horses; against the which he has imponed, as I take it, six French rapiers and poniards, with their assigns, as girdle, hangers, and so: three of the carriages, in faith, are very dear to fancy, very responsive to the hilts, most delicate carriages, and of very liberal conceit.

HAMLET. What call you the carriages?

HORATIO. I knew you must be edified by the margent, ere you had done.

OSRIC. The carriages, sir, are the hangers.

HAMLET. The phrase would be more germane to the matter, if we could carry cannon by our sides; I would it might be hangers till then. But, on; six Barbary horses against six French swords, their assigns, and three liberal-conceited carriages; that's the French bet against the Danish. Why is this 'imponed,' as you call it?

OSRIC. The king, sir, hath laid, sir, that in a dozen passes between yourself and him, he shall not exceed you three hits; he hath laid on twelve for nine, and it would come to immediate trial, if your lordship would vouchsafe the answer.

HAMLET. How if I answer no?

OSRIC. I mean, my lord, the opposition of your person in trial.

HAMLET. Sir, I will walk here in the hall; if it please his majesty, 'tis the breathing time of day with me; let the foils be brought, the gentleman willing, and the king hold his purpose,

I will win for him an I can; if not, I will gain nothing but my shame and the odd hits.

OSRIC. Shall I re-deliver you e'en so?

HAMLET. To this effect, sir; after what flourish your nature will.

OSRIC. I commend my duty to your lordship.

HAMLET. Yours, yours. [*Exit* OSRIC.] He does well to commend it himself; there are no tongues else for 's turn.

HORATIO. This lapwing runs away with the shell on his head.

HAMLET. He did comply with his dug before he sucked it. Thus has he—and many more of the same bevy, that I know the drossy age dotes on—only got the tune of the time and outward habit of encounter, a kind of yesty collection which carries them through and through the most fond and winnowed opinions; and do but blow them to their trial, the bubbles are out.

Enter a LORD.

LORD. My lord, his majesty commended him to you by young Osric, who brings back to him, that you attend him in the hall; he sends to know if your pleasure hold to play with Laertes, or that you will take longer time.

HAMLET. I am constant to my purposes; they follow the king's pleasure: if his fitness speaks, mine is ready; now, or whensoever, provided I be so able as now.

LORD. The king, and queen, and all are coming down.

HAMLET. In happy time.

LORD. The queen desires you to use some gentle entertainment to Laertes before you fall to play.

HAMLET. She well instructs me.   [*Exit* LORD.

HORATIO. You will lose this wager, my lord.

HAMLET. I do not think so; since he went into France, I have been in continual practice; I shall win at the odds. But thou wouldst not think how ill all's here about my heart; but it is no matter.

HORATIO. Nay, good my lord,—

HAMLET. It is but foolery; but it is such a kind of gaingiving as would perhaps trouble a woman.

HORATIO. If your mind dislike any thing, obey it; I will forestal their repair hither, and say you are not fit.

HAMLET. Not a whit, we defy augury; there's a special providence in the fall of a sparrow. If it be now, 'tis not to come; if it be not to come, it will be now; if it be not now, yet it will come: the readiness is all. Since no man has aught of what he leaves, what is 't to leave betimes? Let be.

Enter KING, QUEEN, LAERTES, LORDS, OSRIC, *and* ATTENDANTS
with foils, &c.

KING. Come, Hamlet, come, and take this hand from me.
                              [*The* KING *puts the hand of* LAERTES *into
                                                   that of* HAMLET.

HAMLET. Give me your pardon, sir; I've done you wrong;
But pardon 't, as you are a gentleman.
This presence knows, and you must needs have heard,
How I am punish'd with a sore distraction.
What I have done
That might your nature, honour and exception
Roughly awake, I hear proclaim was madness.
Was't Hamlet wrong'd Laertes? Never Hamlet:
If Hamlet from himself be ta'en away,
And when he's not himself does wrong Laertes,
Then Hamlet does it not; Hamlet denies it.
Who does it then? His madness. If't be so,
Hamlet is of the faction that is wrong'd;
His madness is poor Hamlet's enemy.
Sir, in this audience,
Let my disclaiming from a purpos'd evil
Free me so far in your most generous thoughts,
That I have shot mine arrow o'er the house,
And hurt my brother.
       LAERTES.   I am satisfied in nature,
Whose motive, in this case, should stir me most

To my revenge; but in my terms of honour
I stand aloof, and will no reconcilement,
Till by some elder masters, of known honour,
I have a voice and precedent of peace,
To keep my name ungor'd. But till that time,
I do receive your offer'd love like love,
And will not wrong it.

HAMLET.   I embrace it freely;
And will this brother's wager frankly play.
Give us the foils. Come on.

LAERTES.   Come, one for me.

HAMLET. I'll be your foil, Laertes; in mine ignorance
Your skill shall, like a star i' the darkest night,
Stick fiery off indeed.

LAERTES.   You mock me, sir.

HAMLET. No, by this hand.

KING. Give them the foils, young Osric. Cousin Hamlet,
You know the wager?

HAMLET.   Very well, my lord;
Your Grace hath laid the odds o' the weaker side.

KING. I do not fear it; I have seen you both;
But since he is better'd, we have therefore odds.

LAERTES. This is too heavy; let me see another.

HAMLET. This likes me well. These foils have all a length?

OSRIC. Ay, my good lord.   [*They prepare to play.*

KING. Set me the stoups of wine upon that table.
If Hamlet give the first or second hit,
Or quit in answer of the third exchange,
Let all the battlements their ordnance fire;
The king shall drink to Hamlet's better breath;
And in the cup an union shall he throw,
Richer than that which four successive kings
In Denmark's crown have worn. Give me the cups;
And let the kettle to the trumpet speak,
The trumpet to the cannoneer without,
The cannons to the heavens, the heavens to earth,

'Now the king drinks to Hamlet!' Come, begin;
And you, the judges, bear a wary eye.

HAMLET. Come on, sir.

LAERTES. Come, my lord.   *[They play.*

HAMLET.   One.

LAERTES.   No.

HAMLET.   Judgment.

OSRIC. A hit, a very palpable hit.

LAERTES. Well; again.

KING. Stay; give me drink. Hamlet, this pearl is thine;
Here's to thy health. Give him the cup.

        [Trumpets sound; and cannon shot off within.

HAMLET. I'll play this bout first; set it by awhile.
Come.—*[They play.]* Another hit; what say you?

LAERTES. A touch, a touch, I do confess.

KING. Our son shall win.

QUEEN. He's fat, and scant of breath.
Here, Hamlet, take my napkin, rub thy brows;
The queen carouses to thy fortune, Hamlet

HAMLET. Good madam!

KING. Gertrude, do not drink.

QUEEN. I will, my lord; I pray you, pardon me.

KING. *[Aside.]* It is the poison'd cup! it is too late.

HAMLET. I dare not drink yet, madam; by and by.

QUEEN. Come, let me wipe thy face.

LAERTES. My lord, I'll hit him now.

KING. I do not think 't.

LAERTES. *[Aside.]* And yet 'tis almost 'gainst my conscience.

HAMLET. Come, for the third, Laertes. You but dally;
I pray you, pass with your best violence.
I am afeard you make a wanton of me.

LAERTES. Say you so? come on.   *[They play.*

OSRIC. Nothing, neither way.

LAERTES. Have at you now.

      *[LAERTES wounds HAMLET; then, in scuffling, they
          change rapiers, and HAMLET wounds LAERTES.*

KING.   Part them! they are incens'd.

HAMLET. Nay, come, again.   [*The* QUEEN *falls.*

OSRIC.   Look to the queen there, ho!

HORATIO. They bleed on both sides. How is it, my lord?

OSRIC. How is it, Laertes?

LAERTES. Why, as a woodcock to mine own springe, Osric;
I am justly kill'd with mine own treachery.

HAMLET. How does the queen?

KING.   She swounds to see them bleed.

QUEEN. No, no, the drink, the drink,—O my dear Hamlet!
The drink, the drink; I am poison'd.   [*Dies.*

HAMLET. O villany! Ho! let the door be lock'd:
Treachery! seek it out.   [LAERTES *falls.*

LAERTES. It is here, Hamlet. Hamlet, thou art slain;
No medicine in the world can do thee good;
In thee there is not half an hour of life;
The treacherous instrument is in thy hand,
Unbated and envenom'd. The foul practice
Hath turn'd itself on me; lo! here I lie,
Never to rise again. Thy mother's poison'd.
I can no more. The king, the king's to blame.

HAMLET. The point envenom'd too!—
Then, venom, to thy work.   [*Stabs the* KING.

ALL. Treason! treason!

KING. O! yet defend me, friends; I am but hurt.

HAMLET. Here, thou incestuous, murderous, damnéd Dane,
Drink off this potion;—is thy union here?
Follow my mother.   [KING *dies.*

LAERTES.   He is justly serv'd;
It is a poison temper'd by himself.
Exchange forgiveness with me, noble Hamlet:
Mine and my father's death come not upon thee,
Nor thine on me!   [*Dies.*

HAMLET. Heaven make thee free of it! I follow thee.
I am dead, Horatio. Wretched queen, adieu!
You that look pale and tremble at this chance,

That are but mutes or audience to this act,
Had I but time,—as this fell sergeant, death,
Is strict in his arrest,—O! I could tell you—
But let it be. Horatio, I am dead;
Thou liv'st; report me and my cause aright
To the unsatisfied.

HORATIO.   Never believe it;
I am more an antique Roman than a Dane;
Here's yet some liquor left.

HAMLET.   As thou'rt a man,
Give me the cup: let go; by heaven, I'll have 't.
O God! Horatio, what a wounded name,
Things standing thus unknown, shall live behind me.
If thou didst ever hold me in thy heart,
Absent thee from felicity awhile,
And in this harsh world draw thy breath in pain,
To tell my story.   [*March afar off, and shot within.*
          What war-like noise is this?

OSRIC. Young Fortinbras, with conquest come from Poland,
To the ambassadors of England gives
This war-like volley.

HAMLET.   O! I die, Horatio;
The potent poison quite o'er-crows my spirit:
I cannot live to hear the news from England,
But I do prophesy the election lights
On Fortinbras: he has my dying voice;
So tell him, with the occurrents, more and less,
Which have solicited—The rest is silence.   [*Dies.*

HORATIO. Now cracks a noble heart. Good-night, sweet prince,
And flights of angels sing thee to thy rest!
Why does the drum come hither?   [*March within.*

Enter FORTINBRAS, *the English* AMBASSADORS, *and Others.*

FORTINBRAS. Where is this sight?

HORATIO.   What is it ye would see?
If aught of woe or wonder, cease your search.

FORTINBRAS. This quarry cries on havoc. O proud death!
What feast is toward in thine eternal cell,
That thou so many princes at a shot
So bloodily hast struck?

FIRST AMBASSADOR.   The sight is dismal;
And our affairs from England come too late:
The ears are senseless that should give us hearing,
To tell him his commandment is fulfill'd,
That Rosencrantz and Guildenstern are dead.
Where should we have our thanks?

HORATIO.   Not from his mouth,
Had it the ability of life to thank you:
He never gave commandment for their death.
But since, so jump upon this bloody question,
You from the Polack wars, and you from England,
Are here arriv'd, give order that these bodies
High on a stage be placéd to the view;
And let me speak to the yet unknowing world
How these things came about: so shall you hear
Of carnal, bloody, and unnatural acts,
Of accidental judgments, casual slaughters;
Of deaths put on by cunning and forc'd cause,
And, in this upshot, purposes mistook
Fall'n on the inventors' heads; all this can I
Truly deliver.

FORTINBRAS. Let us haste to hear it,
And call the noblest to the audience.
For me, with sorrow I embrace my fortune;
I have some rights of memory in this kingdom,
Which now to claim my vantage doth invite me.

HORATIO. Of that I shall have also cause to speak,
And from his mouth whose voice will draw on more:
But let this same be presently perform'd,
Even while men's minds are wild, lest more mischance
On plots and errors happen.

FORTINBRAS.   Let four captains

Bear Hamlet, like a soldier, to the stage;
For he was likely, had he been put on,
To have prov'd most royally: and, for his passage,
The soldiers' music and the rites of war
Speak loudly for him.
Take up the bodies: such a sight as this
Becomes the field, but here shows much amiss.
Go, bid the soldiers shoot.

[A dead march. Exeunt, bearing off the bodies;
after which a peal of ordnance is shot off.

Macbeth

INTRODUCTION

Written. 1605–1606 (?)

Published, in the first folio, 1623.

Source of the Plot. Raphael Holinshed tells the story of Macbeth at length in his *Chronicle of Scottish History.* He indicates the character of Lady Macbeth in one line. The real, historical Macbeth was utterly unlike the nervy murderer of the play, but a King of Northern Scotland in his own right, who killed Duncan (King of Southern Scotland) in war, and thereafter ruled the whole of Scotland, with power and wisdom, for seventeen prosperous years. He was killed in battle in Aberdeenshire in 1057, while fighting with Duncan's son.

But Holinshed's *Chronicle,* before reaching the time of Macbeth, tells the story of King Duffe (or Duff) who was murdered in 971 by his castellan Donwald.

Donwald and his wife, being angered by King Duffe, plotted to murder him; the wife, as in so many sagas, being the prime mover. They made the King's guards drunk (the King being then their guest) and sent henchmen to kill the King and carry away his body. This they did. Donwald then killed the King's drunken guards.

In his account of Macbeth, Holinshed makes Banquo a supporter of Macbeth against Duncan. He tells the story of the three witches,

> "either the weird sisters, that is (as ye would say) the goddesses of destiny, or else some nymphs or fairies, indued with knowledge of prophecy,"

and of their prophesying of the future to Macbeth and Banquo.

231

He tells how this prophecy inflamed Lady Macbeth, and how acts of Duncan's, that seemed to make the fulfilment of the prophecy impossible, provoked him into rebellion, so that "he slew the King at Inverness." This was in open war, not by murder nor by guile, but Holinshed does not make this clear.

Shakespeare took these two stories, added to them certain details in Holinshed, and a variety of matter from other sources, and from the mixture of all these, with his genius at its height, created a libel upon the real Macbeth but a masterpiece of poetical glory.

It must be remembered that when *Macbeth* was written many Scotchmen were in London, for King James had become King. It would have been easy for Shakespeare to gather (as he no doubt did) hints from these for other points of use in the play.

The Fable. Macbeth, advised by witches that he is to be a king, is persuaded by his wife to kill his sovereign (King Duncan) and seize the crown. King Duncan, coming to Macbeth's castle for a night, is there killed by Macbeth and his lady. Duncan's sons fly to England. Macbeth causes himself to be proclaimed king.

Being king, he tries to assure himself of power by destroying the house of Banquo, of whom the witches prophesied that he should be the father of a line of kings. Banquo is killed; but his son escapes.

The witches warn Macbeth to beware of Macduff.

Macduff escapes to England, but his wife and children are killed by Macbeth's order.

Macduff persuades Duncan's son, Malcolm, to attempt the recovery of the Scottish crown.

Malcolm and Macduff make the attempt. They attack Macbeth and kill him.

Macbeth must be either the fourth or the fifth of the seven supreme Shakespeare plays. Other men may prefer others of the seven for this or that great quality, but poets, and perhaps most workers in the lovely arts, will usually think *Macbeth* the most glorious, the most poetical.

The theme of the play is delusion, of a kind becoming common in England when the play was written, and a little later very fatal. This is the delusion that will interpret, after worldly inclination, what may have been meant spiritually. Misinterpretation, or prejudiced interpretation of texts, led Puritan England into untold misery. Europe has suffered much and is like to suffer more from ecstatics with hidden craft who can make a half-truth blind a nation.

> . . . to win us to our harm,
> The instruments of darkness tell us truths,
> Win us with honest trifles, to betray 's
> In deepest consequence.

Coming weary and excited from battle, on a day so strange that it adds to the strangeness of his mood, Macbeth hears the hags hail him with prophecy. Life is a strange thing, even at its clearest, and perhaps all of us, at some time, have felt an inner prompting, have known some dream, have had a warning, that has altered life for us, as something sent to us from Powers outside Life. This prompting, so scattered, or however brought, comes to good or evil according to the sun in us. To Macbeth, at first, it is little more than strange, till a first partial fulfilment of the prophecy makes him feel that the veil over the future has been lifted for him; and that Fate means him to be King.

In Shakespeare's conception, Macbeth is a most sensitive, highly-strung, imaginative and gifted man, brave beyond most men in battle, lovely in language beyond all men, but now beset by the thought that Fate means to crown him.

He has not yet begun to think how he may help Fate. Fear that the prompting is all a contriving of the Devil's makes him put it manfully from his mind. Then there comes that talk of Cawdor whose place he holds. That thane of Cawdor was a traitor who has been put to death for treachery. The king had had an "absolute trust" in him; but there is no judging by appearances. This glimpse of the ugliness of treachery makes Macbeth for an instant free of all temptation to it. Then a word stabs him again to the knowledge that if he take no step, the king's young son Malcolm will succeed Duncan. Why should the boy rule? From this point he goes forward, full of all the devils of indecision, but inclining towards righteousness, till his wife, girding and railing at him with definite aim while all his powers are in mutiny, drives him to the act of murder.

The story of the double treachery of the killing of a king, who is also a guest, is so written that we do not feel horror so much as an extraordinary interest in what we can only call the beauty of Macbeth's mind: the beauty is all beset: it is urged, it is tempted, it rallies and tries to escape, and what should be only beauty and wisdom helping it, in Lady Macbeth beside him, quells each rally and bars escape. We see the issue that Macbeth cannot see. We feel the eternal consequence that he for the moment cannot feel overwhelmingly. We feel, as Shakespeare felt, the unimaginable beauty of the victory of goodness here: we can have nothing but pity for the fall.

The horror of the reader or watcher comes later, when it is made plain that the treachery does not end with that old man on the bed, but proceeds in a spreading growth of murder till the man who fought so knightly at Fife is the haunted awful figure who goes ghastly, killing men, women and little children, till Scotland is like a grave. At the end, the "worthy gentleman," "noble Macbeth," having fallen from depth to depth of degradation, is old, sick at heart, friendless, cursed, his wife mad, his subjects rebelling, his enemies in arms, all the birds of murder coming to roost, and his faith in Fortune gone. He sees, too late, that he has been tricked by

> the equivocation of the fiend
> That lies like truth . . .

He dies with courage and fury, fighting not the mortal Macduff, but Fate who has tricked him.

Though all Shakespeare's plays bring surprises, his lovers and admirers must have been startled, as we are, by the beauty and splendour of the verse and of the unknown kingdom that it re-

veals. I have little doubt that nearly all the first two Acts were
written in one marvellous day. That day brought out white-hot
some matchless scenes and incomparable lines.

> And pity, like a naked new-born babe,
> Striding the blast, or heaven's cherubin, hors'd
> Upon the sightless couriers of the air . . .

> Our chimneys were blown down; and, as they say,
> Lamentings heard i' the air; strange screams of death,
> And prophesying with accents terrible . . .

Later in the play, many of the lines of Macbeth are beyond
all praise:

> Duncan is in his grave;
> After life's fitful fever he sleeps well . . .

> Come, sealing night
> Scarf up the tender eye of pitiful day . . .

> Light thickens; and the crow
> Makes wing to the rooky wood . . .

> the time has been,
> That, when the brains were out, the man would die . . .

The inventions of the play are those of a supreme poet: they
have impressed the world. Taking a few prose lines from a
history-book, he created the witches and the devilry in which
they dwell. Taking thought of the talent of the lad who was to
play Lady Macbeth he invented the sleep-walking scene. The
creation of all the murder-scene, and the knocking upon the
door, when the murder has been done, must have shaken many
millions of men and women.

Another great invention, in Act IV, Scene 1, has somehow
been less praised, and has certainly been less emphasised in performance. Macbeth has just questioned the hags for the last time.
He calls Lennox, with the words—

> I did hear
> The galloping of horse: who was't came by?

It was the galloping of messengers with the news that Macduff, who is to be the cause of his ruin, has fled to England. An echo of the galloping stays in the brain, as though the hoofs of some horse rode the night, carrying away Macbeth's luck for ever.

The play divides itself into three parts, the gathering and rushing tide that carries Macbeth to a frightful act; a confusion and welter, perhaps comparable with what is called "slack water" in a tide-way; and then a gathering and overwhelming ebbing that carries the sinner to sea. All must feel the power and wonder of the flood and the ebb; with care in any producer all will feel also the calculated power and wonder of the middle period, in which the justice that has to be done prepares. Shakespeare was fond of such scenes: his method, indeed, made them necessary, and he had in his company men of remarkable talent who made these central scenes triumphant.

The play is frequently performed. There has been a demand of late that the Ghost of Banquo should not be seen by the audience: and that, at the end, the tryrant's bleeding head should not be carried in upon the pike. These things are parts of our greatest poet's greatest mood; by them he threatens, and then shows the doing of justice, poetical justice, upon a shedder of blood. If the modern producer cannot make these terrible signs impressive, let him take to something simpler than this play, that is about the desecration of the holiness of human life.

Sometimes, the play has been performed in Scots costume, with effective use of bagpipes. Any unusual care in the playing of such a poem deserves our praise: few works deserve more care, in the speaking, in the stage-arrangements, in the noises that accompany the action, in the songs, dances and visions of the witches, and in the swift changes at the end, from without Dunsinane to within.

It is the most glorious of our poems: It was poured out in Shakespeare's most marvellous mood; and then, by fatal scissors snipped in The Globe to the shortest play in the canon. Perhaps 700 lines of Shakespeare's masterpiece were there snipped, and later burned.

"Look like the time; bear welcome in your eye,
Your hand, your tongue; look like th' innocent flower,
But be the serpent under't." *Act 1, Scene V*

Two of the greatest living Shakespearian actors—
Maurice Evans as Macbeth and Judith Anderson as Lady Macbeth

DRAMATIS PERSONÆ

DUNCAN, King of Scotland

MALCOLM,
DONALBAIN, } his Sons

MACBETH,
BANQUO, } Generals of the King's Army

MACDUFF,
LENNOX,
ROSS,
MENTEITH, } Noblemen of Scotland
ANGUS,
CAITHNESS,

FLEANCE, Son to Banquo

SIWARD, Earl of Northumberland, General of the English Forces

YOUNG SIWARD, his Son

SEYTON, and Officer attending Macbeth

BOY, Son to Macduff

AN ENGLISH DOCTOR

A SCOTCH DOCTOR

A SERGEANT

A PORTER

AN OLD MAN

LADY MACBETH

LADY MACDUFF

GENTLEWOMAN attending on Lady Macbeth

HECATE and THREE WITCHES

LORDS, GENTLEMEN, OFFICERS, SOLDIERS, MURDERERS, ATTENDANTS, and MESSENGERS. The GHOST of BANQUO, and other APPARITIONS

SCENE. *Scotland; England*

237

Act 1

Scene I. A Desert Heath

Thunder and lightning. Enter three WITCHES.

FIRST WITCH. When shall we three meet again
In thunder, lightning, or in rain?
SECOND WITCH. When the hurlyburly's done,
When the battle's lost and won.
THIRD WITCH. That will be ere the set of sun.
FIRST WITCH. Where the place?
SECOND WITCH.   Upon the heath.
THIRD WITCH. There to meet with Macbeth.
FIRST WITCH. I come, Graymalkin!
SECOND WITCH. Paddock calls.
THIRD WITCH. Anon.
ALL. Fair is foul, and foul is fair:
Hover through the fog and filthy air.   [*Exeunt.*

Scene II. A Camp near Forres

Alarum within. Enter KING DUNCAN, MALCOLM, DONALBAIN,
LENNOX, *with* ATTENDANTS, *meeting a bleeding* SERGEANT.

DUNCAN. What bloody man is that? He can report,
As seemeth by his plight, of the revolt
The newest state.
MALCOLM.   This is the sergeant
Who, like a good and hardy soldier, fought

238

'Gainst my captivity. Hail, brave friend!
Say to the king the knowledge of the broil
As thou didst leave it.

SERGEANT.   Doubtful it stood;
As two spent swimmers, that do cling together
And choke their art. The merciless Macdonwald—
Worthy to be a rebel, for to that
The multiplying villanies of nature
Do swarm upon him—from the western isles
Of kerns and gallowglasses is supplied;
And fortune, on his damned quarrel smiling,
Show'd like a rebel's whore: but all's too weak;
For brave Macbeth,—well he deserves that name,—
Disdaining fortune, with his brandish'd steel,
Which smok'd with bloody execution,
Like valour's minion carv'd out his passage
Till he fac'd the slave;
Which ne'er shook hands, nor bade farewell to him,
Till he unseam'd him from the nave to the chaps,
And fix'd his head upon our battlements.

DUNCAN. O valiant cousin! worthy gentleman!

SERGEANT. As whence the sun 'gins his reflection
Shipwracking storms and direful thunders break,
So from that spring whence comfort seem'd to come
Discomfort swells. Mark, King of Scotland, mark:
No sooner justice had with valour arm'd
Compell'd these skipping kerns to trust their heels,
But the Norweyan lord, surveying vantage,
With furbish'd arms and new supplies of men
Began a fresh assault.

DUNCAN.   Dismay'd not this
Our captains, Macbeth and Banquo?

SERGEANT.   Yes;
As sparrows eagles, or the hare the lion.
If I say sooth, I must report they were
As cannons overcharg'd with double cracks;

So they
Doubly redoubled strokes upon the foe:
Except they meant to bathe in reeking wounds,
Or memorize another Golgotha,
I cannot tell—
But I am faint, my gashes cry for help.

    DUNCAN. So well thy words become thee as thy wounds;
They smack of honour both. Go, get him surgeons.

                          [Exit SERGEANT, *attended.*

    Enter ROSS.

Who comes here?

    MALCOLM.   The worthy Thane of Ross.

    LENNOX. What a haste looks through his eyes! So should he
    look
That seems to speak things strange.

    ROSS.   God save the king!

    DUNCAN. Whence cam'st thou, worthy thane?

    ROSS.   From Fife, great king;
Where the Norweyan banners flout the sky
And fan our people cold. Norway himself,
With terrible numbers,
Assisted by that most disloyal traitor,
The Thane of Cawdor, began a dismal conflict;
Till that Bellona's bridegroom, lapp'd in proof,
Confronted him with self-comparisons,
Point against point, rebellious arm 'gainst arm,
Curbing his lavish spirit: and, to conclude,
The victory fell on us.—

    DUNCAN.   Great happiness!

    ROSS. That now
Sweno, the Norways' king, craves composition;
Nor would we deign him burial of his men
Till he disbursed, at Saint Colme's Inch,
Ten thousand dollars to our general use.

    DUNCAN. No more that Thane of Cawdor shall deceive

Our bosom interest. Go pronounce his present death,
And with his former title greet Macbeth.
  ROSS. I'll see it done.
  DUNCAN. What he hath lost noble Macbeth hath won.

                                      [*Exeunt.*

Scene III.   A Heath

Thunder. Enter the three WITCHES.

  FIRST WITCH. Where hast thou been, sister?
  SECOND WITCH. Killing swine.
  THIRD WITCH. Sister, where thou?
  FIRST WITCH. A sailor's wife had chestnuts in her lap,
And munch'd, and munch'd, and munch'd: 'Give me,' quoth I:
'Aroint thee, witch!' the rump-fed ronyon cries.
Her husband's to Aleppo gone, master o' the Tiger:
But in a sieve I'll thither sail,
And, like a rat without a tail,
I'll do, I'll do, and I'll do.
  SECOND WITCH. I'll give thee a wind.
  FIRST WITCH. Thou'rt kind.
  THIRD WITCH. And I another.
  FIRST WITCH. I myself have all the other;
And the very ports they blow,
All the quarters that they know
I' the shipman's card.
I'll drain him dry as hay:
Sleep shall neither night nor day
Hang upon his pent-house lid;
He shall live a man forbid.
Weary se'nnights nine times nine
Shall he dwindle, peak and pine:
Though his bark cannot be lost,
Yet it shall be tempest-tost.
Look what I have.

SECOND WITCH. Show me, show me.

FIRST WITCH. Here I have a pilot's thumb,
Wrack'd as homeward he did come.   [*Drum within.*

THIRD WITCH. A drum! a drum!
Macbeth doth come.

All. The weird sisters, hand in hand,
Posters of the sea and land,
Thus do go about, about:
Thrice to thine, and thrice to mine,
And thrice again, to make up nine.
Peace! the charm's wound up.

Enter MACBETH *and* BANQUO.

MACBETH. So foul and fair a day I have not seen.

BANQUO. How far is 't call'd to Forres? What are these,
So wither'd and so wild in their attire,
That look not like th' inhabitants o' the earth,
And yet are on 't? Live you? or are you aught
That man may question? You seem to understand me,
By each at once her choppy finger laying
Upon her skinny lips: you should be women,
And yet your beards forbid me to interpret
That you are so.

MACBETH.   Speak, if you can: what are you?

FIRST WITCH. All hail, Macbeth; hail to thee, Thane of
Glamis!

SECOND WITCH. All hail, Macbeth! hail to thee, Thane of
Cawdor!

THIRD WITCH. All hail, Macbeth! that shalt be king hereafter.

BANQUO. Good sir, why do you start, and seem to fear
Things that do sound so fair? I' the name of truth,
Are ye fantastical, or that indeed
Which outwardly ye show? My noble partner
You greet with present grace and great prediction
Of noble having and of royal hope,
That he seems rapt withal: to me you speak not.

If you can look into the seeds of time,
And say which grain will grow and which will not,
Speak then to me, who neither beg nor fear
Your favors nor your hate.

FIRST WITCH. Hail!

SECOND WITCH. Hail!

THIRD WITCH. Hail!

FIRST WITCH. Lesser than Macbeth, and greater.

SECOND WITCH. Not so happy, yet much happier.

THIRD WITCH. Thou shalt get kings, though thou be none:
So, all hail, Macbeth and Banquo!

FIRST WITCH. Banquo and Macbeth, all hail!

MACBETH. Stay, you imperfect speakers, tell me more:
By Sinel's death I know I am Thane of Glamis;
But how of Cawdor? the Thane of Cawdor lives,
A prosperous gentleman; and to be king
Stands not within the prospect of belief,
No more than to be Cawdor. Say from whence
You owe this strange intelligence? or why
Upon this blasted heath you stop our way
With such prophetic greeting? Speak, I charge you.

[WITCHES *vanish.*

BANQUO. The earth hath bubbles, as the water has,
And these are of them. Whither are they vanish'd?

MACBETH. Into the air, and what seem'd corporal melted
As breath into the wind. Would they had stay'd!

BANQUO. Were such things here as we do speak about?
Or have we eaten on the insane root
That takes the reason prisoner?

MACBETH. Your children shall be kings.

BANQUO.   You shall be king.

MACBETH. And Thane of Cawdor too; went it not so?

BANQUO. To the self-same tune and words. Who's here?

Enter ROSS *and* ANGUS.

ROSS. The king hath happily receiv'd, Macbeth,

The news of thy success; and when he reads
Thy personal venture in the rebels' fight,
His wonders and his praises do contend
Which should be thine or his. Silenc'd with that,
In viewing o'er the rest o' the self-same day,
He finds thee in the stout Norweyan ranks,
Nothing afeard of what thyself didst make,
Strange images of death. As thick as hail
Came post with post, and every one did bear
Thy praises in his kingdom's great defence,
And pour'd them down before him.

ANGUS.   We are sent
To give thee from our royal master thanks;
Only to herald thee into his sight,
Not pay thee.

ROSS. And, for an earnest of a greater honour,
He bade me, from him, call thee Thane of Cawdor:
In which addition, hail, most worthy thane!
For it is thine.

BANQUO.   What! can the devil speak true?

MACBETH. The Thane of Cawdor lives: why do you dress me
In borrow'd robes?

ANGUS.   Who was the thane lives yet;
But under heavy judgment bears that life
Which he deserves to lose. Whether he was combin'd
With those of Norway, or did line the rebel
With hidden help or vantage, or that with both
He labour'd in his country's wrack, I know not;
But treasons capital, confess'd and prov'd,
Have overthrown him.

MACBETH. [Aside.] Glamis, and Thane of Cawdor:
The greatest is behind. [To ROSS and ANGUS.] Thanks for your
      pains.
[To BANQUO.] Do you not hope your children shall be kings,
When those that give the Thane of Cawdor to me

Macbeth (Maurice Evans) and
Lady Macbeth (Judith Anderson)

"We fail?
But screw your courage to the sticking-place,
And we'll not fail."   *Act 1, Scene VII*

Promis'd no less to them?

BANQUO. That, trusted home,
Might yet enkindle you unto the crown,
Besides the Thane of Cawdor. But 'tis strange:
And oftentimes, to win us to our harm,
The instruments of darkness tell us truths,
Win us with honest trifles, to betray's
In deepest consequence.
Cousins, a word, I pray you.

MACBETH. [*Aside.*] Two truths are told,
As happy prologues to the swelling act
Of the imperial theme. I thank you, gentlemen.
[*Aside.*] This supernatural soliciting
Cannot be ill, cannot be good; if ill,
Why hath it given me earnest of success,
Commencing in a truth? I am Thane of Cawdor:
If good, why do I yield to that suggestion
Whose horrid image doth unfix my hair
And make my seated heart knock at my ribs,
Against the use of nature? Present fears
Are less than horrible imaginings;
My thought, whose murder yet is but fantastical,
Shakes so my single state of man that function
Is smother'd in surmise, and nothing is
But what is not.

BANQUO. Look, how our partner's rapt.

MACBETH. [*Aside.*] If chance will have me king, why, chance
may crown me,
Without my stir.

BANQUO. New honours come upon him,
Like our strange garments, cleave not to their mould
But with the aid of use.

MACBETH. [*Aside.*] Come what come may,
Time and the hour runs through the roughest day.

BANQUO. Worthy Macbeth, we stay upon your leisure.

MACBETH. Give me your favour: my dull brain was wrought
With things forgotten. Kind gentlemen, your pains
Are register'd where every day I turn
The leaf to read them. Let us toward the king.
Think upon what hath chanc'd; and, at more time,
The interim having weigh'd it, let us speak
Our free hearts each to other.

    BANQUO.   Very gladly.

    MACBETH. Till then, enough. Come, friends.   [*Exeunt.*

Scene IV. *Forres. A Room in the Palace*

Flourish. Enter DUNCAN, MALCOLM, DONALBAIN, LENNOX,
and ATTENDANTS.

DUNCAN. Is execution done on Cawdor? Are not
Those in commission yet return'd?

    MALCOLM.   My liege,
They are not yet come back; but I have spoke
With one that saw him die; who did report
That very frankly he confess'd his treasons,
Implor'd your higheness' pardon and set forth
A deep repentance. Nothing in his life
Became him like the leaving it; he died
As one that had been studied in his death
To throw away the dearest thing he ow'd,
As 'twere a careless trifle.

    DUNCAN.   There's no art
To find the mind's construction in the face:
He was a gentleman on whom I built
An absolute trust.

Enter MACBETH, BANQUO, ROSS, *and* ANGUS.

                  O worthiest cousin!
The sin of my ingratitude even now
Was heavy on me. Thou art so far before

That swiftest wing of recompense is slow
To overtake thee; would thou hadst less deserv'd,
That the proportion both of thanks and payment
Might have been mine! only I have left to say,
More is thy due than more than all can pay.

MACBETH. The service and the loyalty I owe,
In doing it, pays itself. Your highness' part
Is to receive our duties; and our duties
Are to your throne and state, children and servants;
Which do but what they should, by doing everything
Safe toward your love and honour.

DUNCAN. Welcome hither:
I have begun to plant thee, and will labour
To make thee full of growing. Noble Banquo,
That hast no less deserv'd, nor must be known
No less to have done so, let me infold thee
And hold thee to my heart.

BANQUO. There if I grow,
The harvest is your own.

DUNCAN. My plenteous joys
Wanton in fulness, seek to hide themselves
In drops of sorrow. Sons, kinsmen, thanes,
And you whose places are the nearest, know
We will establish our estate upon
Our eldest, Malcolm, whom we name hereafter
The Prince of Cumberland; which honour must
Not unaccompanied invest him only,
But signs of noblesness, like stars, shall shine
On all deservers. From hence to Inverness,
And bind us further to you.

MACBETH. The rest is labour, which is not us'd for you:
I'll be myself the harbinger, and make joyful
The hearing of my wife with your approach;
So, humbly take my leave.

DUNCAN. My worthy Cawdor!

MACBETH. [*Aside.*] The Prince of Cumberland! that is a step

On which I must fall down, or else o'er-leap,
For in my way it lies. Stars, hide your fires!
Let not light see my black and deep desires;
The eye wink at the hand; yet let that be
Which the eye fears, when it is done, to see.   [*Exit.*

DUNCAN. True, worthy Banquo; he is full so valiant,
And in his commendations I am fed;
It is a banquet to me. Let's after him,
Whose care is gone before to bid us welcome:
It is a peerless kinsman.   [*Flourish. Exeunt.*

Scene V. Inverness. Macbeth's Castle

Enter LADY MACBETH, *reading a letter.*

*They met me in the day of success; and I have learned by the
perfect report, they have more in them than mortal knowledge.
When I burned in desire to question them further, they made
themselves air, into which they vanished. Whiles I stood rapt in
the wonder of it, came missives from the king, who all-hailed
me, 'Thane of Cawdor;' by which title, before, these weird
sisters saluted me, and referred me to the coming on of time,
with, 'Hail, king that shalt be!' This have I thought good to deliver thee, my dearest partner of greatness, that thou mightest
not lose the dues of rejoicing, by being ignorant of what great-
ness is promised thee. Lay it to thy heart, and farewell.*
Glamis thou art, and Cawdor; and shalt be
What thou art promis'd. Yet do I fear thy nature;
It is too full o' the milk of human kindness
To catch the nearest way; thou wouldst be great,
Art not without ambition, but without
The illness should attend it; what thou wouldst highly,
That thou wouldst holily; wouldst not play false,
And yet wouldst wrongly win; thou'dst have, great **Glamis,**
That which cries, 'Thus thou must do, if thou have it;'
And that which rather thou dost fear to do

Than wishest should be undone. Hie thee hither,
That I may pour my spirits in thine ear,
And chastise with the valour of my tongue
All that impedes thee from the golden round,
Which fate and metaphysical aid doth seem
To have thee crown'd withal.

Enter a MESSENGER.

                       What is your tidings?
MESSENGER. The king comes here to-night.
LADY MACBETH.   **Thou'rt mad to say it.**
Is not thy master with him? who, were't so,
Would have inform'd for preparation.
MESSENGER. So please you, it is true: our thane is coming;
One of my fellows had the speed of him,
Who, almost dead for breath, had scarcely more
Than would make up his message.
LADY MACBETH.   **Give him tending;**
He brings great news.—[*Exit* MESSENGER.] The raven himself is
    hoarse
That croaks the fatal entrance of Duncan
Under my battlements. Come, you spirits
That tend on mortal thoughts! unsex me here,
And fill me from the crown to the toe top full
Of direst cruelty; make thick my blood,
Stop up the access and passage to remorse,
That no compunctious visitings of nature
Shake my fell purpose, nor keep peace between
The effect and it! Come to my woman's breasts,
And take my milk for gall, you murdering ministers,
Wherever in your sightless substances
You wait on nature's mischief! Come, thick night,
And pall thee in the dunnest smoke of hell,
That my keen knife see not the wound it makes,
Nor heaven peep through the blanket of the dark,

To cry, 'Hold, hold!'

Enter MACBETH.

                     Great Glamis! worthy Cawdor!
Greater than both, by the all-hail hereafter!
Thy letters have transported me beyond
This ignorant present, and I feel now
The future in the instant.
     MACBETH.   My dearest love,
Duncan comes here to-night.
     LADY MACBETH.   And when goes hence?
     MACBETH. To-morrow, as he purposes.
     LADY MACBETH.   O! never
Shall sun that morrow see.
Your face, my thane, is as a book where men
May read strange matters. To beguile the time,
Look like the time; bear welcome in your eye,
Your hand, your tongue: look like the innocent flower,
But be the serpent under 't. He that's coming
Must be provided for; and you shall put
This night's great business into my dispatch;
Which shall to all our nights and days to come
Give solely sovereign sway and masterdom.
     MACBETH. We will speak further.
     LADY MACBETH.   Only look up clear;
To alter favour ever is to fear.
Leave all the rest to me.   *[Exeunt.*

Scene VI. The Same. Before the Castle

Hautboys and torches. Enter DUNCAN, MALCOLM, DONAL-
BAIN, BANQUO, LENNOX, MACDUFF, ROSS, ANGUS, *and* ATTEND-
ANTS.

     DUNCAN. This castle hath a pleasant seat; the air
Nimbly and sweetly recommends itself

Unto our gentle senses.

BANQUO.   This guest of summer,
The temple-haunting martlet, does approve
By his lov'd mansionry that the heaven's breath
Smells wooingly here: no jutty, frieze,
Buttress, nor coign of vantage, but this bird
Hath made his pendent bed and procreant cradle:
Where they most breed and haunt, I have observ'd
The air is delicate.

> *Enter* LADY MACBETH.

DUNCAN.   See, see, our honour'd hostess!
The love that follows us sometime is our trouble,
Which still we thank as love. Herein I teach you
How you shall bid God 'eyld us for your pains,
And thank us for your trouble.

LADY MACBETH.   All our service,
In every point twice done, and then done double,
Were poor and single business, to contend
Against those honours deep and broad wherewith
Your majesty loads our house: for those of old,
And the late dignities heap'd up to them,
We rest your hermits.

DUNCAN.   Where's the Thane of Cawdor?
We cours'd him at the heels, and had a purpose
To be his purveyor; but he rides well,
And his great love, sharp as his spur, hath holp him
To his home before us. Fair and noble hostess,
We are your guest to-night.

LADY MACBETH.   Your servants ever
Have theirs, themselves, and what is theirs, in compt,
To make their audit at your highness' pleasure,
Still to return your own.

DUNCAN.   Give me your hand;
Conduct me to mine host: we love him highly,

And shall continue our graces towards him.
By your leave, hostess.   [*Exeunt.*

Scene VII.   The Same.   A Room in the Castle

Hautboys and torches. Enter, and pass over the stage, a
SEWER, *and divers* SERVANTS *with dishes and service. Then,*
enter MACBETH.

MACBETH. If it were done when 'tis done, then 'twere well
It were done quickly; if the assassination
Could trammel up the consequence, and catch
With his surcease success; that but this blow
Might be the be-all and the end-all here,
But here, upon this bank and shoal of time,
We'd jump the life to come. But in these cases
We still have judgment here; that we but teach
Bloody instructions, which, being taught, return
To plague the inventor; this even-handed justice
Commends the ingredients of our poison'd chalice
To our own lips. He's here in double trust:
First, as I am his kinsman and his subject,
Strong both against the deed; then, as his host,
Who should against his murderer shut the door,
Not bear the knife myself. Besides, this Duncan
Hath borne his faculties so meek, hath been
So clear in his great office, that his virtues
Will plead like angels trumpet-tongu'd against
The deep damnation of his taking-off;
And pity, like a naked new-born babe,
Striding the blast, or heaven's cherubin, hors'd
Upon the sightless couriers of the air,
Shall blow the horrid deed in every eye,
That tears shall drown the wind. I have no spur
To prick the sides of my intent, but only

Vaulting ambition, which o'er-leaps itself
And falls on the other.—

    Enter LADY MACBETH.

                          How now! what news?

LADY MACBETH. He has almost supp'd: why have you left the
    chamber?

MACBETH. Hath he ask'd for me?

LADY MACBETH.   Know you not he has?

MACBETH. We will proceed no further in this business:
He hath honour'd me of late; and I have bought
Golden opinions from all sorts of people,
Which would be worn now in their newest gloss,
Not cast aside so soon.

LADY MACBETH.   Was the hope drunk,
Wherein you dress'd yourself? hath it slept since,
And wakes it now, to look so green and pale
At what it did so freely? From this time
Such I account thy love. Art thou afeard
To be the same in thine own act and valour
As thou art in desire? Wouldst thou have that
Which thou esteem'st the ornament of life,
And live a coward in thine own esteem,
Letting 'I dare not' wait upon 'I would,'
Like the poor cat i' the adage?

MACBETH.   Prithee, peace.
I dare do all that may become a man;
Who dares do more is none.

LADY MACBETH.   What beast was't, then,
That made you break this enterprise to me?
When you durst do it, then you were a man;
And, to be more than what you were, you would
Be so much more the man. Nor time nor place
Did then adhere, and yet you would make both:
They have made themselves, and that their fitness now
Does unmake you. I have given suck, and know

How tender 'tis to love the babe that milks me:
I would, while it was smiling in my face,
Have pluck'd my nipple from his boneless gums,
And dash'd the brains out, had I so sworn as you
Have done to this.

  MACBETH. If we should fail,—
  LADY MACBETH.   We fail?
But screw your courage to the sticking-place,
And we'll not fail. When Duncan is asleep,
Whereto the rather shall his day's hard journey
Soundly invite him, his two chamberlains
Will I with wine and wassail so convince,
That memory, the warder of the brain,
Shall be a fume, and the receipt of reason
A limbeck only; when in swinish sleep
Their drenched natures lie, as in a death,
What cannot you and I perform upon
The unguarded Duncan? what not put upon
His spongy officers, who shall bear the guilt
Of our great quell?

  MACBETH. Bring forth men-children only;
For thy undaunted mettle should compose
Nothing but males. Will it not be receiv'd,
When we have mark'd with blood those sleepy two
Of his own chamber and us'd their very daggers,
That they have done 't?

  LADY MACBETH. Who dares receive it other,
As we shall make our griefs and clamour roar
Upon his death?

  MACBETH. I am settled, and bend up
Each corporal agent to this terrible feat.
Away, and mock the time with fairest show:
False face must hide what the false heart doth know. [*Exeunt.*

Act 2

Scene I. Inverness. Court within the Castle

Enter BANQUO *and* FLEANCE, *with a* SERVANT *bearing a torch before him.*

BANQUO. How goes the night, boy?
FLEANCE. The moon is down; I have not heard the clock.
BANQUO. And she goes down at twelve.
FLEANCE.   I take 't, 'tis later, sir.
BANQUO. Hold, take my sword. There's husbandry in heaven;
Their candles are all out. Take thee that too.
A heavy summons lies like lead upon me,
And yet I would not sleep: merciful powers!
Restrain in me the cursed thoughts that nature
Gives way to in repose.

Enter MACBETH, *and a* SERVANT *with a torch.*

                    Give me my sword.—
Who's there?
MACBETH. A friend.
BANQUO. What, sir! not yet at rest? The king's a-bed:
He hath been in unusual pleasure, and
Sent forth great largess to your offices.
This diamond he greets your wife withal,
By the name of most kind hostess; and shut up
In measureless content.
MACBETH.   Being unprepar'd,

255

Our will became the servant to defect,
Which else should free have wrought.

BANQUO.   All's well.
I dreamt last night of the three weird sisters:
To you they have show'd some truth.

MACBETH.   I think not of them:
Yet, when we can entreat an hour to serve,
We would spend it in some words upon that business,
If you would grant the time.

BANQUO.   At your kind'st leisure.

MACBETH. If you shall cleave to my consent, when 'tis,
It shall make honour for you.

BANQUO.   So I lose none
In seeking to augment it, but still keep
My bosom franchis'd and allegiance clear,
I shall be counsell'd.

MACBETH.   Good repose the while!

BANQUO. Thanks, sir: the like to you.

[*Exeunt* BANQUO *and* FLEANCE.

MACBETH. Go bid thy mistress, when my drink is ready
She strike upon the bell. Get thee to bed.   [*Exit* SERVANT.
Is this a dagger which I see before me,
The handle toward my hand? Come, let me clutch thee:
I have thee not, and yet I see thee still.
Art thou not, fatal vision, sensible
To feeling as to sight? or art thou but
A dagger of the mind, a false creation,
Proceeding from the heat-oppressed brain?
I see thee yet, in form as palpable
As this which now I draw.
Thou marshall'st me the way that I was going;
And such an instrument I was to use.
Mine eyes are made the fools o' the other senses,
Or else worth all the rest: I see thee still;
And on thy blade and dudgeon gouts of blood,
Which was not so before. There's no such thing:

It is the bloody business which informs
Thus to mine eyes. Now o'er the one half-world
Nature seems dead, and wicked dreams abuse
The curtain'd sleep; witchcraft celebrates
Pale Hecate's offerings; and wither'd murder,
Alarum'd by his sentinel, the wolf,
Whose howl's his watch, thus with his stealthy pace,
With Tarquin's ravishing strides, toward his design
Moves like a ghost. Thou sure and firm-set earth,
Hear not my steps, which way they walk, for fear
Thy very stones prate of my whereabout,
And take the present horror from the time,
Which now suits with it. Whiles I threat, he lives:
Words to the heat of deeds too cold breath gives.

> [*A bell rings.*

I go, and it is done; the bell invites me.
Hear it not, Duncan; for it is a knell
That summons thee to heaven or to hell.

Scene II.   The Same

Enter LADY MACBETH.

LADY MACBETH. That which hath made them drunk hath
made me bold,
What hath quench'd them hath given me fire. Hark!
Peace!
It was the owl that shriek'd, the fatal bellman,
Which gives the stern'st good-night. He is about it:
The doors are open, and the surfeited grooms
Do mock their charge with snores: I have drugg'd their possets,
That death and nature do contend about them,
Whether they live or die.

MACBETH. [*Within.*] Who's there? what, ho!

LADY MACBETH. Alack! I am afraid they have awak'd,
And 'tis not done; the attempt and not the deed

Confounds us. Hark! I laid their daggers ready;
He could not miss them. Had he not resembled
My father as he slept, I had done't. My husband!

Enter MACBETH.

MACBETH. I have done the deed. Didst thou not hear a noise?
LADY MACBETH. I heard the owl scream and the crickets cry.
Did not you speak?
MACBETH.   When?
LADY MACBETH.   Now.
MACBETH.   As I descended?
LADY MACBETH. Ay.
MACBETH. Hark!
Who lies i' the second chamber?
LADY MACBETH.   Donalbain.
MACBETH. [*Looking on his hands.*] This is a sorry sight.
LADY MACBETH. A foolish thought to say a sorry sight.
MACBETH. There's one did laugh in 's sleep, and one cried
    'Murder!'
That they did wake each other: I stood and heard them;
But they did say their prayers, and address'd them
Again to sleep.
LADY MACBETH. There are two lodg'd together.
MACBETH. One cried 'God bless us!' and 'Amen' the other:
As they had seen me with these hangman's hands.
Listening their fear, I could not say 'Amen,'
When they did say 'God bless us!'
LADY MACBETH.   Consider it not so deeply.
MACBETH. But wherefore could not I pronounce 'Amen'?
I had most need of blessing, and 'Amen'
Stuck in my throat.
LADY MACBETH. These deeds must not be thought
After these ways; so, it will make us mad.
MACBETH. Methought I heard a voice cry 'Sleep no more!
Macbeth does murder sleep,' the innocent sleep,
Sleep that knits up the ravell'd sleave of care,

The death of each day's life, sore labour's bath,
Balm of hurt minds, great nature's second course,
Chief nourisher in life's feast,—

LADY MACBETH.   What do you mean?

MACBETH. Still it cried, 'Sleep no more!' to all the house:
'Glamis hath murder'd sleep, and therefore Cawdor
Shall sleep no more, Macbeth shall sleep no more!'

LADY MACBETH. Who was it that thus cried? Why, worthy
    thane,
You do unbend your noble strength to think
So brainsickly of things. Go get some water,
And wash this filthy witness from your hand.
Why did you bring these daggers from the place?
They must lie there: go carry them, and smear
The sleepy grooms with blood.

MACBETH.   I'll go no more:
I am afraid to think what I have done;
Look on 't again I dare not.

LADY MACBETH.   Infirm of purpose!
Give me the daggers. The sleeping and the dead
Are but as pictures; 'tis the eye of childhood
That fears a painted devil. If he do bleed,
I'll gild the faces of the grooms withal;
For it must seem their guilt.   [*Exit. Knocking within*

MACBETH.   Whence is that knocking?
How is't with me, when every noise appals me?
What hands are here! Ha! they pluck out mine eyes.
Will all great Neptune's ocean wash this blood
Clean from my hand? No, this my hand will rather
The multitudinous seas incarnadine,
Making the green one red.

    Re-enter LADY MACBETH.

LADY MACBETH. My hands are of your colour, but I shame
To wear a heart so white.—[*Knocking within.*] I hear a knock-
    ing.

At the south entry; retire we to our chamber;
A little water clears us of this deed;
How easy is it, then! Your constancy
Hath left you unattended. [*Knocking within.*] Hark! more
    knocking.
Get on your night-gown, lest occasion call us,
And show us to be watchers. Be not lost
So poorly in your thoughts.
    MACBETH. To know my deed 'twere best not know myself.
                                                [*Knocking within.*
Wake Duncan with thy knocking! I would thou couldst!
                                                      [*Exeunt.*

Scene III.   The Same

Knocking within. Enter a PORTER.

PORTER. Here's a knocking, indeed! If a man were porter of
hell-gate, he should have old turning the key. [*Knocking within.*]
Knock, knock, knock! Who's there, i' the name of Beelzebub?
Here's a farmer that hanged himself on the expectation of
plenty: come in time; have napkins enough about you; here
you'll sweat for 't. [*Knocking within.*] Knock, knock! Who's
there, i' the other devil's name! Faith, here's an equivocator,
that could swear in both the scales against either scale; who
committed treason enough for God's sake, yet could not equivo-
cate to heaven: O! come in, equivocator. [*Knocking within.*]
Knock, knock, knock! Who's there? Faith, here's an English
tailor come hither for stealing out of a French hose: come in,
tailor; here you may roast your goose. [*Knocking within.*]
Knock, knock; never at quiet! What are you? But this place is
too cold for hell. I'll devil-porter it no further: I had thought to
have let in some of all professions, that go the primrose way to

"All hail, Macbeth! Hail to thee, Thane of Glamis!"
Act 1, Scene III
View from the towers of Glamis Castle.

the everlasting bonfire. [*Knocking within.*] Anon, anon! I pray
you, remember the porter. [*Opens the gate.*

Enter MACDUFF *and* LENNOX.

MACDUFF. Was it so late, friend, ere you went to bed,
That you do lie so late?
    PORTER. Faith, sir, we were carousing till the second cock.
    MACDUFF. Is thy master stirring?

Enter MACBETH.

Our knocking has awak'd him; here he comes.
    LENNOX. Good morrow, noble sir.
    MACBETH.   Good morrow, both.
    MACDUFF. Is the king stirring, worthy thane?
    MACBETH.   Not yet.
    MACDUFF. He did command me to call timely on him:
I have almost slipp'd the hour.
    MACBETH.   I'll bring you to him.
    MACDUFF. I know this is a joyful trouble to you;
But yet 'tis one.
    MACBETH. The labour we delight in physics pain.
This is the door.
    MACDUFF.   I'll make so bold to call,
For 'tis my limited service.   [*Exit.*
    LENNOX. Goes the king hence to-day?
    MACBETH.   He does: he did appoint so.
    LENNOX. The night has been unruly: where we lay,
Our chimneys were blown down; and, as they say,
Lamentings heard i' the air; strange screams of death,
And prophesying with accents terrible
Of dire combustion and confus'd events
New hatch'd to the woeful time. The obscure bird
Clamour'd the livelong night: some say the earth
Was feverous and did shake.
    MACBETH.   'Twas a rough night.

LENNOX. My young remembrance cannot parallel
A fellow to it.

Re-enter MACDUFF.

MACDUFF. O horror! horror! horror! Tongue nor heart
Cannot conceive nor name thee!

MACBETH. ⎫
LENNOX. ⎭   What's the matter?

MACDUFF. Confusion now hath made his masterpiece!
Most sacrilegious murder hath broke ope
The Lord's anointed temple, and stole thence
The life o' the building!

MACBETH. What is 't you say? the life?

LENNOX. Mean you his majesty?

MACDUFF. Approach the chamber, and destroy your sight
With a new Gorgon: do not bid me speak;
See, and then speak yourselves.

           [*Exeunt* MACBETH *and* LENNOX.
           Awake! awake!

Ring the alarum-bell. Murder and treason!
Banquo and Donalbain! Malcolm! awake!
Shake off this downy sleep, death's counterfeit,
And look on death itself! up, up, and see
The great doom's image! Malcolm! Banquo!
As from your graves rise up, and walk like sprites,
To countenance this horrror! Ring the bell.   [*Bell rings.*

Enter LADY MACBETH.

LADY MACBETH. What's the business,
That such a hideous trumpet calls to parley
The sleepers of the house? speak, speak!

MACDUFF.   O gentle lady!
'Tis not for you to hear what I can speak;
The repetition in a woman's ear
Would murder as it fell.

Enter BANQUO.

O Banquo! Banquo!
Our royal master's murder'd!

LADY MACBETH. Woe, alas!
What! In our house?

BANQUO. Too cruel any where.
Dear Duff, I prithee, contradict thyself,
And say it is not so.

Re-enter MACBETH *and* LENNOX.

MACBETH. Had I but died an hour before this chance
I had liv'd a blessed time; for, from this instant,
There's nothing serious in mortality,
All is but toys; renown and grace is dead,
The wine of life is drawn, and the mere lees
Is left this vault to brag of.

Enter MALCOLM *and* DONALBAIN.

DONALBAIN. What is amiss?

MACBETH. You are, and do not know 't:
The spring, the head, the fountain of your blood
Is stopp'd; the very source of it is stopp'd.

MACDUFF. Your royal father's murder'd.

MALCOLM. O! by whom?

LENNOX. Those of his chamber, as it seem'd, had done 't:
Their hands and faces were all badg'd with blood;
So were their daggers, which unwip'd we found
Upon their pillows: they star'd, and were distracted; no man's
    life
Was to be trusted with them.

MACBETH. O! yet I do repent me of my fury,
That I did kill them.

MACDUFF. Wherefore did you so?

MACBETH. Who can be wise, amaz'd, temperate and furious,

Loyal and neutral, in a moment? No man:
The expedition of my violent love
Outran the pauser, reason. Here lay Duncan,
His silver skin lac'd with his golden blood;
And his gash'd stabs look'd like a breach in nature
For ruin's wasteful entrance: there, the murderers,
Steep'd in the colours of their trade, their daggers
Unmannerly breech'd with gore: who could refrain,
That had a heart to love, and in that heart
Courage to make 's love known?

    LADY MACBETH.   Help me hence, ho!

    MACDUFF. Look to the lady.

    MALCOLM. [*Aside to* DONALBAIN.] Why do we hold our
      tongues,
That most may claim this argument for ours?

    DONALBAIN. [*Aside to* MALCOLM.] What should be spoken
Here where our fate, hid in an auger-hole,
May rush and seize us? Let's away: our tears
Are not yet brew'd.

    MALCOLM. [*Aside to* DONALBAIN.] Nor our strong sorrow
Upon the foot of motion.

    BANQUO.   Look to the lady:
                      [LADY MACBETH *is carried out.*
And when we have our naked frailties hid,
That suffer in exposure, let us meet,
And question this most bloody piece of work,
To know it further. Fears and scruples shake us:
In the great hand of God I stand, and thence
Against the undivulg'd pretence I fight
Of treasonous malice.

    MACDUFF.   And so do I.

    ALL.   So all.

    MACBETH. Let's briefly put on manly readiness,
And meet i' the hall together.

    ALL.   Well contented.

          [*Exeunt all but* MALCOLM *and* DONALBAIN.

MALCOLM. What will you do? Let's not consort with them:
To show an unfelt sorrow is an office
Which the false man does easy. I'll to England.

DONALBAIN. To Ireland, I; our separated fortune
Shall keep us both the safer: where we are,
There's daggers in men's smiles: the near in blood,
The nearer bloody.

MALCOLM.   This murderous shaft that's shot
Hath not yet lighted, and our safest way
Is to avoid the aim: therefore, to horse;
And let us not be dainty of leave-taking,
But shift away: there's warrant in that theft
Which steals itself when there's no mercy left.   [*Exeunt.*

Scene IV.   The Same. Without the Castle

Enter ROSS *and an* OLD MAN

OLD MAN. Threescore and ten I can remember well;
Within the volume of which time I have seen
Hours dreadful and things strange, but this sore night
Hath trifled former knowings.

ROSS.   Ah! good father,
Thou seest, the heavens, as troubled with man's act,
Threaten his bloody stage: by the clock 'tis day,
And yet dark night strangles the travelling lamp.
Is't night's predominance, or the day's shame,
That darkness does the face of earth entomb,
When living light should kiss it?

OLD MAN.   'Tis unnatural,
Even like the deed that's done. On Tuesday last,
A falcon, towering in her pride of place,
Was by a mousing owl hawk'd at and kill'd.

ROSS. And Duncan's horses,—a thing most strange and certain,—
Beauteous and swift, the minions of their race,

Turn'd wild in nature, broke their stalls, flung out,
Contending 'gainst obedience, as they would
Make war with mankind.

  OLD MAN.   'Tis said they eat each other.

  ROSS. They did so, to the amazement of mine eyes,
That look'd upon 't. Here comes the good Macduff.

  Enter MACDUFF.

How goes the world, sir, now?

  MACDUFF.   Why, see you not?

  ROSS. Is 't known who did this more than bloody deed?

  MACDUFF. Those that Macbeth hath slain.

  ROSS.   Alas, the day!
What good could they pretend?

  MACDUFF.   They were suborn'd.
Malcolm and Donalbain, the king's two sons,
Are stol'n away and fled, which puts upon them
Suspicion of the deed.

  ROSS.   'Gainst nature still!
Thriftless ambition, that wilt ravin up
Thine own life's means! Then 'tis most like
The sovereignty will fall upon Macbeth.

  MACDUFF. He is already nam'd, and gone to Scone
To be invested.

  ROSS. Where is Duncan's body?

  MACDUFF. Carried to Colmekill,
The sacred storehouse of his predecessors
And guardian of their bones.

  ROSS.   Will you to Scone?

  MACDUFF. No cousin, I'll to Fife.

  ROSS.   Well, I will thither.

  MACDUFF. Well, may you see things well done there: adieu!
Lest our old robes sit easier than our new!

  ROSS. Farewell, father.

  OLD MAN. God's benison go with you; and with those
That would make good of bad, and friends of foes! [*Exeunt.*

Act 3

Scene I.   Forres.   A Room in the Palace

Enter BANQUO.

BANQUO. Thou hast it now: King, Cawdor, Glamis, all,
As the weird women promis'd; and, I fear,
Thou play'dst most foully for 't; yet it was said
It should not stand in thy posterity,
But that myself should be the root and father
Of many kings. If there come truth from them,—
As upon thee, Macbeth, their speeches shine,—
Why, by the verities on thee made good,
May they not be my oracles as well,
And set me up in hope? But, hush! no more.

Sennet sounded. Enter MACBETH, *as king;* LADY MACBETH, *as
queen;* LENNOX, ROSS, LORDS, LADIES, *and* ATTENDANTS.

MACBETH. Here's our chief guest.
LADY MACBETH.   If he had been forgotten,
It had been as a gap in our great feast,
And all-thing unbecoming.
MACBETH. To-night we hold a solemn supper, sir,
And I'll request your presence.
BANQUO.   Let your highness
Command upon me; to the which my duties
Are with a most indissoluble tie
For ever knit.

267

MACBETH. Ride you this afternoon?

BANQUO. Ay, my good lord.

MACBETH. We should have else desir'd your good advice—
Which still hath been both grave and prosperous—
In this day's council; but we'll take to-morrow.
Is 't far you ride?

BANQUO. As far, my lord, as will fill up the time
'Twixt this and supper; go not my horse the better,
I must become a borrower of the night
For a dark hour or twain.

MACBETH.   Fail not our feast.

BANQUO. My lord, I will not.

MACBETH. We hear our bloody cousins are bestow'd
In England and in Ireland, not confessing
Their cruel parricide, filling their hearers
With strange invention; but of that to-morrow,
When therewithal we shall have cause of state
Craving us jointly. Hie you to horse; adieu
Till you return at night. Goes Fleance with you?

BANQUO. Ay, my good lord: our time does call upon 's.

MACBETH. I wish your horses swift and sure of foot;
And so I do commend you to their backs.
Farewell.   [*Exit* BANQUO.
Let every man be master of his time
Till seven at night; to make society
The sweeter welcome, we will keep ourself
Till supper-time alone; while then, God be with you!
                    [*Exeunt all but* MACBETH *and an* ATTENDANT.
Sirrah, a word with you. Attend those men
Our pleasure?

ATTENDANT. They are, my lord, without the palace gate.

MACBETH. Bring them before us. [*Exit* ATTENDANT.] To be
    thus is nothing;
But to be safely thus. Our fears in Banquo
Stick deep, and in his royalty of nature
Reigns that which would be fear'd: 'tis much he dares,

Familiar scenes to Shakespeare in his boyhood—the lovely Avon River and the Holy Trinity Church where he is buried.

And, to that dauntless temper of his mind,
He hath a wisdom that doth guide his valour
To act in safety. There is none but he
Whose being I do fear; and under him
My genius is rebuk'd, as it is said
Mark Antony's was by Caesar. He chid the sisters
When first they put the name of king upon me,
And bade them speak to him; then, prophet-like,
They hail'd him father to a line of kings.
Upon my head they plac'd a fruitless crown,
And put a barren sceptre in my gripe,
Thence to be wrench'd with an unlineal hand,
No son of mine succeeding. If 't be so,
For Banquo's issue have I fil'd my mind;
For them the gracious Duncan have I murder'd;
Put rancours in the vessel of my peace
Only for them; and mine eternal jewel
Given to the common enemy of man,
To make them kings, the seed of Banquo kings!
Rather than so, come fate into the list,
And champion me to the utterance! Who's there?
　　　Re-enter ATTENDANT, *with two* MURDERERS.
Now go to the door, and stay there till we call. [*Exit* ATTENDANT.
Was it not yesterday we spoke together?
　　FIRST MURDERER. It was, so please your highness.
　　MACBETH.　　　　　　　　　　　　　　　Well then, now
Have you consider'd of my speeches? Know
That it was he in the times past which held you
So under fortune, which you thought had been
Our innocent self. This I made good to you
In our last conference, pass'd in probation with you,
How you were borne in hand, how cross'd, the instruments,
Who wrought with them, and all things else that might
To half a soul and to a notion craz'd
Say, 'Thus did Banquo.'
　　FIRST MURDERER.　　　You made it known to us.

MACBETH. I did so; and went further, which is now
Our point of second meeting. Do you find
Your patience so predominant in your nature
That you can let this go? Are you so gospell'd
To pray for this good man and for his issue,
Whose heavy hand hath bow'd you to the grave
And beggar'd yours for ever?

    FIRST MURDERER.   We are men, my liege.

    MACBETH. Ay, in the catalogue ye go for men;
As hounds and greyhounds, mongrels, spaniels, curs,
Shoughs, water-rugs, and demi-wolves, are clept
All by the name of dogs: the valu'd file
Distinguishes the swift, the slow, the subtle,
The housekeeper, the hunter, every one
According to the gift which bounteous nature
Hath in him clos'd; whereby he does receive
Particular addition, from the bill
That writes them all alike: and so of men.
Now, if you have a station in the file,
Not i' the worst rank of manhood, say it;
And I will put that business in your bosoms,
Whose execution takes your enemy off,
Grapples you to the heart and love of us,
Who wear our health but sickly in his life,
Which in his death were perfect.

    SECOND MURDERER.   I am one, my liege,
Whom the vile blows and buffets of the world
Have so incens'd that I am reckless what
I do to spite the world.

    FIRST MURDERER.   And I another.
So weary with disasters, tugg'd with fortune,
That I would set my life on any chance,
To mend it or be rid on 't.

    MACBETH.   Both of you
Know Banquo was your enemy.

    SECOND MURDERER.   True, my lord.

MACBETH. So is he mine; and in such bloody distance
That every minute of his being thrusts
Against my near'st of life: and though I could
With bare-fac'd power sweep him from my sight
And bid my will avouch it, yet I must not,
For certain friends that are both his and mine,
Whose loves I may not drop, but wail his fall
Whom I myself struck down; and thence it is
That I to your assistance do make love,
Masking the business from the common eye
For sundry weighty reasons.
    SECOND MURDERER.   We shall, my lord,
Perform what you command us.
    FIRST MURDERER.   Though our lives—
    MACBETH. Your spirits shine through you. Within this hour
      at most
I will advise you where to plant yourselves,
Acquaint you with the perfect spy o' the time,
The moment on 't; for 't must be done to-night,
And something from the palace; always thought
That I require a clearness: and with him—
To leave no rubs nor botches in the work—
Fleance his son, that keeps him company,
Whose absence is no less material to me
Than is his father's, must embrace the fate
Of that dark hour. Resolve yourselves apart;
I'll come to you anon.
    SECOND MURDERER. We are resolv'd, my lord.
    MACBETH. I'll call upon you straight: abide within.
                                  [Exeunt MURDERERS.
It is concluded: Banquo, thy soul's flight,
If it find heaven, must find it out to-night.   *[Exit.*

Scene II. The Same. Another Room in the Palace

Enter LADY MACBETH *and a* SERVANT.

LADY MACBETH. Is Banquo gone from court?

SERVANT. Ay, madam, but returns again to-night.

LADY MACBETH. Say to the king, I would attend his leisure
For a few words.

SERVANT.   Madam, I will.   [*Exit.*

LADY MACBETH.   Nought's had, all's spent,
Where our desire is got without content:
'Tis safer to be that which we destroy
Than by destruction dwell in doubtful joy.

Enter MACBETH.

How now, my lord! why do you keep alone,
Of sorriest fancies your companions making,
Using those thoughts which should indeed have died
With them they think on? Things without all remedy
Should be without regard: what's done is done.

MACBETH. We have scotch'd the snake, not kill'd it:
She'll close and be herself, whilst our poor malice
Remains in danger of her former tooth.
But let the frame of things disjoint, both the worlds suffer,
Ere we will eat our meal in fear, and sleep
In the affliction of these terrible dreams
That shake us nightly. Better be with the dead,
Whom we, to gain our peace, have sent to peace,
Than on the torture of the mind to lie
In restless ecstasy. Duncan is in his grave;
After life's fitful fever he sleeps well;
Treason has done his worst: nor steel, nor poison,
Malice domestic, foreign levy, nothing
Can touch him further.

LADY MACBETH.   Come on;
Gentle my lord, sleep o'er your rugged looks;
Be bright and jovial among your guests to-night.

MACBETH. So shall I, love; and so, I pray, be you.
Let your remembrance apply to Banquo;
Present him eminence, both with eye and tongue:
Unsafe the while, that we
Must lave our honours in these flattering streams,
And make our faces vizards to our hearts,
Disguising what they are.

LADY MACBETH.　　　You must leave this.

MACBETH. O! full of scorpions is my mind, dear wife;
Thou know'st that Banquo and his Fleance lives.

LADY MACBETH. But in them nature's copy's not eterne.

MACBETH. There's comfort yet; they are assailable;
Then be thou jocund. Ere the bat hath flown
His cloister'd flight, ere to black Hecate's summons
The shard-born beetle with his drowsy hums
Hath rung night's yawning peal, there shall be done
A deed of dreadful note.

LADY MACBETH.　　　What's to be done?

MACBETH. Be innocent of the knowledge, dearest chuck,
Till thou applaud the deed. Come, seeling night,
Scarf up the tender eye of pitiful day,
And with thy bloody and invisible hand
Cancel and tear to pieces that great bond
Which keeps me pale! Light thickens, and the crow
Makes wing to the rooky wood;
Good things of day begin to droop and drowse,
Whiles night's black agents to their preys do rouse.
Thou marvell'st at my words: but hold thee still;
Things bad begun make strong themselves by ill:
So, prithee, go with me.　　　　　　　　　　　[*Exeunt.*

Scene III.　The Same. A Park, with a Road leading to the Palace

Enter three MURDERERS.

FIRST MURDERER. But who did bid thee join with us?

THIRD MURDERER. Macbeth.

SECOND MURDERER. He needs not our mistrust, since he delivers

Our offices and what we have to do

To the direction just.

FIRST MURDERER. Then stand with us.

The west yet glimmers with some streaks of day:

Now spurs the lated traveller apace

To gain the timely inn; and near approaches

The subject of our watch.

THIRD MURDERER. Hark! I hear horses.

BANQUO. [*Within.*] Give us a light there, ho!

SECOND MURDERER. Then 'tis he: the rest

That are within the note of expectation

Already are i' the court.

FIRST MURDERER. His horses go about.

THIRD MURDERER. Almost a mile; but he does usually,

So all men do, from hence to the palace gate

Make it their walk.

SECOND MURDERER. A light, a light!

THIRD MURDERER. 'Tis he.

FIRST MURDERER. Stand to 't.

Enter BANQUO *and* FLEANCE, *with a torch.*

BANQUO. It will be rain to-night.

FIRST MURDERER. Let it come down.

[*They set upon* BANQUO.

BANQUO. O, treachery! Fly, good Fleance, fly, fly, fly!

Thou mayst revenge. O slave! [*Dies.* FLEANCE *escapes.*

THIRD MURDERER. Who did strike out the light?

FIRST MURDERER. Was 't not the way?

THIRD MURDERER. There's but one down; the son is fled.

SECOND MURDERER. We have lost

Best half of our affair.

FIRST MURDERER. Well, let's away, and say how much is done.

[*Exeunt.*

Scene IV. The Same. A Room of State in the Palace

A Banquet prepared. Enter MACBETH, LADY MACBETH, ROSS, LENNOX, LORDS, *and* ATTENDANTS.

MACBETH. You know your own degrees; sit down: at first and last,
The hearty welcome.

LORDS.   Thanks to your majesty.

MACBETH. Ourself will mingle with society
And play the humble host.
Our hostess keeps her state, but in best time
We will require her welcome.

LADY MACBETH. Pronounce it for me, sir, to all our friends;
For my heart speaks they are welcome.

Enter FIRST MURDERER, *to the door.*

MACBETH. See, they encounter thee with their hearts' thanks;
Both sides are even: here I'll sit i' the midst:
Be large in mirth; anon, we'll drink a measure
The table round. [*Approaching the door.*] There's blood upon
thy face.

MURDERER. 'Tis Banquo's, then.

MACBETH. 'Tis better thee without than he within.
Is he dispatch'd?

MURDERER. My lord, his throat is cut; that I did for him.

MACBETH. Thou art the best o' the cut-throats; yet he's good
That did the like for Fleance: if thou didst it,
Thou art the nonpareil.

MURDERER.   Most royal sir,
Fleance is 'scap'd.

MACBETH. Then comes my fit again: I had else been perfect;
Whole as the marble, founded as the rock,
As broad and general as the casing air:

But now I am cabin'd, cribb'd, confined, bound in
To saucy doubts and fears. But Banquo's safe?

MURDERER. Ay, my good lord; safe in a ditch he bides,
With twenty trenched gashes on his head,
The least a death to nature.

MACBETH. Thanks for that.
There the grown serpent lies: the worm that's fled
Hath nature that in time will venom breed,
No teeth for the present. Get thee gone; to-morrow
We'll hear ourselves again. [*Exit* MURDERER.

LADY MACBETH. My royal lord,
You do not give the cheer: the feast is sold
That is not often vouch'd, while 'tis a-making,
'Tis given with welcome: to feed were best at home;
From thence, the sauce to meat is ceremony;
Meeting were bare without it.

MACBETH. Sweet remembrancer!
Now good digestion wait on appetite,
And health on both!

LENNOX. May it please your highness sit?
[*The Ghost of* BANQUO *enters, and
sits in* MACBETH's *place.*

MACBETH. Here had we now our country's honour roof'd,
Were the grac'd person of our Banquo present;
Who may I rather challenge for unkindness
Than pity for mischance!

ROSS. His absence, sir,
Lays blame upon his promise. Please 't your highness
To grace us with your royal company.

MACBETH. The table's full.

LENNOX. Here is a place reserv'd, sir.

MACBETH. Where?

LENNOX. Here, my good lord. What is 't that moves your
highness?

MACBETH. Which of you have done this?

LORDS. What, my good lord?

MACBETH. Thou canst not say I did: never shake
Thy gory locks at me.

ROSS. Gentlemen, rise; his highness is not well.

LADY MACBETH. Sit, worthy friends: my lord is often thus,
And hath been from his youth: pray you, keep seat;
The fit is momentary; upon a thought
He will again be well. If much you note him,
You shall offend him and extend his passion:
Feed, and regard him not. Are you a man?

MACBETH. Ay, and a bold one, that dare look on that
Which might appal the devil.

LADY MACBETH.   O proper stuff!
This is the very painting of your fear;
This is the air-drawn dagger which, you said,
Led you to Duncan. O! these flaws and starts—
Impostors to true fear—would well become
A woman's story at a winter's fire,
Authoriz'd by her grandam. Shame itself!
Why do you make such faces? When all's done,
You look but on a stool.

MACBETH. Prithee, see there! behold! look! lo! how say you?
Why, what care I? If thou canst nod, speak too.
If charnel-houses and our graves must send
Those that we bury back, our monuments
Shall be the maws of kites.   [GHOST *disappears.*

LADY MACBETH.   What! quite unmann'd in folly?

MACBETH. If I stand here, I saw him.

LADY MACBETH.   Fie, for shame!

MACBETH. Blood hath been shed ere now, i' the olden time,
Ere human statute purg'd the gentle weal;
Ay, and since too, murders have been perform'd
Too terrible for the ear: the times have been,
That, when the brains were out, the man would die,
And there an end; but now they rise again,
With twenty mortal murders on their crowns,
And push us from our stools: this is more strange

Than such a murder is.

LADY MACBETH.   My worthy lord,
Your noble friends do lack you.

MACBETH.   I do forget.
Do not muse at me, my most worthy friends;
I have a strange infirmity, which is nothing
To those that know me. Come, love and health to all;
Then, I'll sit down. Give me some wine; fill full.
I drink to the general joy of the whole table,
And to our dear friend Banquo, whom we miss;
Would he were here! to all, and him, we thirst,
And all to all.

LORDS.   Our duties, and the pledge.

Re-enter GHOST.

MACBETH. Avaunt! and quit my sight! Let the earth hide thee!
Thy bones are marrowless, thy blood is cold;
Thou hast no speculation in those eyes
Which thou dost glare with.

LADY MACBETH.   Think of this, good peers,
But as a thing of custom: 'tis no other;
Only it spoils the pleasure of the time.

MACBETH. What man dare, I dare:
Approach thou like the rugged Russian bear,
The arm'd rhinoceros, or the Hyrcan tiger;
Take any shape but that, and my firm nerves
Shall never tremble: or be alive again,
And dare me to the desart with thy sword;
If trembling I inhabit then, protest me
The baby of a girl. Hence, horrible shadow!
Unreal mockery, hence!   [GHOST *vanishes.*
                    Why, so; being gone,
I am a man again. Pray you, sit still.

LADY MACBETH. You have displac'd the mirth, broke the good
    meeting,

With most admir'd disorder.

MACBETH.　　　　　　　Can such things be
And overcome us like a summer's cloud,
Without our special wonder? You make me strange
Even to the disposition that I owe,
When now I think you can behold such sights,
And keep the natural ruby of your cheeks,
When mine are blanch'd with fear.

ROSS.　　　　　　　　What sights, my lord?

LADY MACBETH. I pray you, speak not; he grows worse and
worse;
Question enrages him. At once, good-night:
Stand not upon the order of your going,
But go at once.

LENNOX.　　　Good-night; and better health
Attend his majesty!

LADY MACBETH. A kind good-night to all!
　　　　　　　　　[*Exeunt* LORDS *and* ATTENDANTS.

MACBETH. It will have blood, they say; blood will have blood:
Stones have been known to move and trees to speak;
Augurs and understood relations have
By maggot-pies and choughs and rooks brought forth
The secret'st man of blood. What is the night?

LADY MACBETH. Almost at odds with morning, which is which.

MACBETH. How sayst thou, that Macduff denies his person
At our great bidding?

LADY MACBETH.　　　Did you send to him, sir?

MACBETH. I hear it by the way; but I will send.
There's not a one of them but in his house
I keep a servant fee'd. I will to-morrow—
And betimes I will—to the weird sisters:
More shall they speak; for now I am bent to know,
By the worst means, the worst. For mine own good
All causes shall give way: I am in blood
Stepp'd in so far, that, should I wade no more,
Returning were as tedious as go o'er.

Strange things I have in head that will to hand,
Which must be acted ere they may be scann'd.

LADY MACBETH. You lack the season of all natures, sleep.

MACBETH. Come, we'll to sleep. My strange and self-abuse
Is the initiate fear that wants hard use:
We are yet but young in deed.   [*Exeunt.*

Scene V.   A Heath

Thunder. Enter the three WITCHES, *meeting* HECATE.

FIRST WITCH. Why, how now, Hecate! you look angerly.

HECATE. Have I not reason, beldams as you are,
Saucy and overbold? How did you dare
To trade and traffic with Macbeth
In riddles and affairs of death;
And I, the mistress of your charms,
The close contriver of all harms,
Was never call'd to bear my part,
Or show the glory of our art?
And, which is worse, all you have done
Hath been but for a wayward son,
Spiteful and wrathful; who, as others do,
Loves for his own ends, not for you.
But make amends now: get you gone,
And at the pit of Acheron
Meet me i' the morning: thither he
Will come to know his destiny:
Your vessels and your spells provide,
Your charms and every thing beside.
I am for the air; this night I'll spend
Unto a dismal and a fatal end:
Great business must be wrought ere noon:
Upon the corner of the moon
There hangs a vaporous drop profound;
I'll catch it ere it come to ground:

And that distill'd by magic sleights
Shall raise such artificial sprites
As by the strength of their illusion
Shall draw him on to his confusion:
He shall spurn fate, scorn death, and bear
His hopes 'bove wisdom, grace, and fear;
And you all know, security
Is mortals' chiefest enemy.

     [*Song within,* 'Come away, come away,' &c.
Hark! I am call'd; my little spirit, see,
Sits in a foggy cloud, and stays for me.   [*Exit.*
 FIRST WITCH. Come, let's make haste; she'll soon be back
 again.   [*Exeunt.*

Scene VI. *Forres. A Room in the Palace*

Enter LENNOX *and another* LORD.

 LENNOX. My former speeches have but hit your thoughts,
Which can interpret further: only, I say,
Things have been strangely borne. The gracious Duncan
Was pitied of Macbeth: marry, he was dead:
And the right-valiant Banquo walk'd too late;
Whom, you may say, if 't please you, Fleance kill'd,
For Fleance fled: men must not walk too late.
Who cannot want the thought how monstrous
It was for Malcolm and for Donalbain
To kill their gracious father? damned fact!
How it did grieve Macbeth! did he not straight
In pious rage the two delinquents tear,
That were the slaves of drink and thralls of sleep?
Was not that nobly done? Ay, and wisely too;
For 'twould have anger'd any heart alive
To hear the men deny 't. So that, I say,
He has borne all things well; and I do think
That, had he Duncan's sons under his key,—

As, an 't please heaven, he shall not,—they should find
What 'twere to kill a father; so should Fleance.
But, peace! for from broad words, and 'cause he fail'd
His presence at the tyrant's feast, I hear
Macduff lives in disgrace. Sir, can you tell
Where he bestows himself?

LORD.   The son of Duncan,
From whom this tyrant holds the due of birth,
Lives in the English court, and is receiv'd
Of the most pious Edward with such grace
That the malevolence of fortune nothing
Takes from his high respect. Thither Macduff
Is gone to pray the holy king, upon his aid
To wake Northumberland and war-like Siward:
That, by the help of these—with him above
To ratify the work—we may again
Give to our tables meat, sleep to our nights,
Free from our feasts and banquets bloody knives,
Do faithful homage and receive free honours;
All which we pine for now. And this report
Hath so exasperate the king that he
Prepares for some attempt of war.

LENNOX.   Sent he to Macduff?

LORD. He did: and with an absolute, 'Sir, not I,'
The cloudy messenger turns me his back,
And hums, as who should say, 'You'll rue the time
That clogs me with this answer.'

LENNOX   And that well might
Advise him to a caution to hold what distance
His wisdom can provide. Some holy angel
Fly to the court of England and unfold
His message ere he come, that a swift blessing
May soon return to this our suffering country
Under a hand accurs'd!

LORD.   I'll send my prayers with him! [*Exeunt.*

Act 4

Scene I. A Cavern. In the middle, a boiling Cauldron

Thunder. Enter the three WITCHES.

FIRST WITCH. Thrice the brinded cat hath mew'd.
SECOND WITCH. Thrice and once the hedge-pig whin'd.
THIRD WITCH. Harpier cries: 'Tis time, 'tis time.
FIRST WITCH. Round about the cauldron go;
In the poison'd entrails throw.
Toad, that under cold stone
Days and nights hast thirty-one
Swelter'd venom sleeping got,
Boil thou first i' the charmed pot.
ALL. Double, double toil and trouble;
Fire burn and cauldron bubble.
SECOND WITCH. Fillet of a fenny snake,
In the cauldron boil and bake;
Eye of newt, and toe of frog,
Wool of bat, and tongue of dog,
Adder's fork, and blind-worm's sting,
Lizard's leg, and howlet's wing,
For a charm of powerful trouble,
Like a hell-broth boil and bubble.
ALL. Double, double toil and trouble;
Fire burn and cauldron bubble.
THIRD WITCH. Scale of dragon, tooth of wolf,
Witches' mummy, maw and gulf
Of the ravin'd salt-sea shark,

Root of hemlock digg'd i' the dark,
Liver of blaspheming Jew,
Gall of goat, and slips of yew
Sliver'd in the moon's eclipse,
Nose of Turk, and Tartar's lips,
Finger of birth-strangled babe
Ditch-deliver'd by a drab,
Make the gruel thick and slab:
Add thereto a tiger's chaudron,
For the ingredients of our cauldron.

ALL.   Double, double toil and trouble;
Fire burn and cauldron bubble.

SECOND WITCH. Cool it with a baboon's blood,
Then the charm is firm and good.

Enter HECATE.

HECATE.   O! well done! I commend your pains,
And every one shall share i' the gains.
And now about the cauldron sing,
Like elves and fairies in a ring,
Enchanting all that you put in.
          [*Music and a song,* 'Black Spirits,' *&c.*

SECOND WITCH. By the pricking of my thumbs,
Something wicked this way comes.
          Open, locks,
          Whoever knocks.

Enter MACBETH.

MACBETH. How now, you secret, black, and midnight hags!
What is 't you do?

ALL.   A deed without a name.

MACBETH. I conjure you, by that which you profess,—
Howe'er you come to know it,—answer me:
Though you untie the winds and let them fight
Against the churches; though the yesty waves
Confound and swallow navigation up;

Though bladed corn be lodg'd and trees blown down;
Though castles topple on their warders' heads;
Though palaces and pyramids do slope
Their heads to their foundations; though the treasure
Of Nature's germens tumble all together,
Even till destruction sicken; answer me
To what I ask you.

FIRST WITCH.   Speak.

SECOND WITCH.   Demand.

THIRD WITCH.   We'll answer.

FIRST WITCH. Say if thou'dst rather hear it from our mouths,
Or from our masters?

MACBETH.   Call 'em: let me see 'em.

FIRST WITCH. Pour in sow's blood, that hath eaten
Her nine farrow; grease that's sweaten
From the murderer's gibbet throw
Into the flame.

ALL.   Come, high or low;
Thyself and office deftly show.

Thunder. First APPARITION *of an armed Head.*

MACBETH. Tell me, thou unknown power,—

FIRST WITCH.   He knows thy thought:
Hear his speech, but say thou nought.

FIRST APPARITION. Macbeth! Macbeth! Macbeth! beware Macduff;
Beware the Thane of Fife. Dismiss me. Enough.   [*Descends.*

MACBETH. Whate'er thou art, for thy good caution thanks;
Thou hast harp'd my fear aright. But one word more,—

FIRST WITCH. He will not be commanded: here's another,
More potent than the first.

Thunder. Second APPARITION, *a bloody Child.*

SECOND APPARITION. Macbeth! Macbeth! Macbeth!—

MACBETH. Had I three ears, I'd hear thee.

SECOND APPARITION. Be bloody, bold, and resolute; laugh to
  scorn
The power of man, for none of woman born
Shall harm Macbeth.   [*Descends.*
  MACBETH. Then live, Macduff: what need I fear of thee?
But yet I'll make assurance double sure,
And take a bond of fate: thou shalt not live;
That I may tell pale-hearted fear it lies,
And sleep in spite of thunder.

  Thunder. Third APPARITION, *a Child crowned, with a tree
  in his hand.*

                                      What is this,
That rises like the issue of a king,
And wears upon his baby brow the round
And top of sovereignty?
  ALL.   Listen, but speak not to 't.
  THIRD APPARITION. Be lion-mettled, proud, and take no care
Who chafes, who frets, or where conspirers are:
Macbeth shall never vanquish'd be until
Great Birnam Wood to high Dunsinane Hill
Shall come against him.   [*Descends.*
  MACBETH.   That will never be:
Who can impress the forest, bid the tree
Unfix his earth-bound root? Sweet bodements! good!
Rebellion's head, rise never till the wood
Of Birnam rise, and our high-plac'd Macbeth
Shall live the lease of nature, pay his breath
To time and mortal custom. Yet my heart
Throbs to know one thing: tell me—if your art
Can tell so much,—shall Banquo's issue ever
Reign in this kingdom?
  ALL.   Seek to know no more.
  MACBETH. I will be satisfied: deny me this,
And an eternal curse fall on you! Let me know.

Why sinks that cauldron? and what noise is this?   [*Hautboys.*
   FIRST WITCH. Show!
   SECOND WITCH. Show!
   THIRD WITCH. Show!
   ALL. Show his eyes, and grieve his heart;
Come like shadows, so depart.

   A show of Eight Kings; the last with a glass in his hand:
   BANQUO'S GHOST *following.*

   MACBETH. Thou art too like the spirit of Banquo; down!
Thy crown does sear mine eyeballs: and thy hair,
Thou other gold-bound brow, is like the first:
A third is like the former. Filthy hags!
Why do you show me this? A fourth! Start, eyes!
What! will the line stretch out to the crack of doom?
Another yet? A seventh! I'll see no more:
And yet the eighth appears, who bears a glass
Which shows me many more; and some I see
That two-fold balls and treble sceptres carry.
Horrible sight! Now, I see, 'tis true;
For the blood-bolter'd Banquo smiles upon me,
And points at them for his.   [APPARITIONS *vanish.*
                   What! is this so?
   FIRST WITCH. Ay, sir, all this is so: but why
Stands Macbeth thus amazedly?
Come sisters, cheer we up his sprites,
And show the best of our delights.
I'll charm the air to give a sound,
While you perform your antick round,
That this great king may kindly say
Our duties did his welcome pay.
           [*Music. The* WITCHES *dance, and*
                then vanish with HECATE.
   MACBETH. Where are they? Gone? Let this pernicious hour
Stand aye accursed in the calendar!

Come in, without there!

Enter LENNOX.

LENNOX. What's your Grace's will?

MACBETH. Saw you the weird sisters?

LENNOX. No, my lord.

MACBETH. Came they not by you?

LENNOX. No indeed, my lord.

MACBETH. Infected be the air whereon they ride,
And damn'd all those that trust them! I did hear
The galloping of horse: who was 't came by?

LENNOX. 'Tis two or three, my lord, that bring you word
Macduff is fled to England.

MACBETH. Fled to England!

LENNOX. Ay, my good lord.

MACBETH. Time, thou anticipat'st my dread exploits;
The flighty purpose never is o'er took
Unless the deed go with it; from this moment
The very firstlings of my heart shall be
The firstlings of my hand. And even now,
To crown my thoughts with acts, be it thought and done:
The castle of Macduff I will surprise;
Seize upon Fife; give to the edge of the sword
His wife, his babes, and all unfortunate souls
That trace him in his line. No boasting like a fool;
This deed I'll do before this purpose cool:
But no more sights! Where are these gentlemen?
Come, bring me where they are. [*Exeunt.*

Scene II. Fife. Macduff's Castle

Enter LADY MACDUFF, *her* SON, *and* ROSS.

LADY MACDUFF. What had he done to make him fly the land?

ROSS. You must have patience, madam.

LADY MACDUFF. He had none:

His flight was madness: when our actions do not,
Our fears do make us traitors.

ROSS.   You know not
Whether it was his wisdom or his fear.

LADY MACDUFF. Wisdom! to leave his wife, to leave his babes,
His mansion and his titles in a place
From whence himself does fly? He loves us not;
He wants the natural touch; for the poor wren,
The most diminutive of birds, will fight—
Her young ones in her nest—against the owl.
All is the fear and nothing is the love;
As little is the wisdom, where the flight
So runs against all reason.

ROSS.   My dearest coz,
I pray you, school yourself: but, for your husband,
He is noble, wise, judicious, and best knows
The fits o' the season. I dare not speak much further:
But cruel are the times, when we are traitors
And do not know ourselves, when we hold rumour
From what we fear, yet know not what we fear,
But float upon a wild and violent sea
Each way and move. I take my leave of you:
Shall not be long but I'll be here again.
Things at the worst will cease, or else climb upward
To what they were before. My pretty cousin,
Blessing upon you!

LADY MACDUFF. Father'd he is, and yet he's fatherless.

ROSS. I am so much a fool, should I stay longer,
It would be my disgrace, and your discomfort:
I take my leave at once.   [*Exit.*

LADY MACDUFF.   Sirrah, your father's dead:
And what will you do now? How will you live?

SON. As birds do, mother.

LADY MACDUFF.   What! with worms and flies?

SON. With what I get, I mean; and so do they.

LADY MACDUFF. Poor bird! thou'dst never fear the net nor lime,
The pit-fall nor the gin.

SON. Why should I, mother? Poor birds they are not set for.
My father is not dead, for all your saying.

LADY MACDUFF. Yes, he is dead: how wilt thou do for a father?

SON. Nay, how will you do for a husband?

LADY MACDUFF. Why, I can buy me twenty at any market.

SON. Then you'll buy 'em to sell again.

LADY MACDUFF. Thou speak'st with all thy wit; and yet, i' faith,
With wit enough for thee.

SON. Was my father a traitor, mother?

LADY MACDUFF. Ay, that he was.

SON. What is a traitor?

LADY MACDUFF. Why, one that swears and lies.

SON. And be all traitors that do so?

LADY MACDUFF. Every one that does so is a traitor, and must be hanged.

SON. And must they all be hanged that swear and lie?

LADY MACDUFF. Every one.

SON. Who must hang them?

LADY MACDUFF. Why, the honest men.

SON. Then the liars and swearers are fools, for there are liars and swearers enow to beat the honest men, and hang up them.

LADY MACDUFF. Now God help thee, poor monkey!
But how wilt thou do for a father?

SON. If he were dead, you'd weep for him: if you would not, it were a good sign that I should quickly have a new father.

LADY MACDUFF. Poor prattler, how thou talk'st!

Enter a MESSENGER.

MESSENGER. Bless you, fair dame! I am not to you known,
Though in your state of honour I am perfect.
I doubt some danger does approach you nearly:

If you will take a homely man's advice,
Be not found here; hence, with your little ones.
To fright you thus, methinks, I am too savage;
To do worse to you were fell cruelty,
Which is too nigh your person. Heaven preserve you!
I dare abide no longer.   [*Exit.*
  LADY MACDUFF.   Whither should I fly?
I have done no harm. But I remember now
I am in this earthly world, where to do harm
Is often laudable, to do good sometime
Accounted dangerous folly; why then, alas!
Do I put up what womanly defence,
To say I have done no harm?

   Enter MURDERERS.
                          What are these faces?
  MURDERER. Where is your husband?
  LADY MACDUFF. I hope in no place so unsanctified
Where such as thou mayst find him.
  MURDERER.   He's a traitor.
  SON. Thou liest, thou shag-hair'd villain.
  MURDERER.   What, you egg!
Young fry of treachery!   [*Stabbing him.*
  SON.   He has killed me, mother:
Run away, I pray you!   [*Dies.*
              [*Exit* LADY MACDUFF, *crying 'Murder,'*
                  and pursued by the MURDERERS.

Scene III.   *England. Before the King's Palace*

  Enter MALCOLM *and* MACDUFF.

MALCOLM. Let us seek out some desolate shade, and there
Weep our sad bosoms empty.
  MACDUFF.   Let us rather
Hold fast the mortal sword, and like good men
Bestride our down-fall'n birthdom; each new morn

New widows howl, new ophans cry, new sorrows
Strike heaven on the face, that it resounds
As if it felt with Scotland and yell'd out
Like syllable of dolour.

MALCOLM.   What I believe I'll wail,
What know believe; and what I can redress,
As I shall find the time to friend, I will.
What you have spoke, it may be so perchance.
This tyrant, whose sole name blisters our tongues,
Was once thought honest; you have lov'd him well;
He hath not touch'd you yet. I am young; but something
You may deserve of him through me, and wisdom
To offer up a weak, poor, innocent lamb
To appease an angry god.

MACDUFF. I am not treacherous.

MALCOLM.   But Macbeth is.
A good and virtuous nature may recoil
In an imperial charge. But I shall crave your pardon;
That which you are my thoughts cannot transpose;
Angels are bright still, though the brightest fell;
Though all things foul would wear the brows of grace,
Yet grace must still look so.

MACDUFF.   I have lost my hopes.

MALCOLM. Perchance even there where I did find my doubts.
Why in that rawness left you wife and child—
Those precious motives, those strong knots of love—
Without leave-taking? I pray you,
Let not my jealousies be your dishonours,
But mine own safeties: you may be rightly just,
Whatever I shall think.

MACDUFF.   Bleed, bleed, poor country!
Great tyranny, lay thou thy basis sure,
For goodness dare not check thee! wear thou thy wrongs;
The title is affeer'd! Fare thee well, lord:
I would not be the villain that thou think'st
For the whole space that's in the tyrant's grasp,

And the rich East to boot.

MALCOLM. Be not offended:
I speak not as in absolute fear of you.
I think our country sinks beneath the yoke;
It weeps, it bleeds, and each new day a gash
Is added to her wounds: I think withal
There would be hands uplifted in my right;
And here from gracious England have I offer
Of goodly thousands: but, for all this,
When I shall tread upon the tyrant's head,
Or wear it on my sword, yet my poor country
Shall have more vices than it had before,
More suffer, and more sundry ways than ever,
By him that shall succeed.

MACDUFF. What should he be?

MALCOLM. It is myself I mean; in whom I know
All the particulars of vice so grafted,
That, when they shall be open'd, black Macbeth
Will seem as pure as snow, and the poor state
Esteem him as a lamb, being compar'd
With my confineless harms.

MACDUFF. Not in the legions
Of horrid hell can come a devil more damn'd
In evils to top Macbeth.

MALCOLM. I grant him bloody,
Luxurious, avaricious, false, deceitful,
Sudden, malicious, smacking of every sin
That has a name; but there's no bottom, none,
In my voluptuousness: your wives, your daughters,
Your matrons, and your maids, could not fill up
The cistern of my lust, and my desire
All continent impediments would o'erbear
That did oppose my will; better Macbeth
Than such an one to reign.

MACDUFF. Boundless intemperance
In nature is a tryranny; it hath been

Th' untimely emptying of the happy throne,
And fall of many kings. But fear not yet
To take upon you what is yours; you may
Convey your pleasures in a spacious plenty,
And yet seem cold, the time you may so hoodwink.
We have willing dames enough; there cannot be
That culture in you, to devour so many
As will to greatness dedicate themselves,
Finding it so inclin'd.

    MALCOLM.   With this there grows
In my most ill-compos'd affection such
A stanchless avarice that, were I king,
I should cut off the nobles for their lands,
Desire his jewels and this other's house;
And my more-having would be as a sauce
To make me hunger more, that I should forge
Quarrels unjust against the good and loyal,
Destroying them for wealth.

    MACDUFF.   This avarice
Sticks deeper, grows with more pernicious root
Than summer-seeming lust, and it hath been
The sword of our slain kings: yet do not fear;
Scotland hath foisons to fill up your will,
Of your mere own; all these are portable,
With other graces weigh'd.

    MALCOLM. But I have none: the king-becoming graces,
As justice, verity, temperance, stableness,
Bounty, perseverance, mercy, lowliness,
Devotion, patience, courage, fortitude,
I have no relish of them, but abound
In the division of each several crime,
Acting it many ways. Nay, had I power, I should
Pour the sweet milk of concord into hell,
Uproar the universal peace, confound
All unity on earth.

    MACDUFF.   O Scotland, Scotland!

MALCOLM. If such a one be fit to govern, speak:
I am as I have spoken.

MACDUFF. Fit to govern!
No, not to live. O nation miserable,
With an untitled tyrant bloody-scepter'd,
When shalt thou see thy wholesome days again,
Since that the truest issue of thy throne
By his own interdiction stands accurs'd,
And does blaspheme his breed? Thy royal father
Was a most sainted king; the queen that bore thee,
Oft'ner upon her knees than on her feet,
Died every day she liv'd. Fare thee well!
These evils thou repeat'st upon thyself
Have banish'd me from Scotland. O my breast,
Thy hope ends here!

MALCOLM. Macduff, this noble passion,
Child of integrity, hath from my soul
Wip'd the black scruples, reconcil'd my thoughts
To thy good truth and honour. Devilish Macbeth
By many of these trains hath sought to win me
Into his power, and modest wisdom plucks me
From over-credulous haste; but God above
Deal between thee and me! for even now
I put myself to thy direction, and
Unspeak mine own detraction, here abjure
The taints and blames I laid upon myself,
For strangers to my nature. I am yet
Unknown to woman, never was forsworn,
Scarcely have coveted what was mine own;
At no time broke my faith, would not betray
The devil to his fellow, and delight
No less in truth than life; my first false speaking
Was this upon myself. What I am truly,
Is thine and my poor country's to command;
Whither indeed, before thy here-approach,
Old Siward, with ten thousand war-like men,

Already at a point, was setting forth.
Now we'll together, and the chance of goodness
Be like our warranted quarrel. Why are you silent?

MACDUFF. Such welcome and unwelcome things at once
'Tis hard to reconcile.

Enter a DOCTOR.

MALCOLM. Well; more anon. Comes the king forth, I pray
you?

DOCTOR. Ay, sir; there are a crew of wretched souls
That stay his cure; their malady convinces
The great assay of art; but, at his touch,
Such sanctity hath heaven given his hand,
They presently amend.

MALCOLM.   I thank you, doctor.   [*Exit* DOCTOR.

MACDUFF. What's the disease he means?

MALCOLM.   'Tis call'd the evil:
A most miraculous work in this good king,
Which often, since my here-remain in England,
I have seen him do. How he solicits heaven,
Himself best knows; but strangely-visited people,
All swoln and ulcerous, pitiful to the eye,
The mere despair of surgery, he cures,
Hanging a golden stamp about their necks,
Put on with holy prayers; and 'tis spoken,
To the succeeding royalty he leaves
The healing benediction. With this strange virtue,
He hath a heavenly gift of prophecy,
And sundry blessings hang about his throne
That speak him full of grace.

MACDUFF.   See, who comes here?

MALCOLM. My countryman; but yet I know him not.

Enter ROSS.

MACDUFF. My ever-gentle cousin, welcome hither.

MALCOLM. I know him now. Good God, betimes remove

The means that makes us strangers!

ROSS.   Sir, amen.

MACDUFF. Stands Scotland where it did?

ROSS.   Alas! poor country;
Almost afraid to know itself. It cannot
Be call'd our mother, but our grave; where nothing,
But who knows nothing, is once seen to smile;
Where sighs and groans and shrieks that rent the air
Are made, not mark'd; where violent sorrow seems
A modern ecstasy; the dead man's knell
Is there scarce ask'd for who; and good men's lives
Expire before the flowers in their caps,
Dying or ere they sicken.

MACDUFF.   O! relation
Too nice, and yet too true!

MALCOLM.   What's the newest grief?

ROSS. That of an hour's age doth hiss the speaker;
Each minute teems a new one.

MACDUFF.   How does my wife?

ROSS. Why, well.

MACDUFF.   And all my children?

ROSS.   Well too.

MACDUFF. The tyrant has not batter'd at their peace?

ROSS. No; they were well at peace when I did leave 'em.

MACDUFF. Be not a niggard of your speech: how goes 't?

ROSS. When I came hither to transport the tidings,
Which I have heavily borne, there ran a rumour
Of many worthy fellows that were out;
Which was to my belief witness'd the rather
For that I saw the tyrant's power a-foot.
Now is the time of help; your eye in Scotland
Would create soldiers, make our women fight,
To doff their dire distresses.

MALCOLM.   Be 't their comfort
We are coming thither. Gracious England hath
Lent us good Siward and ten thousand men;

An older and a better soldier none
That Christendom gives out.

ROSS.   Would I could answer
This comfort with the like! But I have words
That would be howl'd out in the desert air,
Where hearing should not latch them.

MACDUFF.   What concern they?
The general cause? or is it a free-grief
Due to some single breast?

ROSS.   No mind that's honest
But in it shares some woe, though the main part
Pertains to you alone.

MACDUFF.   If it be mine
Keep it not from me; quickly let me have it.

ROSS. Let not your ears despise my tongue for ever,
Which shall possess them with the heaviest sound
That ever yet they heard.

MACDUFF.   Hum! I guess at it.

ROSS. You castle is surpris'd; your wife and babes
Savagely slaughter'd; to relate the manner,
Were, on the quarry of these murder'd deer,
To add the death of you.

MALCOLM.   Merciful heaven!
What! man; ne'er pull your hat upon your brows;
Give sorrow words; the grief that does not speak
Whispers the o'er-fraught heart and bids it break.

MACDUFF. My children too?

ROSS.   Wife, children, servants, all
That could be found.

MACDUFF.   And I must be from thence!
My wife kill'd too?

ROSS.   I have said.

MALCOLM.   Be comforted:
Let's make us medicine of our great revenge,
To cure this deadly grief.

MACDUFF. He has no children. All my pretty ones?

Did you say all? O hell-kite! All?
What! all my pretty chickens and their dam
At one fell swoop?
  MALCOLM.   Dispute it like a man.
  MACDUFF.   I shall do so;
But I must also feel it as a man:
I cannot but remember such things were,
That were most precious to me. Did heaven look on,
And would not take their part? Sinful Macduff!
They were all struck for thee. Naught that I am,
Not for their own demerits, but for mine,
Fell slaughter on their souls. Heaven rest them now!
  MALCOLM. Be this the whetstone of your sword: let grief
Convert to anger; blunt not the heart, enrage it.
  MACDUFF. O! I could play the woman with mine eyes,
And braggart with my tongue. But, gentle heavens,
Cut short all intermission; front to front
Bring thou this fiend of Scotland and myself;
Within my sword's length set him; if he 'scape,
Heaven forgive him too!
  MALCOLM.   This tune goes manly.
Come, go we to the king; our power is ready;
Our lack is nothing but our leave. Macbeth
Is ripe for shaking, and the powers above
Put on their instruments. Receive what cheer you may;
The night is long that never finds the day   [*Exeunt.*

Act 5

Scene I. Dunsinane. A Room in the Castle

Enter a DOCTOR OF PHYSIC *and a* WAITING-GENTLEWOMAN.

DOCTOR. I have two nights watched with you, but can perceive no truth in your report. When was it she last walked?

GENTLEWOMAN. Since his majesty went into the field, I have seen her rise from her bed, throw her night-gown upon her, unlock her closet, take forth paper, fold it, write upon 't, read it, afterwards seal it, and again return to bed; yet all this while in a most fast sleep.

DOCTOR. A great perturbation in nature, to receive at once the benefit of sleep and do the effects of watching! In this slumbery agitation, besides her walking and other actual performances, what, at any time, have you heard her say?

GENTLEWOMAN. That, sir, which I will not report after her.

DOCTOR. You may to me, and 'tis most meet you should.

GENTLEWOMAN. Neither to you nor any one, having no witness to confirm my speech.

Enter LADY MACBETH, *with a taper.*

Lo you! here she comes. This is her very guise; and, upon my life, fast asleep. Observe her; stand close.

DOCTOR. How came she by that light?

GENTLEWOMAN. Why, it stood by her: she has light by her continually; 'tis her command.

DOCTOR. You see, her eyes are open.

The statue of Shakespeare in the church at Stratford-on-Avon

GENTLEWOMAN. Ay, but their sense is shut.

DOCTOR. What is it she does now? Look, how she rubs her hands.

GENTLEWOMAN. It is an accustomed action with her, to seem thus washing her hands. I have known her to continue in this a quarter of an hour.

LADY MACBETH. Yet here's a spot.

DOCTOR. Hark, she speaks. I will set down what comes from her, to satisfy my remembrance the more strongly.

LADY MACBETH. Out, damned spot! out, I say! One; two: why, then 'tis time to do 't. Hell is murky! Fie, my lord, fie! a soldier, and afeard? What need we fear who knows it, when none can call our power to account? Yet who would have thought the old man to have had so much blood in him?

DOCTOR. Do you mark that?

LADY MACBETH. The Thane of Fife had a wife: where is she now? What! will these hands ne'er be clean? No more o' that, my lord, no more o' that: you mar all with this starting.

DOCTOR. Go to, go to; you have known what you should not.

GENTLEWOMAN. She has spoke what she should not, I am sure of that: Heaven knows what she has known.

LADY MACBETH. Here's the smell of the blood still: all the perfumes of Arabia will not sweeten this little hand. Oh! oh! oh!

DOCTOR. What a sigh is there! The heart is sorely charged.

GENTLEWOMAN. I would not have such a heart in my bosom for the dignity of the whole body.

DOCTOR. Well, well, well.

GENTLEWOMAN. Pray God it be, sir.

DOCTOR. This disease is beyond my practice: yet I have known those which have walked in their sleep who have died holily in their beds.

LADY MACBETH. Wash your hands, put on your night-gown; look not so pale. I tell you yet again, Banquo's buried; he cannot come out on 's grave.

DOCTOR. Even so?

LADY MACBETH. To bed, to bed: there's knocking at the gate.

Come, come, come, come, give me your hand. What's done cannot be undone. To bed, to bed, to bed.   [*Exit.*

DOCTOR. Will she go now to bed?

GENTLEWOMAN. Directly.

DOCTOR. Foul whisperings are abroad. Unnatural deeds
Do breed unnatural troubles; infected minds
To their deaf pillows will discharge their secrets;
More needs she the divine than the physician.
God, God forgive us all! Look after her;
Remove from her the means of all annoyance,
And still keep eyes upon her. So, good-night:
My mind she has mated, and amaz'd my sight.
I think, but dare not speak.

GENTLEWOMAN.   Good-night, good doctor.   [*Exeunt.*

Scene II.   *The Country near Dunsinane*

Enter, with drum and colours, MENTEITH, CAITHNESS, ANGUS,
LENNOX, *and* SOLDIERS.

MENTEITH. The English power is near, led on by Malcolm,
His uncle Siward, and the good Macduff.
Revenges burn in them; for their dear causes
Would to the bleeding and the grim alarm
Excite the mortified man.

ANGUS.   Near Birnam wood
Shall we well meet them; that way are they coming.

CAITHNESS. Who knows if Donalbain be with his brother?

LENNOX. For certain, sir, he is not: I have a file
Of all the gentry: there is Siward's son,
And many unrough youths that even now
Protest their first of manhood.

MENTEITH.   What does the tyrant?

CAITHNESS. Great Dunsinane he strongly fortifies.
Some say he's mad; others that lesser hate him
Do call it valiant fury; but, for certain,

He cannot buckle his distemper'd cause
Within the belt of rule.

    ANGUS.   Now does he feel
His secret murders sticking on his hands;
Now minutely revolts upbraid his faith-breach;
Those he commands move only in command,
Nothing in love; now does he feel his title
Hang loose about him, like a giant's robe
Upon a dwarfish thief.

    MENTEITH.   Who then shall blame
His pester'd senses to recoil and start,
When all that is within him does condemn
Itself for being there?

    CAITHNESS.   Well, march we on,
To give obedience where 'tis truly ow'd;
Meet we the medicine of the sickly weal,
And with him pour we in our country's purge
Each drop of us.

    LENNOX.   Or so much as it needs
To dew the sovereign flower and drown the weeds.
Make we our march towards Birnam.   *[Exeunt, marching.*

Scene III. Dunsinane. A Room in the Castle

Enter MACBETH, DOCTOR, *and* ATTENDANTS.

    MACBETH. Bring me no more reports; let them fly all:
Till Birnam wood remove to Dunsinane
I cannot taint with fear. What's the boy Malcolm?
Was he not born of woman? The spirits that know
All mortal consequences have pronounc'd me thus:
'Fear not, Macbeth; no man that's born of woman
Shall e'er have power upon thee.' Then fly, false thanes,
And mingle with the English epicures:
The mind I sway by and the heart I bear
Shall never sag with doubt nor shake with fear.

Enter a SERVANT.

The devil damn thee black, thou cream-fac'd loon!
Where gott'st thou that goose look?

SERVANT. There is ten thousand—

MACBETH.   Geese, villain?

SERVANT.   Soldiers, sir.

MACBETH. Go, prick thy face, and over-red thy fear,
Thou lily-liver'd boy. What soldiers, patch?
Death of thy soul! those linen cheeks of thine
Are counsellors to fear. What soldiers, whey-face?

SERVANT. The English force, so please you.

MACBETH. Take thy face hence. [*Exit* SERVANT.] Seyton!—I am
    sick at heart
When I behold—Seyton, I say!—This push
Will cheer me ever or disseat me now.
I have liv'd long enough: my way of life
Is fall'n into the sear, the yellow leaf;
And that which should accompany old age,
As honour, love, obedience, troops of friends,
I must not look to have; but, in their stead,
Curses, not loud but deep, mouth-honour, breath,
Which the poor heart would fain deny, and dare not.
Seyton!

Enter SEYTON.

SEYTON. What is your gracious pleasure?

MACBETH.   What news more?

SEYTON. All is confirm'd, my lord, which was reported.

MACBETH. I'll fight till from my bones my flesh be hack'd.
Give me my armour.

SEYTON.   'Tis not needed yet.

MACBETH. I'll put it on.
Send out more horses, skirr the country round;
Hang those that talk of fear. Give me mine armour.
How does your patient, doctor?

DOCTOR.   Not so sick, my lord,

As she is troubled with thick-coming fancies,
That keep her from her rest.

MACBETH.   Cure her of that:
Canst thou not minister to a mind diseas'd,
Pluck from the memory a rooted sorrow,
Raze out the written troubles of the brain,
And with some sweet oblivious antidote
Cleanse the stuff'd bosom of that perilous stuff
Which weighs upon the heart?

DOCTOR.   Therein the patient
Must minister to himself.

MACBETH. Throw physic to the dogs; I'll none of it.
Come, put mine armour on; give me my staff.
Seyton, send out.—Doctor, the thanes fly from me.—
Come, sir, dispatch.—If thou couldst, doctor, cast
The water of my land, find her disease,
And purge it to a sound and pristine health,
I would applaud thee to the very echo,
That should applaud again.—Pull 't off, I say.—
What rhubarb, senna, or what purgative drug
Would scour these English hence? Hear'st thou of them?

DOCTOR. Ay, my good lord; your royal preparation
Makes us hear something.

MACBETH.   Bring it after me.
I will not be afraid of death and bane
Till Birnam forest come to Dunsinane.

DOCTOR. [*Aside.*] Were I from Dunsinane away and clear,
Profit again should hardly draw me here.   [*Exeunt.*

Scene IV.   *Country near Birnam Wood*

Enter, with drum and colours, MALCOLM, *Old* SIWARD *and
his* SON, MACDUFF, MENTEITH, CAITHNESS, ANGUS, LENNOX,
ROSS, *and* SOLDIERS *marching.*

MALCOLM. Cousins, I hope the days are near at hand
That chambers will be safe.

MENTEITH. We doubt it nothing.

SIWARD. What wood is this before us?

MENTEITH. The wood of Birnam.

MALCOLM. Let every soldier hew him down a bough
And bear 't before him: thereby shall we shadow
The numbers of our host, and make discovery
Err in report of us.

SOLDIERS. It shall be done.

SIWARD. We learn no other but the confident tyrant
Keeps still in Dunsinane, and will endure
Our setting down before 't.

MALCOLM. 'Tis his main hope;
For where there is advantage to be given,
Both more and less have given him the revolt,
And none serve with him but constrained things
Whose hearts are absent too.

MACDUFF. Let our just censures
Attend the true event, and put we on
Industrious soldiership.

SIWARD. The time approaches
That will with due decision make us know
What we shall say we have and what we owe.
Thought speculative their unsure hopes relate,
But certain issue strokes must arbitrate,
Towards which advance the war. [*Exeunt, marching.*

Scene V. *Dunsinane. Within the Castle*

Enter, with a drum and colours, MACBETH, SEYTON, *and*
SOLDIERS.

MACBETH. Hang out our banners on the outward walls;
The cry is still, 'They come;' our castle's strength
Will laugh a siege to scorn; here let them lie
Till famine and the ague eat them up;
Were they not forc'd with those that should be ours,

We might have met them dareful, beard to beard,
And beat them backward home.   [*A cry of women within.*
                           What is that noise?
SEYTON. It is the cry of women, my good lord.   [*Exit.*
MACBETH. I have almost forgot the taste of fears.
The time has been my senses would have cool'd
To hear a night-shriek, and my fell of hair
Would at a dismal treatise rouse and stir
As life were in 't. I have supp'd full with horrors;
Direness, familiar to my slaughterous thoughts,
Cannot once start me.

    Re-enter SEYTON.

                           Wherefore was that cry?
SEYTON. The queen, my lord, is dead.
MACBETH. She should have died hereafter;
There would have been a time for such a word.
To-morrow, and to-morrow, and to-morrow,
Creeps in this petty pace from day to day,
To the last syllable of recorded time;
And all our yesterdays have lighted fools
The way to dusty death. Out, out, brief candle!
Life's but a walking shadow, a poor player
That struts and frets his hour upon the stage,
And then is heard no more; it is a tale
Told by an idiot, full of sound and fury,
Signifying nothing.

    Enter a MESSENGER.

Thou com'st to use thy tongue; thy story quickly.
MESSENGER. Gracious my lord,
I should report that which I say I saw,
But know not how to do it.
MACBETH.   Well, say, sir.
MESSENGER. As I did stand my watch upon the hill,

I look'd towards Birnam, and anon, methought,
The wood began to move.

    MACBETH.   Liar and slave!

    MESSENGER. Let me endure your wrath if 't be not so:
Within this three mile you may see it coming;
I say, a moving grove.

    MACBETH.   If thou speak'st false,
Upon the next tree shalt thou hang alive,
Till famine cling thee; if thy speech be sooth,
I care not if thou dost for me as much.
I pull in resolution and begin
To doubt the equivocation of the fiend
That lies like truth; 'Fear not, till Birnam wood
Do come to Dunsinane;' and now a wood
Comes toward Dunsinane. Arm, arm, and out!
If this which he avouches does appear,
There is nor flying hence, nor tarrying here.
I 'gin to be aweary of the sun,
And wish the estate o' the world were now undone.
Ring the alarum-bell! Blow, wind! come, wrack!
At least we'll die with harness on our back.   *[Exeunt.*

Scene VI.   The Same. A Plain before the Castle

Enter, with drum and colours, MALCOLM, OLD SIWARD,
MACDUFF, *&c., and their Army, with boughs.*

    MALCOLM. Now near enough; your leavy screens throw down,
And show like those you are. You, worthy uncle,
Shall, with my cousin, your right-noble son,
Lead our first battle; worthy Macduff and we
Shall take upon 's what else remains to do,
According to our order.

    SIWARD.   Fare you well.
Do we but find the tyrant's power to-night,
Let us be beaten, if we cannot fight.

MACDUFF. Make all our trumpets speak; give them all breath,
Those clamorous harbingers of blood and death.   [*Exeunt.*

Scene VII.   The Same. Another Part of the Plain

Alarums. Enter MACBETH.

MACBETH. They have tied me to a stake; I cannot fly,
But bear-like I must fight the course. What's he
That was not born of woman? Such a one
Am I to fear, or none.

Enter YOUNG SIWARD.

YOUNG SIWARD. What is thy name?
MACBETH.   Thou'lt be afraid to hear it.
YOUNG SIWARD. No; though thou call'st thyself a hotter name
Than any is in hell.
MACBETH.   My name's Macbeth.
YOUNG SIWARD. The devil himself could not pronounce a title
More hateful to mine ear.
MACBETH.   No, nor more fearful.
YOUNG SIWARD. Thou liest, abhorred tyrant; with my sword
I'll prove the lie thou speak'st.
                    [*They fight and* YOUNG SIWARD *is slain.*
MACBETH.   Thou wast born of woman:
But swords I smile at, weapons laugh to scorn,
Brandish'd by man that's of a woman born.   [*Exit.*

Alarums. Enter MACDUFF.

MACDUFF. That way the noise is. Tyrant, show thy face:
If thou be'st slain and with no stroke of mine,
My wife and children's ghosts will haunt me still.
I cannot strike at wretched kerns, whose arms
Are hir'd to bear their staves: either thou, Macbeth,
Or else my sword with an unbatter'd edge

I sheathe again undeeded. There thou shouldst be;
By this great clatter, one of greatest note
Seems bruited. Let me find him, fortune!
And more I beg not.   [*Exit. Alarums.*

Enter MALCOLM *and* OLD SIWARD.

SIWARD. This way, my lord; the castle's gently render'd:
The tyrant's people on both sides do fight;
The noble thanes do bravely in the war;
The day almost itself professes yours,
And little is to do.
        MALCOLM.   We have met with foes
That strike beside us.
        SIWARD.   Enter, sir, the castle.   [*Exeunt. Alarums.*

Re-enter MACBETH.

MACBETH. Why should I play the Roman fool, and die
On mine own sword? whiles I see lives, the gashes
Do better upon them.

Re-enter MACDUFF.

MACDUFF.   Turn, hell-hound, turn!
MACBETH. Of all men else I have avoided thee:
But get thee back, my soul is too much charg'd
With blood of thine already.
        MACDUFF.   I have no words;
My voice is in my sword, thou bloodier villain
Than terms can give thee out!   [*They fight.*
        MACBETH.   Thou losest labour:
As easy mayst thou the intrenchant air
With thy keen sword impress as make me bleed:
Let fall thy blade on vulnerable crests;
I bear a charmed life, which must not yield
To one of woman born.

MACDUFF.   Despair thy charm;
And let the angel whom thou still hast serv'd
Tell thee, Macduff was from his mother's womb
Untimely ripp'd.

MACBETH. Accursed be that tongue that tells me so,
For it hath cow'd my better part of man:
And be these juggling fiends no more believ'd,
That palter with us in a double sense;
That keep the word of promise to our ear,
And break it to our hope. I'll not fight with thee.

MACDUFF. Then yield thee, coward,
And live to be the show and gaze o' the time:
We'll have thee, as our rarer monsters are,
Painted upon a pole, and underwrit,
'Here may you see the tyrant.'

MACBETH.   I will not yield,
To kiss the ground before young Malcolm's feet,
And to be baited with the rabble's curse.
Though Birnam wood be come to Dunsinane,
And thou oppos'd, being of no woman born,
Yet I will try the last: before my body
I throw my war-like shield. Lay on, Macduff,
And damn'd be him that first cries, 'Hold, enough!'

[*Exeunt, fighting.*

Retreat. Flourish. Re-enter, with drum and colours, MAL-
COLM, OLD SIWARD, ROSS, THANES, *and* SOLDIERS.

MALCOLM. I would the friends we miss were safe arriv'd.

SIWARD. Some must go off; and yet, by these I see,
So great a day as this is cheaply bought.

MALCOLM. Macduff is missing, and your noble son.

ROSS. Your son, my lord, has paid a soldier's debt:
He only liv'd but till he was a man;
The which no sooner had his prowess confirm'd
In the unshrinking station where he fought,
But like a man he died.

SIWARD.   Then he is dead?

ROSS. Ay, and brought off the field. Your cause of sorrow
Must not be measur'd by his worth, for then
It hath no end.

SIWARD.   Had he his hurts before?

ROSS. Ay, on the front.

SIWARD.   Why then, God's soldier be he!
Had I as many sons as I have hairs,
I would not wish them to a fairer death:
And so, his knell is knoll'd.

MALCOLM.   He's worth more sorrow,
And that I'll spend for him.

SIWARD.   He's worth no more;
They say he parted well, and paid his score:
And so, God be with him! Here comes newer comfort.

Re-enter MACDUFF, *with* MACBETH's *head.*

MACDUFF. Hail, king! for so thou art. Behold, where stands
The usurper's cursed head: the time is free:
I see thee compass'd with thy kingdom's pearl,
That speak my salutation in their minds;
Whose voices I desire aloud with mine;
Hail, King of Scotland!

ALL.   Hail, King of Scotland!   [*Flourish.*

MALCOLM. We shall not spend a large expense of time
Before we reckon with your several loves,
And make us even with you. My thanes and kinsmen,
Henceforth be earls, the first that ever Scotland
In such an honour nam'd. What's more to do,
Which would be planted newly with the time,
As calling home our exil'd friends abroad
That fled the snares of watchful tyranny;
Producing forth the cruel ministers
Of this dead butcher and his fiend-like queen,
Who, as 'tis thought, by self and violent hands

Took off her life; this, and what needful else
That calls upon us, by the grace of Grace
We will perform in measure, time, and place:
So, thanks to all at once and to each one,
Whom we invite to see us crown'd at Scone.   [*Flourish. Exeunt.*

A GLOSSARY OF WORDS
AND PHRASES

The following abbreviations are used in the Glossary: JC for
Julius Caesar, H for *Hamlet,* M for *Macbeth.* References are listed
by play, act, and scene; e.g. H V, 1 for *Hamlet,* Act V, Scene 1.

ABIDE, pay the penalty for JC III, 1
ABSOLUTE, exact, precise, faultless H V, 1
ABUSE, imposture, deceit H IV, 7
ACHERON, a river in Hell M III, 5
ADDITION, name, reputation H I, 4
ADMIRATION, wonder, amazement H I, 2; III, 2
ADMIRED, amazing M III, 4
AERY (EYRIE), the nest of a bird of prey; also the brood in the
    nest H II, 2
AFFEER'D, confirmed legally M IV, 3
ALCHEMY, a false science that sought to change baser metals into
    gold JC I, 3
AMISS, error, fault, mischief H IV, 5
ANCHOR, anchorite, recluse, hermit H III, 2
ANON, at once, soon H II, 2
ANTIC, strange, odd, ancient H I, 5
APPREHENSIVE, intelligent, perceptive JC III, 1
APPROVE, justify, confirm H I, 29
ARDINT, be off with you, be gone M I, 3
ARGAL, therefore H V, 1
ARRANT, notorious, downright H I, 5
ASSAY, test, challenge H III, 1
AUGURES, predictions M III, 4
AVOUCH, guarantee, evidence H I, 1
AWL, a sharp-pointed tool JC I, 1

BADGED, marked as with a badge M II, 3
BASIS, the base of a statue JC III, 1

315

BATTEN, thrive, grow fat H III, 4
BAY'D, brought to bay like a hunted animal JC III, 1
BEAVER, the lower portion of the face guard of a helmet H I, 2
BELDAMES, hags M III, 5
BELLMAN, the town crier M II, 2
BELLONA'S BRIDEGROOM, the spouse of the Roman goddess of
    war, here meaning Macbeth M I, 2
BENISON, blessing M II, 4
BENT, inclination H II, 2
BILBOES, iron fetters H V, 2
BISSON, blind H II, 2
BLANK, the white spot in the center of the target H IV, 1
BLAZON, publication, revelation, proclamation H I, 5
BLOOD-BOLTERED, stained with clots of blood M IV, 1
BODEMENTS, omens M IV, 1
BODKIN, a short, pointed weapon, a dagger H III, 1
BORE, importance H IV, 6
BORNE IN HAND, handled, treated, deceived H II, 2; M III, 1
BOSOM INTEREST, dearest concern M I, 2
BOURNE, boundary H III, 1
BRINDED, streaked, brindled M IV, 1
BRUIT, report noisily H I, 2
BURNING ZONE, the sun H V, 1
BUTTON, bud H I, 3

CANKER, canker worm H I, 3
CAPABLE, susceptible of feeling H III, 4
CAP-A-PE, from head to foot H I, 1
CARD, the chart or face of the compass H V, 1
CARRIAGE, the hanger of a sword H V, 2
CASING, enveloping, surrounding M III, 4
CAST, shade of color, tinge H III, 1
CATAPLASM, plaster, poultice H IV, 7
CAT I' THE ADAGE, the cat in the proverb that liked fish but not
    getting its jaws wet M I, 7
CAUTEL, trickery or craftiness H I, 3
CAUTELOUS, suspicious, crafty JC II, 1
CENSURE, opinion, judgment H I, 3
CHAPLESS, without a jaw H V, 1

CHARACTER, inscribe, brand, stamp H I, 3
CHARIEST, most careful and cautious H I, 3
CHAUDRON, entrails M IV, 1
CHOKE THEIR ART, impede each other's skill M I, 2
CHOLER, anger, wrath JC IV, 3; H III, 1
CHOPINE, high-heeled and thick-soled shoes H II, 2
CHOPPY, chaffed M I, 3
CICATRICE, scar H IV, 3
CLEPE, call, name H I, 4
CLEPT, called M III, 1
CLIMATURES, regions H I, 1
COBBLER, one who mends shoes, a botcher, a bungling workman
   JC I, 1
COFFER, treasury JC III, 2
COIL, noisy disturbance, fuss, ado H III, 1
COLDLY SET, underrate H IV, 3
COLLECTION, inference H IV, 5
COLOSSUS, the great statue at Rhodes which spanned the harbor,
   one of the seven wonders of the ancient world JC I, 2
CO-MART, joint bargain or agreement H I, 1
COMPOSITION, terms of peace M I, 2
COMPT, accounted for, in trust M I, 6
CONCEIT, fantastic imagination H III, 4
CONSCIENCE, reflection, speculation H III, 1
CONSONANCY, agreement, harmony H II, 2
CONTUMELY, insolence, contempt H III, 1
CONVOY, conveyance H I, 3
COP'D, encountered, met H III, 2
CORSE, corpse, body JC III, 1
COTED, passed by, outstripped H II, 2
COZ, cousin, kinsman M IV, 2
CRACK THE WIND OF, to break down, to overwork H I, 3
CRACKS, charges M I, 2
CRANTS, garlands, wreaths H V, 1
CROWNER, coroner H V, 1
CURB, bend, bow, cringe H III, 4

DANSKERS, Danes H II, 1
DELATED, conveyed, entrusted H I, 2

DEAREST, worthiest, closest H I, 2
DINT, blow, stroke JC III, 2
DISAPPOINTED, unprepared H I, 5
DOLE, grief H I, 2
DOUT, do out, quench, extinguish H IV, 7
DRABBING, frequenting women H II, 1
DRACHMA, a coin JC III, 2
DRIFT OF CONFERENCE, roundabout methods H III, 1
DROSSY, frivolous, cheap H V, 2
DUCAT, a gold coin H III, 4
DULL THY PALM, make your friendliness too common H I, 3

EAGER, keen, sharp, also acid, sour H I, 4; I, 5
ECSTASY, madness, excitement, emotion H III, 1; M IV, 3
EDGE, keenness, desire H III, 1
EISEL, vinegar H V, 1
EMULATE, ambitious H I, 1
ENGLAND, the king of England H IV, 3
ENTERTAINMENT, reception, treatment H II, 2
ESCOTED, paid for H II, 2
ET TU BRUTE, And you, Brutus JC III, 1
ETERNAL JEWEL, the soul M III, 1
EXCREMENTS, outgrowths like hair H III, 4
EXIGENT, pressing need JC V, 1
EXTRAVAGANT AND ERRING, wandering, roving H I, 1
EYASES, young hawks H II, 2

FALSE, defective, out of tune JC IV, 3
FARDELS, bundles, burdens H III, 1
FEE-GRIEF, private sorrow M IV, 3
FELL, cruel, fierce H V, 2
FELLIES, rims of a wheel H II, 2
FINGERED, stole H V, 2
FLAW, sudden blast or gust of wind H V, 1
FLEER, mock, sneer JC I, 3
FOIL, blunted rapier H V, 2
FOREST OF FEATHERS, hat with plumes H III, 2
FORGED PROCESS, false report H I, 5
FORM, a long bench or seat JC III, 2

FILED, defiled, stained M III, 1

FOISON, abundance, plenty M IV, 3

FUST, to become musty or stale H IV, 4

GAGED, pledged H I, 1

GAIN-GIVING, misgiving H V, 2

GALLED, sore, irritated H I, 2

GALLOW GLASS, heavily armed Irish soldiers M I, 2

GERMEN, germ, seed M IV, 1

GIB, tomcat H III, 4

GIN, snare, trap M IV, 2

GIS, Jesus H IV, 5

GLAZE, stare JC I, 3

GLOBE, head, skull H I, 5

GOLDEN COUPLETS, yellow chickens or young birds H V, 1

GOLGOTHA, a place of the skull, from the New Testament M I, 2

GOOD KISSING CARRION, dead flesh good to kiss H II, 2

GOOD NOW, exclamation of entreaty H I, 1

GOOSE, a tailor's pressing iron M II, 3

GOOSE QUILLS, pens or satirical writings H II, 2

GORGE, stomach H V, 1

GORGON, the Medura who petrified anyone who looked on her M II, 3

GOUTS, drops M II, 1

GRAYMALKIN, name for a cat M I, 1

GROSS AND SCOPE, general or overall view H I, 1

GROUNDLINGS, audience in the pit of the theatre H III, 2

GULES, red, bloody H II, 2

GYVES, shackles, fetters H IV, 7

HANDSAW, heron H II, 2

HARPIER, the third Witch's familiar, a possible variation of Harpy M IV, 1

HARROWS, tears or wounds H I, 1

HATCHMENT, escutcheon, coat of arms H IV, 5

HAUTBOY, wooden, wind instrument, oboe H III, 2; M IV, 1

HEBONA, henbane, a narcotic poison, or the yew H I, 5

HECATE, goddess of the underworld M II, 1

HENT, grasp, grip, course H III, 3

HERMIT, a beadsman who prayed for a noble benefactor **M I, 6**
HEYDAY, wildness, wantonness H III, 4
HIC ET UBIQUE, here and everywhere H I, 5
HOT AT HAND, hard to rein in or control JC IV, **2**
HOWLET, owlet M IV, 1
HUGGER-MUGGER, secrecy H IV, 5
HURLY BURLY, confusion, uproar M **I, 1**
HUSBANDRY, thrift, economy H I, 3
HYPERION, the Sun God M I, 2
HYRCANIAN BEAST, the tiger H II, **2**

IDES OF MARCH, March 15 JC I, 2
'ILD, yield, reward H IV, 5
IMPARTMENT, communication H I, **4**
IMPOND, staked H V, 2
IMPOSTHUME, abscess, sore H IV, 4
IMPRESS, enforced services H I, 1
INCARNADINE, redden M II, 2
INCONTENENCY, debauchery H II, 1
INSTANT, present moment M I, 5
IT, its H I, 2

JADE, a vicious, worthless horse JC IV, 2
JIGGING, a contemptuous word for rhyming JC IV, **3**
JIG-MAKER, clown, comedian H III, 2
JOINTRESS, a widow who holds an estate in jointure with **another**
     H I, 2
JUMP, exactly, precisely; also hazard, risk H I, 1; M I, 7

KERN, a light-armed Irish foot-soldier M I, 2; M V, 7
KIBE, sore on the heel, chilblain H V, 1

LAWLESS RESOLUTES, determined outlaws H I, 1
LAZAR, leper H I, 5
LETHE, a lake or river in the infernal regions that gave **forgetful**-
     ness to those who drank of it H I, 5; JC III, 1
LETS, hinders, restrains H I, 4
LIMBECK, vessel used for distilling M I, 7

LIMITED, appointed M II, 3
LOGGATS, a game something like bowls H V, 1
LOON, lout, stupid rascal M V, 3
LUPERCAL, a February feast in honor of Lupercus, the Roman god Pan JC I, 1

MACHINE, body H II, 2
MAGGOT-PIES, magpies M III, 4
MARGENT, marginal explanation or note H V, 2
MARRY, the name of the Virgin Mary used as an oath or interjection H I, 4
MARTLET, the house-martin bird M I, 6
MATED, bewildered, overcome M V, 1
MAZZARD, head, skull H V, 1
MEAN, method, means, way JC III, 1
MEMORIZE, make memorable M I, 2
METAPHYSICAL, supernatural M I, 5
METTLE, disposition, temperament JC I, 2
MICHING MALLECHO, secret wickedness H III, 2
MILCH, moist H II, 2
MIND'S CONSTRUCTION, no art to find the mind's construction in the face, no way to discover how a man's mind is working by his face M I, 4
MOBLED, muffled H II, 2
MOE, more JC II, 1
MOIETY COMPETENT, equal or equivalent amount H I, 1
MOIST STAR, the Moon H I, 1
MOTE, speck or trifle H I, 1
MOUNTEBANK, quack, one who mounts a bench to proclaim his wares H IV, 7
MOW, grimace H II, 2
MUTINES, mutineers, rebels H V, 1

NAPKIN, handkerchief H V, 2
NEAT, ox or cow JC I, 1
NEMEAN LION, a mythical monster slain by Hercules H I, 4
NERVE, sinew H I, 4
NIGHTGOWN, dressing gown M II, 2

NIOBE, daughter of Tantalus, turned into stone for her boasting about her children who were slain by the gods. The stone is supposed to weep. H I, 2

NONCE, for the once H IV, 7

NUMBERS, verses H II, 2

OBSCURE BIRD, the owl M II, 3

OBSEQUIOUS, mourning H I, 2

OLD, plenty of M II, 3

ORDINANT, arranging, directing H V, 1

ORTS, fragments of food, scraps, leftovers JC IV, 1

PADDOCK, toad H III, 4; M I, 1

PAJOCK, peacock H III, 2

PALTER, trifle, quibble JC II, 1; M V, 7

PARDON, permission H I, 2

PARTISAN, long-handled spear H I, 1

PATCH, fool, clown M V, 3

PATH, pursue one's course JC II, 1

PENTHOUSE LID, eyelid M I, 3

PERDIE, *par Dieu,* by God, verily, indeed H III, 2

PERPEND, ponder, consider H II, 2

PETAR, bomb, explosive shell H III, 4

PHYSICS, remedies M II, 3

PICKED, refined, dainty H V, 1

PICKERS AND STEALERS, the hands H III, 2

POINT, at point, complete and ready H I, 2

PONIARD, dagger H V, 2

PORPENTINE, porcupines H I, 5

POSSET, hot milk spiced with liquor M II, 2

POSTERS, speedy travelers M I, 3

POSY, motto on a ring H III, 2

PRAETOR, a Roman magistrate JC I, 3

PRENOMINATE, before-mentioned H II, 1

PRESENT, immediate H IV, 3

PRIMY, in its prime, youthful H I, 5

PROBATION, proof H I, 1

PURSY, fat, corpulent H III, 4

QUALITY, the profession of acting H II, 2
QUELL, slaughter, murder M I, 7
QUEST, inquest H V, 1
QUESTION, subject, conversation H I, 1
QUIDDITIES, subtleties H V, 1
QUILLETS, tricks in argument H V, 1

RACK, cloud H II, 2
RANKER, larger, greater H IV, 4
RAVIN, devour greedily M II, 2
RAZED, slashed H III, 2
RECKS NOT HIS OWN REDE, disregards his own advice H I, 3
RECORDER, a flutelike instrument H III, 2
REGION, the sky H II, 2
REECHY, dirty, rancid H III, 4
REPAST, feed H IV, 5
REPLICATION, reply H IV, 2
RETROGRADE, contrary, opposed H I, 2
RIVALS, partners or associates H I, 1
RIV'D, torn, broken JC IV, 3
ROMAGE, bustle, turmoil H I, 1
RONYON, a mangy or scabby creature M I, 3
ROOD, the Cross H III, 4
ROUND, directly, frankly, plain-spoken H II, 2; III, 4
ROUSE, revel, noisy mirth H I, 2
RUMP-FED RONYON, fat-rumped good-for-nothing M I, 3
RUSSET, homespun woolen cloth of reddish brown or grey color
  H I, 1

SALLET, spiciness, indecency H II, 2
SANS, without H III, 4
SAW, a saying, maxim H I, 5
SCHEDULE, scroll, document JC III, 1
SCONCE, head H V, 1
SCOTCH, cut, gash M III, 2
SCRIMERS, fencers H IV, 7
SEELING, blending M III, 2
SENNET, series of trumpet notes M III, 1

SHAG-EARED, with long hair about the ears M IV, 2
SHARP UP, collected without regard to selection H I, 1
SHENT, shamed, reproached H III, 2
SHOUGHS, lap-dog M III, 2
SHUT UP, concluded the day M II, 1
SIMPLE, a medicinal plant or herb H IV, 7
SITH, since H IV, 4
SKIRR, scour M V, 3
SLAB, half solid, sticky M IV, 1
SLEAVE, a skein of silk threads M II, 2
SMATCH, taste JC V, 5
SOMETHING FROM, somewhat away from M III, 1
SOOTH, truth M I, 2
SORT, agree with H I, 1
SPLENETIVE, irascible, easily angered H V, 1
SPRINGES, snares H I, 3
STAMP, coin M IV, 3
STATIST, statesman H V, 1
STITHY, forger, smithy H III, 2
STOMACH, adventures H I, 1
STRAWS, trifles H IV, 5
SUPPOSAL, estimate, conjecture H I, 2
SWOOPSTAKE, sweepstake, indiscriminately H IV, 5
SWOUND, swoon JC I, 2

TABLES, writing tablets H I, 5
TARRE, set on, incite H II, 2
TENT, search, prove, try H II, 2
TERMAGANT, a boisterous Saracen god H III, 2
TESTY, impetuous, rash JC IV, 3
TETTER, a skin eruption H I, 5
THANE, Scottish title of nobility, chief of clan, an earl's son M I, 2
THUNDER-STONE, thunderbolt JC I, 3
TICKLE O' THE SERE, on the hair trigger, easily set off H II, 2
TOIL, net H III, 2
TOILS THE SUBJECTS, causes the subjects or people of the land
   to work nights H I, 1
TOY IN BLOOD, a passing fancy H I, 3
TRAINS, traps, bait M IV, 3

TRAMMEL UP, confine us in a net M I, 7
TRAVELLING LAMP, the sun M II, 4
TRISTFUL, sorrowing H III, 4
TRUE-PENNY, honest fellow H I, 5
TRUNCHEON, staff or baton H I, 2
TURK, turn Turk or go to the bad H III, 2

UNANEL'D, without extreme unction H I, 5
UNBATED, unblunted H IV, 7
UNHOUSELED, not having received Holy Communion H I, 5
UNSEAMED HIM FROM THE NAVE TO THE CHAPS, laid him
   open from the navel to the jaw M I, 2
UNYOKE, be done with it H V, 1
UPON OUR FIRST, directly he had heard us H II, 2
UPSPRING, new, recent H I, 4
UTTERANCE, the utmost, to the death M III, 1

VAILED, lowered, downcast H I, 2
VALANCED, fringed, bearded H II, 2
VAST, emptiness, waste H I, 2
VENTAGES, wind holes, stops H III, 2
VIZARD, mash M III, 2
VOID, empty, vacant JC II, 4

WANTON, unrestrained M I, 4
WARRANTISE, authority H V, 1
WASSAIL, deep drinking, reveling M I, 7
WATER-RUG, shaggy water-dog M III, 1
WEAL, commonweal, the state M V, 2
WHORESON, term of abuse H V, 1
WIT, wisdom H II, 2
WRACK, ruin H II, 1; M I, 3

YAW, move unsteadily, to deviate from a straight course H V, 2
YESTY, foaming, frothy M IV, 1

GREAT ILLUSTRATED CLASSICS

Adam Bede—*Eliot*
The Arabian Nights
Around the World in 80 Days—*Verne*
Autobiography of Benjamin Franklin
Ben-Hur—*Wallace*
The Black Arrow—*Stevenson*
Black Beauty—*Sewell*
The Call of the Wild—*London*
Captains Courageous—*Kipling*
Christmas Tales—*Dickens*
Comedies I—*Shakespeare*
Comedies II—*Shakespeare*
A Connecticut Yankee in King Arthur's Court—*Clemens*
The Cruise of the Cachalot—*Bullen*
David Copperfield—*Dickens*
The Deerslayer—*Cooper*
Dr. Jekyll and Mr. Hyde—*Stevenson*
Emma—*Austen*
Famous Tales of Sherlock Holmes—*Doyle*
Five Tales—*Melville*
From the Earth to the Moon—*Verne*
Great Expectations—*Dickens*
Green Mansions—*Hudson*
Gulliver's Travels—*Swift*
Hawthorne's Short Stories—*Hawthorne*
Henry Esmond—*Thackeray*
Histories I—*Shakespeare*
Histories II—*Shakespeare*
The House of the 7 Gables—*Hawthorne*
Huckleberry Finn—*Clemens*
The Hunchback of Notre-Dame—*Hugo*
Ivanhoe—*Scott*
Jane Eyre—*Brontë*
A Journey to the Centre of the Earth—*Verne*
Kenilworth—*Scott*
Kidnapped—*Stevenson*
Kim—*Kipling*
King Arthur—*Malory*
Last Days of Pompeii—*Bulwer-Lytton*
The Last of the Mohicans—*Cooper*
Lord Jim—*Conrad*
Lorna Doone—*Blackmore*
The Luck of Roaring Camp—*Harte*
The Man in the Iron Mask—*Dumas*

The Mill on the Floss—*Eliot*
The Moonstone—*Collins*
The Mysterious Island—*Verne*
The Odyssey—*Homer*
Oliver Twist—*Dickens*
The Oregon Trail—*Parkman*
The Pathfinder—*Cooper*
Père Goriot—*Balzac*
The Pilot—*Cooper*
The Pioneers—*Cooper*
The Prairie—*Cooper*
Pride and Prejudice—*Austen*
The Prince and the Pauper—*Clemens*
Pygmalion (and other plays)—*Shaw*
Quentin Durward—*Scott*
Quo Vadis—*Sienkiewicz*
The Red Badge of Courage—*Crane*
The Return of the Native—*Hardy*
The Rise of Silas Lapham—*Howells*
Robinson Crusoe—*Defoe*
The Scarlet Letter—*Hawthorne*
The Scarlet Pimpernel—*Orczy*
Sense and Sensibility—*Austen*
Silas Marner—*Eliot*
The Sketch Book—*Irving*
The Spy—*Cooper*
A Tale of Two Cities—*Dickens*
Tales—*Poe*
The Talisman—*Scott*
Tess of the D'Urbervilles—*Hardy*
The Three Musketeers—*Dumas*
Tom Sawyer—*Clemens*
Tragedies I—*Shakespeare*
Tragedies II—*Shakespeare*
Treasure Island—*Stevenson*
20,000 Leagues Under the Sea—*Verne*
Two Years Before the Mast—*Dana*
Typhoon—*Conrad*
Uncle Tom's Cabin—*Stowe*
Up From Slavery—*Washington*
Walden—*Thoreau*
The Way of All Flesh—*Butler*
The White Company—*Doyle*
White Fang and Other Stories—*London*
The Wreck of the Grosvenor—*Russell*
Wuthering Heights—*Brontë*

GREAT ILLUSTRATED CLASSICS—TITANS

Afloat and Ashore—*Cooper*
Anna Karenina—*Tolstoy*
Autobiography of Benvenuto Cellini
Barnaby Rudge—*Dickens*
Bleak House—*Dickens*
The Cloister and the Hearth—*Reade*
Crime and Punishment—*Dostoevsky*
Dombey and Son—*Dickens*
Don Quixote—*Cervantes*
Everybody's Plutarch
Little Dorrit—*Dickens*

Martin Chuzzlewit—*Dickens*
Nicholas Nickleby—*Dickens*
The Old Curiosity Shop—*Dickens*
Our Mutual Friend—*Dickens*
Pickwick Papers—*Dickens*
Short Novels of Henry James—*James*
Tom Jones, A Foundling—*Fielding*
Twenty Years After—*Dumas*
Vanity Fair—*Thackeray*
Westward Ho!—*Kingsley*